D0206470

Light Within The Shadows is an artist's triptych spanning three continents and a historical primer on Pnina Granirer's life: her early years at the heart of Europe in Romania before, during, and after the Second World War under the Nazis and the Communists, where her family and Jewish community in Brăila were immunized by a Romanian concoction of kindness and corruption, and the connivings of a canny mother with an eye for recycling designer clothes and making deals with devils.

For me, the standouts of the book are its moments of graphic memory, some sensory, some sensationally sad and curious. After confiscating her father's library of leather-bound books, a Nazi official has them stacked on the shelves in his office, not to be read, but to make them look good and him important. A fabulous black woman, Lulu Belle, staring at me out of a surreal drawing across the counter of her antique curio shop in Urbana, Illinois.

Although Pnina Granirer calls the book her "visual diary," many fine, sensory turns of phrase lingered after I finished reading it . . . "the perfume of pencils," for example. Anyone who can come up with that and revive my own memories of ink wells and my wooden desk and lead (graphite) in the pencil I held between my childish fingers has me involved with all five senses in her life story.

George McWhirter
Professor Emeritus of Creative Writing, UBC
Author of numerous works of fiction and poetry

. . . During a year in Montreal, her camaraderie with artists living bohemian lives devoted exclusively to their art made her question the effect on her work of her own conventional life as a wife and now the mother of one small child. Her doubts were reinforced by talking to other female artists and by attending a workshop in 1980 with Judy Chicago, whose sensational work *The Dinner Party* was drawing crowds. Judy Chicago's statement that no woman artist can ever make it big if she has a family resonated and propelled Granirer into her most ambitious work so far.

The Trials of Eve examines the subjugation of women, beginning with the creation myth in the first two chapters of Genesis. . . .

The written text is only part of what this book has to offer, for each step in Granirer's career is illustrated with her work — from the drawings she made of places and people in Israel and the midwest to the ambitious paintings of her final period. The paintings, many from *The Carved Stones* series, are reproduced in full colour. The visual component adds a rich dimension to this artist's account of living and creating through eight decades of monumental upheaval and change.

Excerpt from Joan Givner's article
in *BC Book World* Summer Edition 2017

Granirer writes with a painter's eye, vividly evoking cities from Jerusalem to Paris to Montreal and landscapes from the coastal sand dunes of Israel to the far north of Canada.

Granirer shares her creative process and how it relates to her life experience in three very different cultures with their different opportunities and limitations.

This thoughtful and fascinating memoir would appeal to anyone interested in the creative life and how it was lived by one gifted and determined artist through the vicissitudes of the 20th century and into the 21st.

Graham Good
Professor Emeritus of English, University of British Columbia
Author of *The Observing Self* and *Humanism Betrayed*

Light Within The Shadows

To Edith —
who loves art
with best wishes

Philna

LIGHT
WITHIN THE
SHADOWS

A Painter's Memoir

PNINA
GRANIRER

GRANVILLE ISLAND
PUBLISHING

Library and Archives Canada Cataloguing in Publication

Granirer, Pnina, 1935–, author
   Light within the shadows : a painter's memoir / Pnina Granirer.

ISBN 978-1-926991-84-9 (softcover)

   1. Granirer, Pnina, 1935–. 2. Women painters—Canada—Biography. 3. Painters—Canada—Biography. I. Title.

ND249.G713A2 2017   759.11   C2017-902304-7

Book editors: Pat Dobie & Kyle Hawke
Copy editing and indexing: Bookmark: Editing & Indexing
Book designer: Omar Gallegos

All artworks without provenance are part of the artist's personal collection.
Cover image: Child's Journey — detail | 1975 | dyptich
Photo of the artist: Peppa Martin

Granville Island Publishing Ltd.
212 – 1656 Duranleau St. Granville Island
Vancouver, BC, Canada V6H 3S4

604-688-0320 / 1-877-688-0320
info@granvilleislandpublishing.com
www.granvilleislandpublishing.com

Second printing in 2018
Printed in Canada on recycled paper

To everything there is a season
and a time to every purpose under the heaven:
A time to be born and a time to die . . .
A time to love and a time to hate;
a time of war and a time of peace.

Ecclesiastes 3

For me — it is a time to remember.

Shadows, photograph by Pnina Granirer

Luminous spots of remembrance and dark areas of forgetfulness
weave the unreliable, but only too real tapestry of our memories
— light within the shadows.

Contents

Introduction

And for the most part [the young] live in hope; for hope is of the future and remembrance of the past and for the young the future is long and the past short. And the old live in memory rather than in hope; for the rest of their life is short and hope is of the future, memory of past things.

Aristotle
The Art of Rhetoric

A day came when I knew a profound change had taken place in my life. Time had reversed itself quietly, stealthily, without warning. Suddenly, alarmingly, the future became but a short path ahead, as the past cast its long shadow behind. Simple words — like 'later', 'next year', 'tomorrow', 'not now' — became risky, unsure and speculative. Words such as 'now' acquired a sudden gravitas not considered before.

Children perceive the universe through a magic lens of unbound optimism and limited life experience. They live in the moment, blissfully unaware of the past and unconcerned with the future. Each day brings new skills, experience and knowledge. The past is remote for the young, who believe they are immortal and are anxious to embark on the vast uncharted ocean of hope and possibilities that is the future. In contrast, for the old the future has shrunk to a sliver of unreliable time; it is the past that looms large now, rich with experience and history, stretching deep into time, old roots preventing the tree from falling.

And so, we start searching.

The years stretch like signposts seen through the rear window of a speeding car. Ten, twenty, thirty — decade after decade. Too soon, the road nears its end and a mist of uncertainty hides the few posts left ahead. A deep desire to revisit the well-travelled road arises in the pilgrim's heart.

This is how, at the closing of my seventh decade, I found myself brushing away the cobwebs of time, sifting through memories and yellowed documents and trying to conjure the ghostly figures of my family living with the harsh realities of life as Jews in Romania.

I regret all the questions not asked of the dead and I mourn for all the missed answers. I shall never know how these people, wordlessly staring at me from old photographs, lived their lives. What were their thoughts and how did they cope?

I am grateful to my parents, who protected me and gave me a happy childhood in the midst of tragedy, turmoil and danger.

Some of the stories in this book were passed on to me by family and friends, others pulled from my own memory, making this account an imperfect one; for memories are fickle. Many gaps are filled in by sheer imagination, others left blank. Those few documents and photographs salvaged from the past helped jog my memory, bringing to life the actors in the play.

It all began with the old photo album in my parents' flat, quietly lying behind the glass doors of the small cabinet under the television set. The tattered red covers and the grey string holding them together had seen better days, but inside this old album lay a treasure trove of memories — black-and-white photographs of my grandparents, uncles and aunts, cousins and friends had been carefully inserted into triangular corners glued to the album's black pages. These images were the few survivors from a large collection that had to be abandoned when we left Romania. Our tormentors not only robbed us of our possessions while extracting a hefty price for our freedom, but also, in a last symbolic gesture, they attempted to rob us of our memories as well.

I was well into my fifties when I took the album home and spent long moments looking at the pictures that later became the inspiration for a body of works I called *Family Portraits*. But now, in my eighties, paintings are not enough. I need words that, akin to moles digging deep into the fertile soil of the past, will find the hidden roots and tell the story.

Roots are like anchors. During a storm, trees may be pulled out of the ground, their shallow roots exposed. Deep-rooted trees, however, may survive the storms. And should they still snap in the wind and fall, their roots will remain hidden in their subterranean home, testimony to the life of the fallen tree.

And so it is with people.

The Jews have a long and ancient history stretching across millennia. But as individuals, relatively few can go far back into the past. The threads of continuity have been lost, cut short. They were catastrophically severed by lives interrupted whether through wanderings — from place to place, from country to country and from continent to continent — or through changed names and disappearances in violent upheavals, murder and persecution.

How far could I peer into my family's history to find the untold stories? My parents spoke little about the past. When they did, it was mostly about their recent personal experiences. Beyond that, almost total silence: a thick blanket stretching across time into nothingness.

I began my search by assembling the few family photographs and the carefully-preserved brittle documents in my possession and researching the history of those times in books and on the Internet. Still, there were numerous gaps in my knowledge. I turned to cousins living in Israel and New York, hoping they could provide some of the missing pieces of the puzzle. As new information was gleaned over long phone conversations, I realized that, like me, my cousins remembered little beyond their own generation.

The number three has been decisive in my story. My life is akin to a play in three acts performed in three different languages, on stages set on three continents. And many of my paintings are in three panels — triptychs. As I began this memoir, it presented itself in the shape of a play in three acts conceived by an impatient playwright with no clear script. I was unprepared for the creative difference between painting and writing. In painting, the details are seen in their entirety throughout the creative process. The writer, on the other hand, covers page after page with words and sentences that have to be read one by one and never seen at a single glance. The singular element foreign to painting, but inextricably linked with writing, is the element of time. One needs a certain time to read a book, while a painting may be seen in seconds, minutes or hours, according to the viewer's wishes. The hackneyed phrase that 'an image is worth one thousand words' may well be true, but along with my paintings, now I need those thousand words to tell my stories. This memoir is an attempt to shine some light into the nooks and crannies of a journey that pointed me inexorably towards a final destination: art.

ACT I
ROMANIA

Chapter 1

Beginning

I was born in my parents' bed on April 11, 1935, just as the grandfather clock in our house struck three. Had I believed in magic, I might easily imagine that a fairy godmother was present at the exact moment of my birth, one who would protect me from the impending storm about to draw Europe in a vortex of death and destruction.

One month earlier, on March 16, in violation of the Treaty of Versailles Adolf Hitler had announced German rearmament and reintroduced compulsory military service. On September 15, the Nuremberg Laws went into effect in Germany, stripping German Jews of their citizenship rights. The Nazis used a pseudoscientific theory for racial discrimination against Jews: people were classified as Jews if they descended from three or four Jewish grandparents, even if some of their family had converted to Christianity. A person with one or two Jewish grandparents was a *mischling*, a crossbreed of 'mixed blood', many of whom ended up in the death camps along with full-blooded Jews.

I was definitely born a Jew. My parents decided that I would remain an only child since the world had become too dangerous a place for Jewish children. Obviously, they did not believe in fairy tales. Years later, my mother casually mentioned undergoing thirteen abortions rather than bring another child into those dangerous times.

By 1935, the fascist Legion of the Archangel Michael, better known as the Iron Guard, dominated the political scene in Romania. Led by Corneliu Codreanu, it was responsible for some of the most brutal persecutions of Romanian Jews, starting with the massacre of prominent members of the Jewish community in Bucharest.

These facts were unknown to me since my parents never discussed them in my presence. I learned the gory details years later when I read *The Silent Holocaust: Romania and Its Jews* by I.C. Butnaru, which I found in a pile of discounted books in the gift shop of the United States Holocaust Memorial Museum in Washington, DC. Full of trepidation, not having ever encountered any books discussing the fate of the Romanian Jews, I bought it and began reading. It was a shocking revelation. I had been unaware of the extent of the destruction perpetrated by the Romanians themselves against their own Jewish population. It had been a 'silent' Holocaust indeed — Romania has consistently denied its part in the ruthless annihilation of its Jews, putting the blame on the Germans.

In 1940, the first pogrom by the Iron Guard raged in Bucharest. Ion Gigurtu's cabinet adopted Romania's equivalent to the Nuremberg Laws, forbidding Jewish-Christian intermarriage and defining Jews by racial criteria.

I was five years old. My parents and grandparents were all Jewish.

Chapter 2

Memory Snapshots

Memory . . . is the diary that we all carry about with us.

Oscar Wilde
The Importance of Being Earnest

MEMORY SNAPSHOT ONE: FIRST IMAGE OF BEAUTY

The rhythmic tinkling of bells on the necks of the horses pulling the open sleigh through heavy snow is music to my ears as I sit between my parents, covered with blankets against the cold. I look up and around me as the sleigh swiftly travels through a white fairyland of snow and ice. Trees throw their arms up to the sky like worshippers carved in a delicate wood engraving. Rich patterns of shimmering snow hang over the treetops like curtains of lace lovingly woven by a benevolent magician while a silver blanket with mauve shadows covers a silent, enchanted world. Everywhere below and above, millions of diamonds sparkle as the sun reflects in the white crystals. This forest is truly an enchanted place, a place of beauty carved in my childish memory.

I am very young, perhaps three years old. The war has not yet started. The time and place will be lost in time, but the image will survive inside my mind.

Memory Snapshot Two: First skill

The shiny red ribbon I clutch in my small, awkward fingers is as slippery as a silvery fish. My helper patiently shows me how to hold the ribbon, how to slip it through the knot and then pull tight to create a neat bow.

After a few trials, suddenly success! I proudly show the bow to everyone who is willing to look. First triumph of dexterity — my first skill acquired through hard work, carved in memory.

I am still very young, not yet four years old. The helper is my nanny, *Fräulein* Mina. She will soon be gone. And the war is about to begin.

Memory Snapshot Three: First taste of the forbidden

Fräulein Mina, my German Catholic nanny, takes me to church. I am entranced by the mystery and the beauty of the place. The stained-glass windows glow in rich red, blue and gold, the silver chalice and the mysterious perfume of incense, the robes and the music — all these make me feel as if I have stepped into a fairy tale where miracles can happen. I try to ignore the tortured, bleeding body of the man hanging on the cross, not understanding why he is there among all the lavish displays of richness and beauty. I don't ask. It is a secret between my nanny and me. I love secrets.

But this is not the right place for a Jewish girl. Mother finds out and puts a stop to these pleasant escapades.

First knowledge of the forbidden, carved in memory.

Memory Snapshot Four: First fear

November 11, 1940. A deafening noise like a roaring engine races through the house. Everything is shaking: the walls, the windows, the objects on shelves and tables. Books fall off the bookcase, there is the sound of broken glass, the lamps on the ceiling swing wildly.

Is a powerful giant, a huge vengeful golem, heavily treading through the rooms destroying everything in his way? As mother scoops me from my bed, the plaster from the ceiling comes crashing down in a waterfall of solid white matter. Dust is everywhere. The large bronze sculpture of Aphrodite in the entrance hall lies on the floor like a metal corpse. Everyone is rushing and screaming, "Earthquake! Earthquake!" My throat chokes on the overwhelming panic of the world collapsing around me.

Then, quiet. It is over. The house still stands.

First fear, carved in memory. The year is 1940. The war lurks like a viper about to spring.

MEMORY SNAPSHOT FIVE: FIRST ASSERTION OF PRINCIPLE

1940. The war is on. In Germany, Hitler has embarked on his mad crusade to destroy the Jews and conquer the world, but the world keeps quiet. Chamberlain has ignored the clear message of Hitler's book, *Mein Kampf,* and Czechoslovakia has been sacrificed on the altar of appeasement.

Everybody is glued to the radio — anxiety, like a spreading plague, is written on worried faces. I don't understand why everyone whispers when I enter the room. What are they hiding from me? *Fräulein* Mina disappears from my life, like a deleted icon on a computer screen. Where did she go? My mother tells me that a German person is not allowed to work for a Jewish family. I miss her a lot.

I am five years old and my language is German. My *Brothers Grimm* fairy tales, printed in spiky Gothic letters, with their beautiful illustrations of ogres, princes and princesses, are my favourite treasures. But no more, I announce, gravely pulling myself up to the height of my five-year-old frame, "I won't speak German anymore, because the Germans are killing our people. From now on, I shall speak Romanian only." From now on, the world is a changed place.

First awareness of the weight of principles, carved in memory.

One wonders why certain images are saved in the hidden folds of one's brain, while others vanish as if wiped out by a wet cloth moving across the blackboard of memory. Here are a few more snapshots that survived intact.

Memory Snapshot Six: First encounter with enchantment

My love of mountains and forests begins with an early memory from when I was less than five years old.

My parents, grandparents, aunts and uncles all walk in the forest, leaning on beautifully-carved wooden sticks common in the Carpathians. Unexpectedly, I find myself alone in the centre of a small clearing enclosed by tall fir trees. The grass, dotted with little daisies like so many fallen stars, is soft underfoot. It is quiet, so quiet that I can hear my heart beating. Only the melodious song of a bird, hidden among the branches, breaks this silence — and then is gone. I cannot see the sun, but its rays penetrate the canopy and create a spectacular show of brilliant white beams where tiny insects dance, fluttering and shining like drops of liquid gold. It is one of the happiest memories of my life. Sometimes I wonder if it really happened.

Memory Snapshot Seven: First awareness of social tact

The whole family is walking together on a well-worn path near a resort in the Carpathians. Jenica, my grandmother's sister, is with us. There is much talking and joking. Someone tells a joke that seems to be unbearably funny and everybody bursts into laughter. We all stop walking. It is impossible to proceed while everyone is bent over, laughing uncontrollably. I am standing near Aunt Jenica, who is leaning against a wall, tears of laughter streaming down her cheeks. Being the smallest in the group and therefore the closest to the ground, I notice a shocking sight: a small puddle has materialized at my aunt's feet and it is growing by the minute, as she shakes with laughter. She cannot stop and desperately tries to keep her legs together to arrest the flow, with no success. Everybody sees it, but tactfully ignores the accident and we all walk on.

MEMORY SNAPSHOT EIGHT: FIRST AWARENESS OF TRUE LOVE

To my mother's dismay, a large number of pigeons take up residence in our yard. She constantly complains about the noise and the droppings that cover the small terrace, but I love those birds and watch their courtship rituals for hours on end. They go like this: the male raises his head high, emits loud grunts and puffs up his chest until it resembles a small balloon, greatly increasing his size in width and height. He repeatedly circles the seemingly indifferent female, his head bobbing up and down, his voice getting louder and louder. It looks like hard work to me, as he keeps this up for a long time. I never know how the female signals her acceptance. She seems quite bored and is busily pecking some grain off the ground and paying no attention to her hard-working suitor. But then suddenly, *poof!* There he is, right on top of her, energetically doing what he meant to do all along. This activity is of such short duration that it could be missed if one blinked.

Pigeons remain faithful forever.

One day, we hear a great commotion, a desperate flapping of wings and loud cries, unlike any we have heard before. Rushing out, we see a hawk clutching a dove in his talons, high in the air. We yell and throw stones at the predator until he finally decides that the whole affair is not worth his while, drops his prey and flies away. Sadly, it is too late — the poor pigeon is dead. Her mate grieves day after day, cooing softly and sadly. He stops eating and dies soon after of a broken heart.

I'll never cease to marvel that seventy years later, I can still remember these events of my childhood. In the midst of the greatest disaster experienced by my people in Europe, my family existed in a bubble of precarious and temporary safety. Perhaps the fairy godmother present at my birth was real after all.

Chapter 3

The Play Begins

*All the world's a stage. And all the men
and women merely players.*

William Shakespeare
As You Like It

Before the curtain goes up, let me describe the stage set and the historic elements woven in the fabric of the play about to open.

The first act began in Moldova, a piece of land in Eastern Europe which had changed hands numerous times like a coveted toy pulled from hand to hand by greedy children. Europe was no stranger to such shifts in real estate. Entire countries were split up after senseless wars and put together again by new rulers who knew very little about the local populations and cared even less about their history, their culture and their wishes. Names of countries were changed and foreign languages imposed. Without moving from one's birthplace, one could suddenly be living in a different country, forced to speak a different language and having to swear allegiance to different rulers.

Moldova, a large landlocked area east of the Carpathian Mountains and wedged between Romania and the Ukraine, was such a place. Like a constantly oscillating yo-yo, the eastern part of Moldova was seized from the Turkish Ottoman Empire, annexed by the Russian Empire in 1812 and renamed Bassarabia. In 1918, it was briefly independent, only to be annexed by the Soviet Union as the Autonomous Moldavian Soviet Socialist Republic in 1924. As an ally of Germany, Romania re-conquered Bassarabia in 1941, only to lose it again to the Russians before the end of the war. Finally, in 1991, in yet another historical twist, this tortured land declared its independence and reinstated the Romanian language. It's enough to make one's head spin!

During those seismic upheavals, the Jews were the perennial losers. Rabid anti-Semitism left them as defenseless as leaves blowing in the wind, with no protection, rights or citizenship.

At the International Congress of Berlin of 1878, ending the Russo-Turkish war, the nations of Europe recognized the difficult situation of Jews and other minorities and forced Romania to accept all its ethnic population as full citizens. Grudgingly, the country removed the article in its constitution banning Jewish citizenship but, in reality, they did all they could to make the naturalization process extremely cumbersome, requiring approval of Parliament in each individual case and a personal petition from the applicants with proof they did not hold any other citizenship, with the result that very few Jews were naturalized.

Knowing the historical facts helps to gain a better understanding of the times, but dry statistics do not pull at the emotional heartstrings. For me, the general history became personal only when I held in my hands the fragile documents my father had saved. Only now, after learning the history, do those documents become real, telling the story of what it meant for a Jewish family to acquire and hold on to Romanian citizenship. My great-grandparents and their families had lived during these troubled times in this dangerous and unforgiving land. The difficult past was a closed book they never mentioned. It is nothing short of miraculous to me when I meet people who can trace their ancestry far back in time and who can search for their family's roots at the local church or town hall. Few Jews can do so.

Chapter 4

My Father's Side

The oldest document in my possession is the death certificate of Marcus Solomon, my father's grandfather. It was issued in the city of Bârlad, commune of Tutova in Romanian Moldova, dated January 7, 1913. In the text, handwritten in violet ink in tall, spiky cursive writing, I find the names of his parents, my great-great-grandparents Slomi and Beila Solomon, whom no one has ever mentioned — they too are lost to memory, joining the great army of ghosts who left no footprints behind.

Marcus Solomon was a storekeeper. From the fragile document, we learn that Marcus died at home, in 1913, at the age of fifty-seven, leaving behind his wife Etla and his son Iosif, born in 1880.

Iosif's birth certificate mysteriously describes him as being "of Ottoman protectorate", explaining my father's puzzling remark that our family came from Turkey.

Iosif later married Estera Graif. These were my grandparents.

This is the end of my family's history on my father's side, the farthest I could go in my search. Beyond these names, never mentioned by my father, there is a gaping hole.

From the same trove of handwritten documents, we learn that Iosif, also a storekeeper, died in 1917, at the age of thirty-four, at the Hospital No.1 of Contagious Diseases. What the document does not tell us is that he had been serving as a Romanian soldier in WWI and had died of typhoid fever, leaving behind his wife Estera and their two young children. Lascar was seven years old and Maria, his little sister, was five.

Lascar Solomon was my father.

Lascar   Estera and Iosif Solomon   Iosif

In the only photograph I have of Iosif and Estera together, the unsmiling couple is formally posing for their engagement picture in 1909. They shall have only eight years of marriage to enjoy, but for the moment they are together, just about to start a new life. Estera is seated, dressed in a long dark skirt and a high-necked white blouse with long sleeves, her hands demurely crossed in her lap. She looks directly into the camera. Her shiny black hair, raised high above her head like a crown, frames an oval face with pleasing symmetrical features. Estera is a very handsome woman indeed. Iosif is standing next to her looking grave, his arm leaning protectively on the back of her chair. He is wearing a three-piece suit and a shirt with a high stiff-necked collar. His receding hairline belies his young age but his regular features and small moustache suggest that he was an attractive young man.

Both are in their early twenties but seem much older due to their formal clothes and stiff pose. I never met my grandfather Iosif, but I could see his good looks and wavy hair mirrored in my father's face.

The photograph of my grandparents became a ghostly couple in my painting. The curtains slowly open on the first act of the play.

Reflections — detail
1983 | mixed media on paper | 30 × 22 in | 76 × 56 cm

Chapter 5

My Mother's Side

Life is the art of drawing without an eraser.

John W. Gardner
quoted in *Cracking the Code of Our Physical Universe*
by Matthew M. Radmanesh

I know little about grandfather Leon, my mother's father. Conversations with him were brief and to the point — he never spent any significant time with his grandchildren. We vaguely knew that he came from somewhere in Moldova, one of those Eastern European lands that history tossed back and forth like a soccer ball between Turkey, Russia and Romania.

Leon was in his early twenties and living in Brăila when he married Perla Paulina Loebel and opened the small dry goods store he called 'La Moldoveanu', reflecting his Moldovan origin. The formal photograph on the right was probably taken at the time

Leon as a young man

of his marriage. Four daughters, Any, Reghina, Carola and Frida, were born to the young couple in quick succession in the cramped house above the store on Strada Regală.

Carola was my mother.

Paulina's Story

When Paulina became pregnant for the fifth time, she panicked at the possibility of adding yet another girl to the family. Her story is the sad, universal tale of unwanted pregnancies that women still experience all over the planet. A trusted midwife was secretly summoned to help dispose of the baby.

I never learned the details of the traumatic events of that fateful day, but could easily imagine the woman's arrival at the house. I see her climbing the stairs leading to the small bedroom where Paulina is lying on the double bed. I can almost hear the woman's voice uttering reassuring words, almost sense Paulina's anxiety and distress. Did the midwife use the age-old 'tool', the proverbial coat hanger, for this purpose? I never asked. All I know is that things went horribly wrong. It is not difficult to imagine the woman's fumbling hands trying to stabilize her 'instruments', her attempts to calm Paulina and finally, finally, her realization that the battle was lost, as her patient lay in her bed bleeding to death.

Paulina died that day, leaving her four small daughters motherless. The story of that tragic day has haunted me like a recurring nightmare. As a young girl, I kept thinking of those dark moments with a sense of panic, fear and doom. My childish imagination conjured a dark room dominated by the bed on which a young woman with black hair lay twisting in agony on the crumpled blood-stained sheets while the midwife desperately tried to stem the flow of blood. I imagined the screams filling the room and the terror of the woman who had been using the cold, hard coat hanger, helplessly watching as life oozed out of her patient. My mother, eight years old at the time of her mother's death, became an orphan at the same age as I was when she told me the story.

Curiously, she never recounted anything else about Paulina's life. It seemed that this traumatic death was the only memory she had of her own mother.

I was named Paula, in honour of my dead grandmother.

In my imagination, I conjured countless deaths and suffering in childbirth and abandoned babies. I even went so far as to imagine that I was a foundling who had lost her mother and was not my own parents' daughter.

And I was terrified of dying in childbirth myself.

One day I came across the only photograph of the grandmother I never knew and whose name, Pnina, the Hebrew translation of Perla, I now bear. She poses alone, dressed in a dark, long high-necked dress, her body turned sideways, but facing the viewer. Her black hair frames a full face, one with high cheekbones, heavy dark eyebrows and a sensuous, unsmiling mouth. She is in her early twenties, but looks older and is regal in her bearing. I recognize her thick eyebrows and high cheekbones in my own face.

Paulina, my mother's mother

Brought to life on a sheet of Fabriano paper, the grandmother I never knew stands erect, resembling an unworldly apparition about to vanish into the void, her severe gaze directed somewhere outside the frame. Billowing curtains are about to close, ending her brief appearance as a cameo in the play. Three rows of black-and-white roses grow silently under her feet — a last offering from the granddaughter she never lived to see.

Portrait of Grandmother as a Young Woman is my salute to this woman who gave birth to my mother and her sisters. Hers is the sad, but not unusual, story of women who made their own difficult choices and paid with their lives.

Portrait of Grandmother as a Young Woman
1983 | mixed media on paper | 30 × 22 in | 76 × 56 cm

Chapter 6

A 'Blended' Family

Life calls the tune, we dance.

John Galsworthy
Five Tales

Having lost his young wife, Leon was left alone to manage his business while taking care of his four small, motherless daughters. Raising the girls alone proved too difficult. He appealed to a well-connected matchmaker whose registry reached far and wide, including Jewish communities in other towns.

While this drama unfolded in Brăila, a similar scenario in reverse took place in the Moldovan city of Tecuci, home of the Solomons, my father's parents.

Iosif and Estera's happy marriage had been cut short when Iosif died and Estera was left alone to run the store and raise her two children.

How an enterprising matchmaker succeeded in making the connection between these two widowers living in different cities, how they met and how they decided to set up a new household together is not known. A deal was made and so it came to pass that Estera Solomon arrived in Brăila with her two children, Lascar and Maria, to become Estera Herscovici.

Soon after this marriage, a child was born: a boy named Friedrich and nicknamed 'Fridirel'. There were now seven children to care for.

What was life like in this large family? What kind of games did they play? What schools did they go to? How did Leon's daughters relate to their new stepmother and her children? None of them are still alive, except for ninety-year-old Fridirel, now Freddy, who lives in Tel-Aviv.

This formal family picture below was probably taken in 1924, after Freddy's birth. Leon, only forty years old, looks more like the grandfather of the new baby. Estera, although still a beautiful woman, is overweight and has lost her youthful looks. Estera's children, Lascar and Maria, are on the far left, followed by Frida, the youngest sister. Any, already a well-developed adolescent, stands in the centre, with Reghina and Carola on the right. The girls are identically dressed in Tyrolean dresses, save Any, who wears a fancy adult dress and a string of pearls. My mother, Carola, is thirteen years old and Any, at almost seventeen, is only months away from being married off.

Not unlike other family pictures, this photograph conveys a happy image. It is also a screen that conceals the conflicts, loves and tensions of everyday life.

My parents' blended family, from left to right: Maria, Lascar, Frida, Estera, Any, Friedrich, Leon, Reghina, Carola

There were more photographs in the old album. In one of them, four girls dressed in their best outfits are posing for a group picture.

They sit close together, staring pensively into the camera. Carola leans on the edge of a white bench with a curved, slatted high back, hugging little Frida, who is comfortably nested against her shoulder, while Reghina stands behind. Any sits by herself on an upholstered chair holding a book in her lap, perhaps to show off her love of learning.

Four sisters: Any, Reghina, Carola and Frida

In this other black-and-white picture, Carola, then a small girl of four or five, her round face framed by neatly combed straight dark hair gathered by two ribbons, perches on a chair too high for her. Her older sister Any, stands next to her — looking serious, almost angry, and slightly bored. Photography was a slow process: the small girls had to hold their pose for a long time, making a long-lasting smile difficult. Both girls have their dark bangs combed in a straight line across their foreheads. Both would become blondes as adults.

Any and Carola

19

Two Sisters
1983 | mixed media on paper | 30 × 22 in | 76 × 56 cm

Chapter 7

A Love Story

Who, being loved, is poor?

Oscar Wilde
A Woman of No Importance

My parents married for love. What's so special about this, you may ask. Nothing really, except that the year was 1933, when most Jewish marriages were done through the services of a matchmaker and love was not mentioned in any of these transactions. Also special, because of one small detail: the two lovers were brother and sister.

"What? Have I heard you correctly?" you ask in horror. "Did you say 'brother and sister'?" Well, yes, in a way, but not quite. I should have said stepbrother and sister. Blended family and all that, you know…

Marry for love? Unheard of! Outrageous! Impractical! Not done!

My mother relished retelling the story whenever the opportunity arose. It was a Jewish *Romeo and Juliet* tale, with all the drama, rejections, suspense and tribulations of a Shakespearean tragedy, but with a fairytale-like happily-ever-after ending.

Here is another gem, a rare element in any marriage: one might say with utmost certainty that the lovers knew each other well

Young Lascar before his father's death

before tying the knot. Following a childhood spent together under the same roof, there were no surprises in store about one another's character and temperament.

Few photos of my father as a child survive. In one of the earliest, he is five years old, not yet fatherless and wearing a white sailor suit.

We see him again as an adolescent of seventeen or so (long before 'teenager' appeared in the lexicon). He sits next to his mother, who is hugging his little brother. Lascar is serious, almost grim, wearing his lyceum, or high school, uniform and a cap with a shiny black visor. This relaxed pose is taken outdoors next to a tree, unlike the earlier stiff studio-posed photographs. Estera is smiling with real pleasure in the company of her two sons. By this time, she has put on weight and acquired a matronly look very different from the young and beautiful fiancée in the photographs of years past.

Lascar, Estera and Fridirel

Lascar became a handsome young man with big dreams. His charm lay in the features he had inherited from his father: a straight nose, blue-green eyes the colour of cedar leaves, and wavy light-brown hair that he always tried to smooth down by wearing a ridiculous black hair-net while sleeping. He managed to keep his good looks until he died in Vancouver at the age of eighty-three.

Lascar showed musical talent in his youth, but when

he asked his parents for violin lessons, they felt that it was more appropriate for a young man to play the piano. And so he did. He became so proficient that he was employed as an accompanist to silent movies in the local movie theatre. A particular section of "Rosamunde" by Schubert that my father later played for me was the music of choice for scary episodes. To this day, my father stands next to me whenever I hear it.

I have fond memories of the concerts we played in my parents' bedroom, with my father at the piano and me on the accordion, my mother the only person in the audience.

After graduating from the lyceum, Lascar expressed his wish to become an engineer.

"An engineer?" his stepfather said. "I need you in the store to be my accountant and this is what you'll study!"

And so it was.

Carola's wish to learn English was also rejected by her parents, who made her study French instead.

In those times, the family structure was strict and hierarchical. Parents had absolute power over their children's lives, imposing on them what they should study, if anything at all. They chose the partners for their sons and daughters, expecting them to obey without argument — in short, the parents made all the major decisions. The children's wishes were irrelevant.

Carola's sisters had been married off to wealthy men through the services of a matchmaker and she was expected to follow their example. However, she and Lascar had other plans: they were in love and dreamed of getting married, in direct opposition to their parents' plans that involved only financial security — and not romance.

Carola Herscovici

Since Lascar and Carola both were their children, Estera and Leon saw such a marriage as a useless transfer of dowry money literally from one pocket into another, instead of benefiting the family with an influx of new funds from an outside candidate.

A matchmaker was called in, resulting in the introduction of an older well-to-do man as Carola's prospective husband. In contrast to Lascar, who was only one year older than her, the new candidate was most unappealing in her eyes: he was short, showing the beginning of a small belly and his glistening scalp was ominously peeking through his thinning hair. She vetoed the match after the first meeting, only to be offered another similar choice soon after.

My parents' wedding picture

Here the story reaches its melodramatic peak. Carola threatened to run away, announcing that she was prepared to jump into the Danube and drown — she could not swim. Lascar bought a gun and threatened to shoot himself. Faced with such fierce opposition, the parents conceded and the two lovers were allowed to marry at last. It seems that mothers and fathers do not always know best. The future would show that this match was truly made in heaven.

The price for a young couple's rebellion against parental authority was high. Unlike her sisters, Carola did not receive a dowry. Maria was given a house, while her brother and stepsister got nothing and they never owned their own home in Brăila.

With my mother's tireless retelling, this story became a parable of the power of love over money. It was not surprising that her constant moralizing on this theme irritated her sisters, who came to resent her. Not missing any opportunity to point out that her happiness was due to love and not money spread a frosty blanket over their relationship, which lasted for many years.

Not having experienced true love had surely affected my mother's sisters, who did not appreciate Carola's harping on her own happiness. On the other hand, not having her sisters' financial security had most probably allowed the snake of envy to inject its poison in my mother's ears as well. Only when Any and Frida visited Carola in Vancouver during the last decade of their lives did the sisters finally make their peace. But did all these squabbles really matter in the long run? My parents married for love!

Chapter 8

The House

You can go other places, all right — you can live on the other side of the world, but you can't ever leave home.

Sue Monk Kidd
The Mermaid Chair

Houses are secret realms of fantasy and imagination for children.

When I was five, we moved to a big house on Strada Grădinii Mare, the Street of the Big Garden, built by an Italian architect whose initials are enshrined to this day on the wrought-iron gate. Our Greek landlords were the Litzikas, who had rented out their house and moved away. I never saw Mr. Litzika. It was only his wife who returned from time to time to check on their belongings locked away in a few of the rooms. I was consumed with curiosity about the mysterious contents of these forbidden rooms but was never allowed to peek inside.

There was no art to speak of in our house. Except for a black-and-white etching of my mother's portrait, there was nothing. No pictures anywhere, not even posters. Family photographs, yes, quite a few of them, but nothing one could call 'art'. If there was a museum in our town, I was not aware of it and art was not a subject of discussion. There were only a few sculptural items in our house that I do remember, the most prominent one being an armless bronze sculpture of Aphrodite standing in the entrance hall.

Then there was the small ceramic fisherman sitting on a side table in the dining room. Dressed in Tyrolean shorts held up by decorated suspenders and a green hat atop his curly hair, he perched at the edge of a small pond, holding a fishing rod. Although intended to hold water, perhaps even a few goldfish, the miniature pond had never been used for this purpose. Instead, the dry cavity was filled to the brim with a great untidy pile of black-and-white photographs. The little fisherman was fated to stare wistfully into a fish-free pond and be content with inventing stories about the people in the photographs, his useless fishing rod catching only memories. I have no doubt that the long hours I spent sifting through this rich repository of visual family history, with the little fisherman as my sole companion, have given shape to many of my memories.

The third item that held a particular fascination for me was found in the house of my aunt Maria and uncle Sammy. A plump porcelain Buddha, elegantly decorated with patterns of blues, yellows, pinks and gold, was enthroned on a dresser in their bedroom. He sat cross-legged and stared directly into one's eyes, a perpetual smile on his painted red lips. He was dressed in a white, lavishly-patterned loose gown edged with gold trim. His head and dainty white hands were attached to the body with hidden wires that allowed a gentle up-and-down movement when lightly touched. But the greatest attraction was the sharp red tongue that would pop out of the dainty mouth when the head bobbed up and down. I always thought that this Buddha was precious, coming from an exotic, mysterious and far-away land. I never missed a chance to touch its head and hands and watch the tongue bobbing, the hands moving and the head nodding as if to say "Yes, yes, yes."

A prosaic but vivid memory of beauty was the empty chocolate box on the table in my room. I have no recollection of its contents or origin, but the image on the lid is entrenched in my memory. A garden such as I had never seen before appeared on the cover with masses of flowers in riotous blues, purples, whites and yellows hanging over low stone walls. The paths in this garden were lined with flowering bushes in splashes of brilliant reds, pinks and mauves. In the background, a glimpse of water shimmered in the sun. This garden was the closest vision to paradise I could imagine. I wanted to be there, to walk among these flowers and immerse myself in this rich tapestry. Was this real? Could such flowers possibly grow on Earth? And if they did exist, where did they grow?

While writing these lines about my old home, I became possessed by a strong desire to see it again. Fortunately, we live now in a world in which the human brain has opened up the whole Earth with the invention of the Internet. Full of trepidation, I sat down in front of my computer and clicked on Google Earth. Would the house on Strada Grădinii Mare still be there? Had Google unleashed its motorized snoops on the streets I used to walk as a child and if so, could I hitch a ride with them? I typed in the location and watched in awe as the map of the city appeared on my screen. I clicked again and in the blink of an eye I was on the street leading to the house. I followed the arrows that virtually walked me along the Strada Golești, turned the corner towards the Grădina Publică, the public garden, and there it was: the same massive foundation stones, the windows with their decorative carved stone gables and the wrought-iron gate. I could clearly see the two windows of my room in the corner of the house, next to the windows of my parents' bedroom.

Our house on Strada Grădinii Mare

Strada Golești was a long street lined with acacia trees laden with clusters of fragrant white flowers hanging down like lacy decorations. I knew that street well. I used to walk it every day on my way to Sancta Maria, the private Catholic school I began attending in the third grade, where the nuns ran the only non-Jewish school that accepted Jewish students during the war.

Across the street, directly facing our house, was the public garden. As I grew older, this garden became my private green space. My cousin Gabi and I often played in the shade of its trees and skipped about on the large, leafy paths. One of our favourite games was scooping up one of the numerous snails leaving behind its sticky trail in the grass. The moment we picked it up, the snail would disappear inside its little house. Our game consisted of singing a rhyming ditty that begged the small creature to come out and show us its tiny horns. We had to be patient and wait until the snail forgot where it was and timidly crawled out of its safe residence, painting a silvery path across our outstretched palms.

Snails were beautiful and mysterious creatures for us, a miracle of nature. They were self-sufficient and well-protected in the turban-like homes they carried on their backs, decorated with elegant, brown and beige swirls. It never occurred to us to think of them as garden pests!

Irises growing in the roundabout in the centre of our yard provided Gabi and I with a wonderful game. Plucking out the long sword-like leaves of the flowers, we pretended they were elegant epées for duelling over fair ladies. One of us, usually myself, took on the part of the gallant knight in shining armour, which suited me just fine. Gabi played the part of the damsel in distress, waiting for me, the brave warrior, to save her from whatever danger she was in.

Our house was L-shaped, with the kitchen at the back facing the large courtyard and the gate to the street. The front entrance was reached from the courtyard. At the top of five low marble steps, a handsome carved wooden door with sandblasted decorative glass panels opened into a vestibule dominated by the bronze Aphrodite. The walls and high ceilings throughout the house were painted in soft, creamy pastel colours and finished with curvaceous Art Nouveau decorations along the ceilings. The tall bedroom windows facing the street were covered at night with heavy wooden shutters.

On one side of the large dining room was a door leading onto a long poorly-lit hallway that connected the main part of the house with what must have once been the servants' quarters and the kitchen. A few of the doors along this hallway were always locked, hiding mysterious objects belonging to Madame Litzika.

The hallway ended in two flights of stairs near the kitchen: one descending into a cool and dark cellar, the second climbing up to the attic, a large space stretching the length of the house, full of dust and cobwebs hanging from heavy rafters. Onions and potatoes, the only vegetables available during the cold winter months, were stored in the cellar in wooden boxes filled with sand.

Towards the end of the war, whenever the screaming sirens announced the approaching American planes, we would scramble down the stairs into the cellar and cower in the darkness at the sound of falling bombs, our hearts beating like the flapping wings of terrified birds. After a while, the hysterical sound of sirens, the deep quivering bass of the approaching planes and the grand finale of explosions became a recurring and familiar nightmare.

Impossible as it may seem, despite the worry and the uncertainty of war, I remember the nine years spent in this house as happy ones. I felt secure, never doubting that my mother was endowed with magical powers to stave off any possible calamity.

A rare oasis in the eye of the hurricane, Brăila was a city where most Jews would somehow survive the disasters of war.

Chapter 9

Coloured Pencils: First Foray into Art Business

Every artist was first an amateur.

Ralph Waldo Emerson
Letters and Social Aims: Progress of Culture

Children are fertile fields awaiting planting. Every word, any gesture, a smile or a frown, a gift offered, a stern or loving look, a melody, a whiff of perfume, a taste of food — all these fall like windblown seeds into the furrows of the child's soul where they grow into vigorous plants or wither without a trace, creating the adult person the child will become.

It might have been my birthday on the morning when I saw a small package on the table in my room, wrapped in shiny gold paper and elegantly tied with red ribbon. Inside I found a slim metal container of coloured pencils with the brand, 'Koh-i-Noor', after the famous diamond, boldly printed on the lid. Opening the box, I saw a wondrous sight: snugly lying side-by-side like babies in a cradle were smartly-sharpened pencils in all the colours of the rainbow. If colour could be music, these hues — ranging from white to brilliant yellows to lively oranges, from flaming reds to warm browns — would be a heavenly orchestra!

There were pink, red and purple pencils, light and dark green ones and a gamut of blues, getting darker and darker until they reached the black pencil at the edge of the box. The yellows were like graceful piccolos and the oranges were violins; the reds evoked energetic trumpets, while the pinks and violets were like romantic lutes and harps; then came the velvety cello blues, followed by the green drums. Lastly, the darkest blues and blacks filled my ears with the deep, reassuring sound of the bass. How wonderful! I shall be the composer who creates music with colours instead of musical instruments!

What is more, over this wondrous array of hues hovered the delicious smell of freshly sharpened pencils. Even now, my heart skips a beat when I encounter coloured pencils on the shelf of an art supply store or when I smell the distinctive perfume of newly sharpened pencils. A feeling I can only describe as pleasure, delight, anticipation and excitement takes hold of me and I instantly remember that day.

Was this gift the seed that made me fall in love with art? Were my first childish drawings of fairytale princes and princesses, magic dragons, little dwarves, mushrooms, elves and flowers the early heralds of my future as an artist, triggered by this wonderful gift from my parents?

I used the pencils with great care, sharpening them when they became blunt, always returning them in the right order to their home in the box and often sniffing the perfume of the sharpened leads when the box was open.

The illustrations in my fairy tales became an inspiration for myself and my Gentile friend Mary Banos. We began drawing our own version of the stories, without a thought to the dark side of vicious ogres and scary dragons. Quite the contrary, a shiver of excitement ran down our spines when the valiant prince saved the princess from her tormentors and everyone lived happily ever after.

Our first exhibition was soon ready. We stuck the finished drawings on the walls and proudly invited our parents to the *vernissage*. I should mention that these exhibitions were always a smashing success!

Not only was I making art, I was also an avid collector. Whenever I could, I would buy the shiny cheap pictures that were like the hockey cards or stickers that kids collect in Canada today. I pasted them carefully in a large scrapbook and spent many hours turning the pages and admiring them. The variety of colours and shapes gave me never-ending pleasure. There were stickers of flowers: bouquets of forget-me-not, lilac, daisies, roses and lilies. There were bunnies, ponies, cherubs, angels and cute maidens. I had assembled an impressive collection of the prettiest and most sentimental kitsch imaginable. I could never get enough of those pink angels, little girls with straw hats and curly hair, puppies and kittens. My greed for enlarging this collection knew no bounds, but the meagre resources of a second-grader were never enough to satisfy my collector's passion.

While pondering my lack of funds, an exciting thought flashed through my mind: if my friends were willing to buy the small mass-produced sticker images, they might like to acquire real 'originals' drawn by me. I could trace the illustrations from my fairy tales, colour them by hand with my precious Koh-i-Noor pencils and offer them for sale. Plagiarism, you say? The word was Chinese to me.

Picture making became a consuming passion in the seventh year of my life. Not just a passion, but also a naïve belief that others might get as excited as myself about the images I was creating.

Where would I find the young collectors wanting to acquire those rare and precious images? In my own school, of course! And why were they so rare and so special? Because one could get them from one source only: me!

And so, in grade two, I enthusiastically embarked on this artistic business adventure. I loved tracing the beautiful illustrations from the Brothers Grimm and Charles Perrault fairy tales — blonde princesses and knights in shiny armour, vicious dragons spewing columns of orange flames from their huge nostrils, and dangerous sorcerers wearing tall pointy hats and flowing black robes intoning powerful spells by waving their magic wands.

After copying the outline, I coloured the drawings in hues of my own choice. It didn't take me long to build up a substantial portfolio.

The first collection was ready. Now I had to find the best way to market it.

The school was in an old building with creaky brown wooden floors. The classrooms were upstairs, accessible by a wide staircase, the obvious location for my business venture. I saw myself standing at the top of those stairs, holding my drawings up for sale and wondering if anyone would buy. Happily, I had found a captive market! My schoolmates loved the drawings and were willing to pay the bargain price I charged. Business was brisk. I sold cheap, for just a few *lei*, and my friends were snapping them up.

It was exciting while it lasted. I don't remember how long I managed to keep my first 'gallery' in operation and I don't recall how the news of my flourishing endeavour reached my mother. The result was a business disaster — my mother nipped my career as a young entrepreneurial artist in the bud and my great adventure came to a screeching halt. I filed this mishap away as an example of a great injustice, as I could not understand what was wrong with my marketing initiative. Ironically, today my efforts would most probably be labeled as a 'start-up'.

Ten years later in Israel, when I painted cuckoo clocks and lampshades for children's rooms to help my parents through difficult times, they heartily welcomed my efforts. But that would happen on another continent in the second act of the play.

Years would pass before I would become a 'real' illustrator and a serious painter. Instead of tracing the illustrations from my books, I would be drawing my own.

It all began with a small box of Koh-i-Noor coloured pencils . . .

Chapter 10

My Cousin and I

Childhood is the one story that stands by itself in every soul.

Ivan Doig
The Whistling Season

In an early photograph, my cousin Gabi and I are sixteen months old; squinting at the sun, we sit on the sand wearing identical sun hats and little beach suits with colourful anchor patterns.

Year after year, photographs show us wearing similar dresses. With only two weeks between us, we were inseparable and as close as sisters. We played and went to school together

Gabi and I in identical costumes

and shared deep and important secrets. Before telephones were forbidden to Jews, we would call each other every morning and discuss what to wear so that we could be clad in similar attire. We continued this custom even after the war. Since ready-made clothes were unknown at the time, Madame Feinstein, the seamstress who worked for our parents, sewed us identical dresses.

Gabi and I were about eleven or twelve years old when we got into 'show business' creating a performance to which 'the public', or our families, was invited. It was great fun writing the poems and songs to be performed. We became playwrights, directors, actors, musicians and stage managers all at once and rehearsed the show with great enthusiasm. We wrote invitations, made up a poster and even produced admission tickets. The show was not free — oh no! We took our work as performers quite seriously and had to be paid, just as any performing artists.

When the day of the performance arrived, we stood at the entrance to welcome the crowds of spectators and later we morphed into ushers who showed the eager public to their seats. The performance took place at my house and the guests arrived on time. Our parents and a few aunts and uncles made their way up the five marble stairs leading to the vestibule where we stood selling tickets. Oh, yes, I forgot to mention the colourful programs that we made beforehand listing the details of the great performance. These were free with admission.

I am sorry to say that I don't remember any of the songs or skits we performed that day, but I do remember the applause and, most of all, our immense pleasure and excitement.

In my early youth, I was keenly aware that good looks had not been included in the gift package left behind by my imaginary fairy godmother. All in life being relative, I could not avoid comparing myself to my beautiful cousin Gabi, whose small upturned nose and red lips set in a pleasing oval face made her a delight to behold. Protected by long eyelashes, her eyes were emerald pools of liquid green. One felt compelled to hug her delicate doll-like body and to forgive her any misdeeds or naughty tricks. Being taller and slightly overweight, I felt big and clumsy standing next to her. I had no way of knowing that at age fifteen I would stop growing and Gabi would shoot up like a flower fertilized by a loving gardener, growing rapidly until the situation was inversed: she grew into a tall beauty, while I became the petite person I was meant to be.

Chapter 11

My Room, My Kingdom

It is a happy talent to know how to play.

Ralph Waldo Emerson
Emerson in His Journals

My room was my domain, my refuge and my kingdom — where I played, read, dreamt wild plots and strange adventures and painted my pictures. In winter, before I fell asleep, the high stove of green shiny tiles in the corner would be stoked with wood and I'd watch the reflection of the flames dancing on the ceiling until my eyes closed. In the morning, in the now icy-cold room, my mother would wake me up and slide warm socks on my feet beneath the covers.

The furniture in my room was painted green. My bed was a divan, the Turkish word describing a low, wider-than-usual daybed with an upholstered roll at the head. Each night my mother made my bed with the sheets and the pillow stored in a large box behind the divan. In the morning, after airing the sheets on the open window, she would return them to the box and my bed became a divan again.

A square table covered with a floor-length tablecloth occupied the centre of the room. Gabi and I spent many happy hours hiding with our toys in the womblike space under the table, pretending that we were in distant lands and having great adventures. We made up countless stories and intricate plays in which our dolls were the principal actors. It was difficult to leave that world when my mother called, ordering us back to reality.

Make-believe and fairy tales were my favourite games. There was no television in Romania, so imagination ran wild. Among a large number of lavishly-illustrated children's books, I loved the Brothers Grimm tales printed in the spiky German-Gothic type, the La Fontaine fables and the Charles Perrault stories of *Cinderella* and *Sleeping Beauty*. The cruelty of these tales did not bother us at all — they were just stories!

The Adventures of Max and Moritz, written by William Busch in 1865, long before the age of political correctness, stands out in my memory. Seven rollicking stories in lively rhyme tell the adventures of two wicked boys who play unspeakably-evil tricks on everyone in town. When a farmer they cheated finally catches them, the story reaches its climax. The farmer takes Max and Moritz to the miller, who grinds them into coarse millet, later to be eaten up by a pair of geese. These dreadful depictions of the boys being ground up did not strike us as cruel at all. We thought it was a funny and a well-deserved punishment for those imps. As a delightful revenge, the story ended with these lines:

> *Through the place in short there went*
> *One wide murmur of content:*
> *"God be praised! The town is free*
> *From this great rascality!"*

Chapter 12

What am I? Jewish Identity

Pessimism is a luxury that a Jew can never allow himself.

Golda Meir
quoted in *The Observer* (December 29, 1974)

Being Jewish was an inescapable fact of life. As a very young child, I did not understand its meaning although it was clear to me that whatever it was, it made us different from other people and included an element of latent danger.

The hushed adult conversations about dire things happening or about to happen around us did not mean much to me. I was blessed with the happy ignorance of a young child whose world was limited to the narrow confines of the family. However, as I grew older and the time for school arrived, this otherness became apparent. In 1940, Jewish children were banned from public schools, thus setting them apart. Growing up in a secular family with a socialist father uninterested in religious matters, I had not considered myself different and began developing a sense of injustice.

My grandfather Leon, a tall, slightly-overweight balding man with a greying moustache, visited the synagogue only for the high holidays, accompanied by the family. Even then, prayer was probably not the main reason he frequented the holy place. He spent most of the time schmoozing with friends, more interested in the social interaction than in communicating with God. And on Yom Kippur, the Day of Atonement, the holiest day of fast and repentance in the Jewish religion, I would spy him in the kitchen getting a quick snack before setting off to the synagogue.

The Days of Awe, the days between and including Rosh Hashanah and Yom Kippur, are all about repentance and forgiveness. To atone for sins against God, prayer was enough. But to atone for sins against another person, one had first to seek reconciliation with that person, righting the wrongs committed against them if at all possible. That had to be done before Yom Kippur.

The bizarre ritual of atonement, the *Kapparah*, was observed in my grandparents' house, but not in mine. A live cock (or was it a hen?) was brought inside, its legs tied together, frantically flapping its wings and cackling wildly. The hapless bird was held upside-down above our heads and moved in a circular motion while Hebrew prayers asking for forgiveness were chanted over the screeching of the distraught fowl. This was the convenient way of transferring our sins onto the innocent rooster, leaving us free of past misdemeanours and ready to embark upon new sins. Much as I tried, I could not think of any sins that we children were guilty of. We considered this ritual a weird and entertaining aspect of the holiday.

The few religious activities I remember took place at my grandparents' house. *Hanukkah* was mentioned in passing and the Seder or the Passover meal was just a big meal, with no reading of the *Haggadah*, the ancient text that tells the story of the flight of the Israelites from Egypt. There was no discussion about the significance of the holiday when we all gathered around the large table in the dining room. We all sat around the table and just ate. I loved the crisp and crunchy matzah and the chicken soup with matzah balls.

I don't remember any religious instruction or discussion about Judaism until after the war, a year before we went to Israel, when a teacher was hired to teach me Hebrew. My mother was an ardent Zionist — our Jewishness was expressed not by religion, but by the optimistic yearning for a place where Jews could escape the dangers facing them in Europe, for the safety of their own country.

Each December, I was invited to help my friend Mary decorate her Christmas tree. How I envied her for having a tree! I remember the pleasure of cutting out the shapes of angels, of dipping them in silver glitter and of carefully inserting the colourful wax candles into ornamental tin candleholders clipped onto the fragrant branches of the tree. This was a truly creative activity since most of the decorations were made by hand.

Only once, after much nagging and begging, was I allowed to have my own small Christmas tree. We set it up in the tight place between the head of my bed and the wall. I dressed it up with glittering ropes of silver and gold, hung on its branches richly coloured shiny globes and cutouts of little angels, slivers of moons and golden stars. The last touch were the candles in their ornate candleholders, flickering on the green foliage. The beauty of the decorated little tree gave me no end of joy. I was grateful to my parents for allowing me this non-Jewish pleasure.

Were these very first exhibitions of drawings and the joy of dipping cardboard angels in shiny glitter signposts of my future as a painter? I am convinced that humans are attracted to beauty like bees to flowers, the need for it built into our genes. A person deprived of beauty will seek it in every possible way and be miserable without it. Ornamentation, bodily decoration and communion with nature express the human need for beauty. Art, of course, is the ultimate expression of the search for beauty and spirituality that only humans employ.

Chapter 13

Life with the Nuns

It is a miracle that curiosity survives formal education.

Albert Einstein
Albert Einstein, Philosopher-Scientist

After finishing grade two, Gabi and I were enrolled in grade three at the Sancta Maria Institute, a Catholic school for girls. This was the same school my mother and my aunt Any had attended in their youth. The institute, run by nuns, was the only non-Jewish school accepting Jewish girls during the war.

We all wore simple uniforms: a dark blue top with a small round white collar, a pleated dark blue skirt and white knee-high socks. A smart French beret sporting the shiny school emblem completed this outfit. No quandary of what to wear, no posturing with fancy clothes. We were all equal.

Each morning after breakfast and a hot chocolate, I walked to school carrying my leather bag crammed with notebooks, manuals, pencils, erasers and whatever else was needed. Sometimes my father accompanied me and sometimes I walked on my own. I greatly enjoyed the long walk to school, particularly in spring when the blooming acacia trees turned the street into a perfumed garden.

Life at the school was centred on prayer. The nuns fervently believed that, in response to their supplications, the Allied planes had not bombed Brăila as heavily as they had other cities and were convinced of having a straight line to God. I wonder if they suspected their Bucharest counterparts of not having prayed enough or thought that God was too busy listening to the Brăila nuns and forgot to direct the planes away from Bucharest. The Bucharest nuns had obviously not succeeded in reaching God's ear as efficiently as their Brăila counterparts, resulting in fierce bombing of the capital during the last year of the war.

Much time was spent on prayer: prayer before the bell rang, prayer at the end of class, prayer again before the next class, prayer, prayer and more prayer. As a result of these endless prayer sessions, the few Jewish girls in the school became keenly aware of being different and felt excluded from the rest of the girls. With time and perhaps with the intervention of our parents, we were allowed to be silent during prayer and to put our hands palms down on the desk instead of holding them together in prayer mode. During religion class, we were allowed to go to the gym for physical education or embroidery lessons.

The very same gym was the scene of my most unpleasant and humiliating memory from the years spent at Sancta Maria. On one of the days when the Jewish girls were in the gym during Bible class, a teacher walked in, her face puckered in an angry scowl. In a harsh voice that cut the silence like a knife, she informed us that there had been a theft in the school. Since we were the only ones not in class when the object was stolen, it was clear that one of us was the culprit. We were stunned, but were given no chance to protest.

"On your knees," barked the teacher. "You'll stay there until the thief stands up and confesses!"

Red with shame and embarrassment, we dropped to our knees, tears streaming down our faces. The doors opened soon after and in walked a large crowd of girls from other classes expressly sent to have a look at the 'thieves'. They marched around and around the small row of Jewish girls kneeling on the hard floor, smirking and laughing at our discomfort. Our humiliation was complete.

It was soon discovered that the owner herself had misplaced the 'stolen' object, but the scar of the painful experience of total helplessness in the face of false accusation stayed with me.

At Sancta Maria, rows of well-worn wooden desks with inkwells in the middle were lined up in the classroom. Discipline was rigorous. The students had to sit up, backs straight and arms folded behind the back for good posture. The theory was right, but alas, it did not help my posture in the least!

The teachers were all nuns. When the class teacher walked in, we sprang to our feet and greeted her in unison, "Good day, Mother Alfonsa!" This performance was repeated when she walked out at the end of class, after the usual prayer. Study was taken very seriously. Not only science and humanities were considered important, we also spent much time and effort acquiring the now lost art of cursive penmanship. I loved the calligraphy classes when we used a pen with a shiny flat nib dipped into the inkwell on our desk, then carefully wiped it clean and put it away at the end of the lesson. I remember fondly the horizontal rectangular notebooks, each page with light blue lines in two sizes: a narrow one for lower script and a wider-spaced one for capital letters. The letter we had to practice each day was featured at the top of the sheet and had to be repeated the whole length of the line down to the bottom of the page until we had achieved perfection.

The preferred teaching tools were repetition and memorization. Sometimes they worked wonders, such as learning the multiplication table by heart. It was simple. No need to analyze or understand the reason for the results of seven times eight, for example. No, all we had to do was memorize, memorize, memorize. Of course, this took many hours and endless tests, both oral and written, but in the end, it worked. The multiplication table became a killer app in our young brains — by clicking on an invisible mouse we could bring up results in a flash. To this day, although I have not spoken Romanian for many years, whenever I need to multiply numbers, they come up instantly — in Romanian.

Talking in class was forbidden unless answering the teacher. I am sure that everyone living in today's enlightened world would regard this kind of discipline as barbaric, but I allow myself the suspicion that teachers may feel a pang of envy at the loss of their authority and ability to enforce discipline.

As punishment for whatever the teachers considered overstepping the boundaries, we had to write a certain sentence such as "I shall not talk in class" or "I won't forget my homework" one hundred times, or perform some other inane and time-consuming activity. Did this improve our performance as students? I frankly can't tell, but it was better than the old strap method!

The years spent at the Sancta Maria Institute also had positive aspects. This was where I was first introduced to ancient history. Exotic Greek gods like Zeus and Aphrodite, Eros and Athena and names like Thucydides, Aristophanes, Socrates, Alexander of Macedonia and the twins Romulus and Remus, who were raised by a she-wolf and went on to found Rome — had a huge impact on my imagination. I have retained a fascination and a deep interest in the distant past and its mythology, kindled by the teachers who taught at Sancta Maria. This interest surfaced time and again in my work as an artist later in life, when images such as Nike, the goddess of victory, featured prominently in some of my paintings.

In good weather, we spent the noon-hour break exercising in the school courtyard. That meant walking arm in arm in pairs, around and around until the bell rang. This kind of 'recreation' brings to mind images of prison convicts walking around the prison grounds, but for us it was the norm. It was all connected with the ideas of order and discipline the nuns were so fond of. We used the same courtyard for physical education, which involved games such as volleyball. None of the teachers ever wore gym clothes — in fact, the nuns were not even allowed to bathe in the nude, their bodies having to be covered at all times. It was quite a sight to behold: the young nuns playing volleyball — black habits, veils and long skirts flopping wildly about as they jumped to catch the ball — bringing to mind large black birds taking off into the wind, but never getting off the ground. I can't imagine how sweaty they must have been when the weather was hot!

During cold or rainy weather, we walked arm in arm in pairs along the hallways inside the school. Up and down, up and down, no shouting allowed, talking in whispers. Since the school was also a lyceum, there were a large number of older girls who joined the younger students for this 'recreation'. The closed space of the hallways, the tall windows shut tight against the cold and the lack of air circulation created a fetid smell that I found so unpleasant that I wished I had a mask to cover my nose.

When I was twelve years old, I fell completely and utterly in love with Mother Alfonsa, my favourite homeroom teacher. I adored her every word, tried to please her in every way and worshipped her every move. I saw her as more elegant, gracious and beautiful than all the other nuns. The starched white cowl descending in a semi-circle around her shoulders enhanced her smooth skin and ready smile. I admired her friendly but firm way of dealing with her students and was entranced by the dimple on her chin and her light blue-grey eyes. To top it all off, she was also our art teacher, the subject I loved most.

As a token of admiration for this beloved teacher, I wrote a poem in French, entitled "Ma Mère," which I solemnly offered her. She accepted it and I was in seventh heaven!

Later that year, I secretly drew her portrait in pencil on a small sheet of paper. I waited for an opportune moment and, gathering my courage, handed it to her with bated breath. Disaster! Catastrophe! Imagine my horror when Mother Alfonsa took one look at my offering and then calmly, right in front of me, tore it apart — first in half, then in quarters. She could not, she said, accept a portrait of her own image. This kind of vanity was totally opposed to the oath of modesty she had taken, she said.

"You should never do it again," she added. "This is quite unacceptable."

And she handed me the torn pieces.

French was a required language in the school and English was optional. I did take English for just one year before I left the school and still remember my struggle with the 'th' sound that does not exist in either Romanian or French. Our teacher came up with an original solution for conquering this challenge. Holding a pencil between our teeth, we had to utter the sound of the letter 't' — we were, in fact, learning to lisp. It worked.

Creativity and originality were firmly discouraged during art class at Sancta Maria. Art lessons consisted mainly of producing exact copies of the Old Masters' paintings. This method familiarized me with some of the Dutch and other classical painters and their way of working. I learned much about painting by copying them.

Only when I drew maps for the geography class was I given more freedom. I enjoyed drawing maps in colour and inserting small drawings of landscapes and of people dressed in the national costumes a lot.

Seven years later, I would draw real maps while serving in the Israeli Army.

Chapter 14

The War Years

They think not there how much of blood it costs.

Dante Alighieri
Paradiso

"Dear God, please make the Allies win the war!"

Each night, I would kneel by my bed, put my hands together and repeat these words, "Please God, make the Allies win the war! Please God, make the Allies win the war!"

I was five years old when the war began and nine years old when it ended. Like acrid smoke seeping through a burning building, the war crept in slowly, spreading insidiously into hidden crevices of our lives. For a young child, the foul cloud becomes visible only when it invades the lungs and its nasty smell pervades aspects of everyday life. When parents exchange worried looks and speak about unspeakable things in hushed voices, children become aware of unusual and threatening events happening around them. Secure in the knowledge that their parents will always protect them though, children do not perceive the reality of war and its dangers through the same dark lens as their caregivers.

Such events are shapeless for a child. They blend into a patchwork quilt of constant anxiety, a foreboding of evil and a feeling of danger. Incidents are remembered one by one, disconnected. And yet, life continues. My first encounter with the dark shadows of war was as sudden as a door slamming shut: losing *Fräulein* Mina, my beloved nanny. From that point on, our life would change in ways we could not yet imagine.

Small incremental changes began to occur as new laws against the Jews were enacted day by day. Jews were not allowed to own telephones and radios, so our telephone disappeared and the radio was hidden. Jews were not allowed to own cars — although few owned any, my father's passion for cars had always been a source of family jokes. In 1938, he had somehow managed to buy a beautiful green second-hand Lincoln convertible that he was immensely proud of. As the restrictions on Jews multiplied, it was clear that this car would be 'requisitioned' — actually, stolen by a prominent local fascist who particularly favoured green, the signature colour of fascism. Blessed with foresight, my father sold his car to Prince Bibescu, a member of the royal family who was not an anti-Semite and who willingly helped his Jewish friends.

My father's library shelves, lined with beautiful leather-bound books of French classic literature, did not fare as well. We received the polite visit of an official posing as a cultured Nazi officer, who felt that most of these books would be better placed in his own library. It was not a love of books that turned him into a book thief. He believed that the smooth brown leather bindings with the book titles stamped in gold letters would add class to his office. Without much ado, most of my father's classical literature was requisitioned, leaving empty shelves in his library. I remember the uniformed man in our house, pointing to the books he wanted and carting them away.

Helping themselves to Jewish property was widely practiced by the representatives of the new order, but to the terrible and violent persecution of Jews in other cities, we were fortunate to suffer only plunder and to remain in our house instead of being deported. All Jewish men without exception, were ordered to do 'public works', such as shovelling snow on city streets. After a few months of this degrading labour, some money changed hands and my father was exempted. Others were not so lucky. Sammy, Gabi's father, was sent to a labour camp from which he returned only after becoming quite ill and Herman, my grandfather's brother, was sent to another labour camp not too far from Brăila. Desperate to see his family, he took the chance of coming home on a Sunday for a few hours without the necessary permit. He was caught, arrested and, as punishment, sent to one of the infamous and much-dreaded camps in Transnistria, across the Dniester River. He survived and returned to Brăila at the end of the war, ill and barely alive, after walking all the way home.

Despite the danger, a few decent people in Brăila came to the help of their Jewish neighbours whenever they could. One such person was the general prosecutor of the local court, Nicu Oprişan. According to the story told me by my uncle Freddy, cousins of my grandfather in Bucharest had adopted and raised two orphan Christian boys, Nicu Oprişan being one of them. Although the family was Jewish, they respected his roots and raised him as a Christian. Oprişan remained forever grateful and, using his official position, did his best to protect the Jews of Brăila. When some Jewish merchants were arrested and taken to the fascist Legionnaire headquarters, or the Green House, so named after the fascists' chosen colour, where they were beaten and threatened with deportation if they did not give up their businesses, Oprişan ordered the merchants to be freed, knowing that without his intervention they would face grave danger.

As a young child living in a relatively safe town, I was oblivious to the snowball of terrifying events rolling out of control down a slope covered with deep layers of hatred and murderous intent. Ironically, the fate of the seven or eight hundred thousand Romanian Jews during the war is still generally unknown, as the Romanian Holocaust has been eclipsed by the well-documented slaughter perpetrated by the Germans in other countries. It is little known that the Romanians killed about half of their Jewish population through their own anti-Semitic orgies and have consistently denied their evil deeds, blaming them on Germany.

I realized how shallow and incomplete my own knowledge had been when I read Butnaru's *The Silent Holocaust: Romania and Its*

Jews. By then, I was already in my early sixties and living in Canada. I was shocked at my own ignorance and horrified by the details of the tragic history of my own people in the country of my birth.

Brăila, my own town, had been relatively safe during the war. Even so, there are only about seventy Jews living there now from a population of 10,000–20,000 before the war. Most were fortunate to leave through immigration.

Being an active member of the Nazi Axis powers, Romania was heavily bombed by both the British and the American Allies towards the end of the war. Blackouts were introduced and severely enforced. Strips of paper had to be glued on the windows to prevent the glass shattering during the bombings. This was quite a tedious and time-consuming affair since sticky tape was unknown and the paper had to be dampened to activate the glue before being attached to the glass. People made up creative designs for their windows in an attempt to transform the ugly strips into decorative patterns.

There was a sinister ritual to those bombings. First came the strident wailing of the sirens sounding louder and louder, penetrating every pore, entering the chest, spreading to the brain and finally dropping like a stone in the stomach, our hearts racing like rabbits fleeing a cruel and determined hunter. The shrill sound of the falling bombs filled the air with urgency and fear, urging us to run, to find shelter fast. The brain *screamed*, "Run, run, run!" propelling us towards the cellar. It was forbidden to turn on the light lest it attract the attention of the approaching planes, so the house was pitch black. Quivering flashlights showed us the way through the long unlit hallway and down the stairs to the cellar.

Then the wait began. Soon, in the dark and deafening silence, we heard a deep rhythmic pulse like the beating heart of a murderous giant. The droning of the planes came nearer and nearer, flying inexorably closer and closer above our heads. Their deadly purpose became urgent and all encompassing. Will they drop the bombs here? Will we be hit? I could hear my heart thumping, almost exploding in my chest. It was almost a relief when the ground shook with the loud BOOOOM of an exploding bomb. We covered our heads with our arms, as if this gesture could save us from harm.

Usually, the bombers flew overhead towards more important targets. Except once.

It was early evening and I was lying in bed with my mother, recovering from the whooping cough, when the alarm sounded. Mother screamed at my father to run to the shelter alone since she was afraid to take me out of bed to the cold cellar. As my father crossed the room toward the door, we heard the dreaded whistle of the falling bomb and a split second later came the explosion. The bomb had landed directly in the public garden across the street. The house shook, the windows rattled and the room filled with smoke. A splinter penetrated the window and the heavy wooden shutters and flew straight across the room hitting the opposite wall and missing my father's head by a finger. Then it fell at his feet, burning a hole in the carpet. This was the closest we ever came to being hurt.

Luck was still on our side.

We were deeply torn during these frightening moments. Our intense hope for an Allied victory achieved by bombing Romania into submission was balanced by the fear that the very planes that were defeating our enemies might destroy us first.

Chapter 15

Family

Grown-ups are complicated creatures, full of quirks and secrets.

Roald Dahl
Danny the Champion of the World

MY MOTHER

My mother had the personality of a fierce fighter. She had strong convictions of what was right or wrong and firmly believed that she had the duty to always, always, tell the truth, regardless of whether it hurt people's feelings. "Truth always rises up, like oil on water," she would say. My mother was very fond of flinging proverbs about and had a ready quote for almost any situation, much like an expert baker tossing pizza dough in the air. Truth may have been important; however, in case of emergency, little white lies were allowed.

Frivolous activities in times of crisis elicited my mother's remark, "The house is burning and grandma is combing her hair." When I asked too many questions, she would reprimand me with another maxim: "Don't stick your nose where your pot is not boiling." I was puzzled by her oft-spoken proverb, "The clothes do not the man make," meaning that it is the person and not the attire that is important, because she herself loved to dress as well as possible.

Her response to rumours and gossip was the expected, "There is no smoke without fire." One of her sayings, "Self-praise smells bad," damaged my modest ego forever, eroded my budding self-confidence and made me allergic for life to people who boast excessively about their accomplishments. "Don't blow your own horn," finished the job.

Some of the maxims flung about by my mother demonstrate deep wisdom acquired through life experience. Take luck, for instance. This elusive element, yielding decisive power over life and death, success or failure, happiness or misery, cannot be bought or brought about. Luck controls our destiny like an invisible master puppeteer pulling invisible strings. My mother would often quote the proverb, "Mother, with luck make me born and into fire have me thrown!" Luck would conquer even fire, in her view.

During Communist rule, when she was struggling to free my grandfather from prison or arrange my father's escape, my mother had to find her way to the right officials to achieve her goal. The road to their door was long and dangerous with many hurdles on the way. This was when my mother used the maxim, "until you get to God, you'll be eaten up by the Saints."

Merciless when hearing of the downfall of someone she did not respect and wearing a righteous smile on her lips, my mother would say, "As you make your bed, so you must sleep. Nah! They deserved what they got!"

MY GRANDPARENTS

My grandparents, Leon and Estera, were benign figures of my childhood, comprising a reliable anchor. Although we saw them often, the interactions were shallow.

My grandfather, or 'Tata Mare' (Big Daddy), loved to play backgammon, called *tablé* in Romanian. This called for a special ritual: the rectangular wooden box was ceremoniously brought out and carefully opened so as not to spill out its contents. The round black-and-white wooden chits were speedily and noisily arranged in the right order on the long triangles inside the box and the dice were rolled by each of the players to determine who would start the game. Throwing the dice was quite an art — held in both fists, they were rattled with gusto and then thrown with a flourish on the wooden surface. From then on the game proceeded at a lively pace, the chits being moved from side to side with great speed and loud banging, piled up in small mounds and exclaimed over when a dramatic move occurred. I had to be very careful and watch my moves like a hawk since the unspoken truth of the game was that grandfather could not bear to lose. I had to cleverly maneuver the game in such a way that he would always win — not an easy task if the dice happened to land in my favour. I had to concoct silly mistake-riddled moves and pretend to regret them, as Tata Mare triumphantly declared that these moves were irreversible. The wisdom of allowing unimportant battles to be lost might be a useful lesson for diplomats in learning how to secure favourable results in negotiations.

Tata Mare was notoriously tightfisted. After the weekly Sunday noon dinner, he would retire for his siesta. My cousin Gabi and I sat quietly during the whole meal, these being the times when children were to be seen but not heard. We would look forward to the much-awaited ritual that took place as soon as Tata Mare began snoring. Grandma, or as we called her, 'Mama Mare' (Big Mother), would beckon us to the head of the table. She would quietly hug us and slip a few coins into our hands. This special treat was for buying tickets at the movie theatre down the street, sometimes even for two consecutive shows! Of course, this delightful secret was strictly between Grandma and us.

Most of the films being shown at the Trianon cinema were Russian movies celebrating the victories of the Red Army and the heroism of its soldiers over the Nazis. This was after the war when the euphoria of liberation was prevalent. Watching the battle scenes in the dark movie theatre, we would join in the wild cheering and applause celebrating victory over the Germans each time the famous Katyusha cannons appeared on the screen mowing down the enemy.

MY GRANDPARENTS' HOUSE

My grandfather's dry-goods store faced the street while the living quarters were on the second floor. To the left of the store was a wide wooden gate. When it was open, horse-drawn carts carrying merchandise for the store could enter the unexpectedly huge yard behind it.

Using the small side door to gain access to the living quarters, one had to step over a raised sill, a common European feature. I was always anxious at this point, since I knew that on the other side of the gate awaited my nemesis — a large, majestic black turkey resplendent in shiny ebony feathers, puffing and huffing like a trained guard dog, shiny red beads loosely hanging around its neck, its talons ready to tear apart any intruder. I would flee in terror when faced by its spread wings and threatening snorts.

This turkey was not the only menacing presence behind the gate. A large white goose would flap its huge wings and stretch out its neck, hissing loudly with its sharp protruding tongue, ready to attack whoever dared trespass on its domain.

A third danger lurked upstairs in the shape of a small chihuahua. There was a small balcony by the back stairs where this little bundle of nastiness whiled away his time. One day, he became exceedingly upset at something in the yard below, perhaps a cat or the goose. He began to bark, his voice rising to a strident crescendo, his small body jerking with anger, hysteria engulfing him like a tidal wave, until he gave way to his fury and actually jumped off the balcony to attack the object of his ire. Oops! He forgot that a chihuahua was not a bird and fell to his death.

POOOFF!

This was an end worthy of the Wicked Witch of the West herself!

SEX

In today's open and permissive culture, with young children receiving sex education in public schools and seeing sexual imagery all around them, it is difficult to imagine that seventy years ago, sex was a mysterious and forbidden territory. Of course, we thought about it and imagined all sorts of answers to our questions, but there were no manuals to read and no one to ask. For younger children, the answer to "Where do babies come from?" was still the stork story.

Gabi and I spent many secret moments acting out romantic scenes inspired by books we read, particularly by French authors like Victor Hugo or Alexandre Dumas. Gabi was always the beautiful maiden and I was always the dark, tall and handsome lover. We sensed that there was something sinful and a whiff of the forbidden about these games, so we tried to make sure that there was nobody home to discover us. The only real experience we had with anything remotely connected with sex was an unfortunate incident when we were ten or eleven years old. We had just been to the movies at the Trianon Theatre and were heading back to Gabi's home. Just as we were about to cross one of the ubiquitous dark filthy alleys serving as unofficial public urinals, a man suddenly appeared from the shadows, flashing his huge penis and making obscene gestures. Terrified, we ran as fast as we could away from this menacing figure. We had never seen a penis before and after this experience we did not want to ever see one again.

I owe most of my sex education to Tzilly, my grandparents' housekeeper. A thin woman with sharp features and dark hair, she always wore an apron over her everyday clothes. While grandmother Estera spent most of her days in the store working as cashier and business overseer, Tzilly had the run of the house. Once in a while, she would take me aside and deliver all sorts of fascinating and titillating information. The first important fact I learned from her was the most basic one: how babies were made. She told me many exciting and delightfully sinful stories about how men and women make love.

However, she did not tell me a most important detail which in my innocence I had not guessed, although it was common knowledge among the rest of the family: Tzilly was my grandfather's mistress. My grandmother had been riddled with gout for a long time. I don't remember her ever being slim or attractive or even moving without leaning heavily on her walking stick. She had not aged well and my grandfather, then in his sixties, began living with Tzilly even before my grandmother's death. This was the dark family secret kept well away from us children, who never suspected or imagined that such a thing was possible.

Chapter 16

The Last Day of War

Geography is destiny.

Abraham Verghese
Cutting for Stone

In April of 1944, when I turned nine years old, the situation seemed desperate. There had been whispered stories of atrocities against the Jews, of people disappearing and of imminent deportations. Rumours of various calamities about to happen circulated widely. At the same time, however, it was clear that the Red Army was fast approaching the Romanian border and Germany was losing the war.

Something felt different when I woke up on the morning of August 23, 1944. It was a beautiful summer day. There was a change in the air that was almost palpable, a change from the constant feeling of dread that had been hovering over us for the last few years.

Since Jews were not allowed to possess radios or telephones, we had no inkling of the dramatic events that were unfolding, but something was most definitely different. We sensed that unusual things were happening, without knowing what they were.

Across the street, the city's public garden was green and inviting. It was difficult to imagine that anything out of the ordinary could occur. Mid-morning, my father called us and wordlessly pointed to the window. Peeking through the shutters, we saw an unusual sight: helmeted German soldiers, their rifles pointing ahead, were noiselessly running single file towards the train station, like in a clip from a silent movie. They were no longer the threatening and cocky conquerors we were accustomed to. Not strutting, confident and arrogant, but frightened and defeated.

"Something is going on," my father said. "Let's go up to the water tower in the big garden and have a look."

We rushed through the wide alleys shaded by tall chestnut trees, skirted the large turnabout where the tall red calla lilies grew in abundance like flaming torches oblivious to human folly. We arrived at the highest structure in town, the water tower overlooking the Danube River. I don't recall how we climbed the stairs leading to the top but I do remember the terrible sight we saw.

In the distance along the Danube was Galați, the large port which was Brăila's twin city. A thick column of smoke filled the sky above the city and flames were bursting from below in a wild bouquet of hellish fires: Galați was burning. The distance dulled the sound and fury of the explosions, but we saw the smoke rising in a menacing black column, uncanny in its silence. Since Galați was a bigger and more important port than Brăila, the German High Command had been stationed there. Now in retreat, they were enacting their brutal 'scorched earth' policy.

Unbeknownst to us, Romania's twenty-three-year-old King Mihai had been secretly negotiating with the approaching Soviets for some time. He knew that Germany and the Axis had lost the war even though their policy was to fight on until the end. He understood that each day of fighting would increase the number of casualties and the damage to Romanian cities and decrease the chances of signing an armistice that would avoid a total and abject surrender. The young king summoned Ion Antonescu, Romania's self-styled 'Führer', to the royal palace and asked him to sign an armistice with the Russians. Antonescu angrily refused, shouting that he would not listen to orders from "a child." King Mihai called in his guards to arrest him — and the putsch was over. The army and administration were loyal to the young king and Romania joined the Allies, shortening the war by months.

The king, who was eighteen at the onset of the war, had been powerless to change any of the Nazis' anti-Semitic policies. However, he and his mother, Queen Elena, had been in close contact with the Jewish community through the chief rabbi of Romania who had kept them informed of the actions against the Jews. The queen met often with Antonescu and managed to have some anti-Jewish measures and orders rescinded. The Yad Vashem Holocaust Museum in Israel later recognized her role in saving many thousand Jewish lives by awarding her the title of 'Righteous Gentile'.

On that fateful day in August 1944, not long after the last German soldier had vanished, we heard loud engines and the neighing of horses. A massive flood of jeeps, light tanks and other equipment poured into our street. The Russian soldiers manning these instruments of war were very different from the Germans. We watched as a large group of horses led by their riders entered the garden across the street, followed by a cloud of shiny green horseflies.

Within minutes, what seemed like a whole battalion stopped in front of our gates. A communication and intelligence unit of Soviet soldiers descended on our doorstep and jeeps, trucks and motorcycles appeared out of nowhere, along with men milling about and shouting orders in an unfamiliar language.

We opened the wrought-iron gates and it seemed as if the whole Red Army poured in. It was the 'invasion' we had been praying for! We were ecstatic. The Germans were gone. The Red Army had saved us! The war was over.

The Russian uniforms were different from those of the Germans. They were high-necked, long khaki tunics held around the waist by a wide leather belt. A diagonal strap crossed the soldiers' chests and their riding pants were tucked into dusty boots. They smelled strongly of DDT, sweat and *makhorka*, a cheap tobacco. Their heads were shaven in an attempt to avoid lice and the typhoid fever they caused.

The intelligence unit that settled in our yard along with all sorts of machinery and even a few horses, was like a swarm of ants disturbed by a careless visitor. We stood in awe watching them through the kitchen window when we heard some of them yelling and gesticulating as if asking for a drink. We thought they were calling for vodka and got worried, but then we realized that they were calling *voda*, meaning water. Of course, we rushed out and offered them as much water as they wanted. Our happiness at having these Russian saviours in our yard was overwhelming!

Since there was enough space in our house, the Romanian officer who had been billeted with us was exchanged for a Russian *kapitan*, whose name, amazingly, was Berliner. I never knew his first name and I don't remember in what language we communicated, perhaps German. He was a gentle, soft-spoken Jewish man and he stayed with us for a while. In the heat of liberation we were, of course, immensely and deliriously grateful to the Red Army. Unfortunately, the new Communist order did not turn out to be the Nirvana we had been hoping for. Soon after he moved in, *Kapitan* Berliner, at tremendous personal risk, quietly advised us to leave Romania as fast as we could. We were confused. We had just been liberated. Why would we want to leave?

Later that day, we learned that the rumours we had heard had been true: cattle cars designed to take the Jewish population deep into Germany had been waiting at the train station the very day the Red Army entered our town. Even while obviously losing the war and needing the trains for their own retreating army, the killing of the Jews remained the Nazis' priority.

But now, on August 23, 1944, we were free! Unfortunately, this was not the case for the hundreds of thousands of Hungarian Jews and many others in Central Europe, who perished during the months up to May 8, 1945 when Germany finally collapsed. Geography had saved us.

To this day, I find it difficult to comprehend the incredible luck of our liberation and survival. We were free while the war still went on. We were free while most Hungarian Jews were being killed in Auschwitz. We were free while untold numbers of Jewish people were forced on death marches and died horrible deaths during those last eight months of the war waged by the Nazi murderers.

The day after that fateful night of August 23, 1944, Gabi and I slept at our grandparents' house, sharing the wide divan below the window facing the street. We were fast asleep when suddenly, in the stillness of the night, we awoke to the sound of powerful explosions. The loud booms came in quick succession, louder and louder, the windows rattling at the terrifying sound that seemed to be close by. We pulled the covers over our heads, shivering with fear and hugging one another. Had the Germans come back? Were we going to be killed? Where were our parents? Had the war started again?

When the terrible din showed no signs of abating, I suggested that perhaps we should peek through the window and see what was happening. Slowly, with fear in our hearts, we stuck our heads out from under the blanket and pulled aside a corner of the heavy drapes covering the window.

What a sight! Through the crisscross patterns of the anti-aircraft strips, the sky was ablaze with fireworks! A rich, glittering tapestry of gold, silver, reds, blues and greens was noisily spluttering, booming and exploding into fountains of light like a rain of stardust washing out the night in a magical display.

"Fireworks!" we shouted.

They were fireworks! The Germans were not back! It was a celebration! Hurray, hurray!

We did not know whether to laugh at our stupidity or cry with happiness. There was nothing to worry about — the Germans were gone for good and a new era of happiness was beginning.

Or so we thought.

Chapter 17

The Aftermath of War

The streets swarm with Red Army soldiers and officers and equipment of all kinds whizzes all over town. Stories abound of people being stopped and ordered to *davai cias*, 'give watch', and soldiers wearing watches from wrist to elbow are a common sight. With the arrival of the cooler autumn weather, a new kind of widespread davai appears: men are stopped on sidewalks and ordered to *davai palton*, 'give coat'. This fashionable robbery was funny since the soldiers could not possibly wear those heavy, long, mostly black winter coats. Was this strategic wardrobe planned for their return home?

The writer and journalist Mihail Sebastian, born Iosif Hechter in Brăila and later living in Bucharest, kept a journal throughout the war years. This is what he wrote about the first weeks of occupation by the Red Army:

> *Bewilderment, fear, doubt. Russian soldiers rape women (Dina Cocea told me yesterday). Soldiers who stop cars in the street, order the driver and*

passengers out, then get behind the wheel and disappear. Looted shops. This afternoon three burst into Zaharia's, rummaged through the strongbox, and made off with some watches. (Watches are the toy they like most.)

Journal, 1935-1944: The Fascist Years

One night, I had a dream.

I am staring out of the bathroom window into the yard, when suddenly my uncle, who has not been heard from since being deported to Transnistria and has been given up for dead, appears before my eyes. I watch him as he slowly makes his way towards the main entrance. He looks tired and worn out, unshaven, his hair long and unkempt, his tattered clothes hanging loosely on his thin frame, but I recognize him immediately.

The next morning, I recounted the dream to my parents and my uncle's wife, Aunt Esther, who had lived with us since his deportation. They sadly shook their heads at this improbable scenario.

May one dare to believe in miracles? Are dreams prescient? A few days later, precisely as I had seen him in my dream, my uncle walked through the gate: thin, haggard, wearing torn and dirty clothes. Alive.

There was a tragi-comic continuation to the story that later became part of the family lore. On a chilly autumn day not long after his return, my uncle left to run some errands, dressed in a heavy overcoat. Imagine our surprise when he returned wearing nothing but his underwear and shivering in the cold weather. He had been stripped of his clothes, thus joining the ranks of people robbed by the Russian soldiers roaming the streets. *Davai cias* and *davai palton* were some of the first Russian words that we learned.

I thought that was funny, but being only nine years old, I knew nothing of the gory details of war and of the brutality and cruelty of the Romanian soldiers who forced their way into the

Ukraine as keen allies of the Nazis. I knew nothing of the killings and the burnings, of the mistreatment of civilians and the looting of Russian villages and towns. Of course, even being aware of the role Romania had played against their Russian opponents did not stop people from muttering that stealing watches and clothes was uncouth behaviour on the part of the new allies. They dismissed the anger of the Red Army soldiers who had experienced the destruction of their land and people by Romanian troops. Revenge is a stranger to ethics and plunder is as old as war itself.

The shift in power occurred after August 23, 1944. The common joke was that former fascists had changed their green shirts for red ones and now called themselves communists. This was the time when the dreaded Securitate, the Romanian secret service, was formed under the direction of the NKVD, the Soviet secret service. The Communist Party was still quite small in numbers, but its ranks swelled as if by magic.

One of the first rulings introduced by the new régime outlawed anti-Semitism. This was most commendable but there was a problem: people's feelings and thoughts cannot be legislated. This law improved our status as Jews and brought the official persecution to an end, but it did not eradicate the centuries-old prejudices entrenched in the Romanian psyche. Anti-Semitism went underground, popping up in deeds that were nasty but not life threatening as in the past.

Pre-Internet, news filtered out slowly to the general public. First to arrive were rumours about extermination camps followed by the testimonies of the survivors themselves. Only later would the official confirmation come. The magnitude of the destruction brought upon Europe slowly became clear, like a blurred image sharpened by the camera lens.

As children, we were not supposed to hear or know any of that, so we danced merrily on the rose-coloured floor of the new age following the armistice, euphoric with the joy of escape and survival from looming hell.

These were exciting times, especially for a nine-year-old girl. Seeing myself as a character in a fairy tale with a happily ever-after ending became a great adventure. But then, why did my parents still seem worried? Why were the grown-ups talking in whispers about leaving Romania if the war was over? And why did I hear new, exciting words cropping up in hushed conversations, words such as 'boat', 'captain', 'voyage', 'Turkey'?

Many Jews, among them my mother, understood that the efforts of the Jewish population to fit in as good citizens were useless. We would always and forever be the 'other' and subject to the fickle changes of the winds of history. After the horrors of the Holocaust, it was strongly felt that there was only one solution for Jews — to have a country of their own, ending two thousand years of exile and persecution.

In 1947, my father decided that 'Solomon' was not a good name to have if one wanted to get ahead in life and he officially changed our family name from 'Solomon' to 'Savin'.

My mother became an active Zionist fundraiser for Keren Kayemeth Lelsrael, the Jewish National Fund that was raising money to plant trees and buy land in Palestine. The little blue box in which people could deposit small contributions was prominently displayed in our house.

When Zionist activities were legalized, I joined Gordonia, a socialist youth organization located across the street from Gabi's house. We were idealistic teenagers, excited to be working towards a common goal of historical proportions. We attended meetings, lectures, ceremonies and dances and, most importantly, led an intense social life. I threw myself wholeheartedly into these activities that offered us a promise of hope for the future. The astonishing rebirth of Hebrew was seen as a true miracle. We sang Hebrew songs with great enthusiasm without understanding any of the words. Their meaning would become clear only after I arrived in Israel.

One day a large round object appeared, enthroned upon a table in our dining room and I learned that this intriguing device was a maritime compass. It was encased in a beautiful box of polished wood and covered with a glass lid that protected the hands of the compass and its mysterious numbers and signs. My parents and their friends stood around the table scrutinizing this strange object and talking about 'the boat'. How exciting! I was told, under an oath of silence that we would sail to Turkey and then on to Israel, on a boat that had been hired by a group of friends.

My excitement knew no bounds and the secrecy of it all made me feel trusted and grown-up. Before falling asleep at night, I lay in bed imagining myself on the deck of a mighty ship, my hair blowing in the wind, the star-studded black sky spread out like a velvet canopy covered with diamonds reflected in the immense mirror of the sea.

Alas, this dream voyage, like most dreams — with the exception of my dream about my uncle — was not meant to be. Believing in miracles does not always make them happen.

Just in time, the small group of wannabe sailors discovered that the 'mighty ship' of my dreams was but a leaky vessel, too dangerous to sail on. The beautiful maritime compass vanished and life went on with no adventure in sight.

Chapter 18

Brave New World

After all, what is an individual?

Aldous Huxley
Brave New World

My father was a committed socialist, believing in social justice, equality and freedom of speech. One of the books from his substantial library of socialist luminaries that made a lasting impression on me was *The Foundations of Christianity* by the Czech-German philosopher Karl Kautzky, a thick book that I often read with great interest. I was fascinated by Kautzky's unusual interpretation of Christianity, better explained, in his view, by historical materialism than by divinity.

Everything I read in those books made sense to me. The world was a harsh and cruel place, but socialism offered ways of improving humanity's lot through social justice, fairness and the right division of wealth. In contrast, the brand of communism imposed after the war began to look more and more like just another reign of terror. To idealists like my father, socialism offered a milder, more acceptable version of social justice. But as we soon found out, there was no place for socialism or any other ideas under communism. Shortly after the victorious Red Army liberated us from the fascists, the harsh realities of communism took hold in everyday life.

A new kind of terror seeped into our lives. In only two or three short years following our liberation, everything had changed drastically. Like the pendulum on a grandfather clock, we moved from the ecstasy of liberation to the despair of oppression, from the giddy happiness of our rescue from fascism to the deep gloom of living under yet another repressive dictatorship. America was wildly popular in post-war Romania. Franklin Delano Roosevelt became a folk hero even though it was the Red Army who had liberated us from the fascists rather than the Americans. Roosevelt was so beloved that, after his death, people named their newborn sons after him — in my town, one child was named Franklin Delano Ciuraru.

I don't recall any baby being named Stalin or Lenin . . .

America represented a world of freedom, playfulness, well-being and affluence. Without having met any American soldier in the flesh, we couldn't get enough of the handsome, friendly, nonchalant, gum-chewing, young US soldiers seen in the abundant post-war movies. "Yankee Doodle Dandy" was on everyone's lips and was especially popular with young people, who would whistle it with gusto. However, as the dark shadow of communism spread over the country, this beloved song was forbidden. Humming the cheery tune exposed one to stern inquiry by the dreaded secret police, who would accuse the singer of subversive connections to the imperialist, capitalist and decadent West.

It did not take long for the new communist order to show its true face. Slowly, insidiously, fear spread. Speaking freely or criticizing any of the institutions or new laws and regulations became dangerous. The slightest hint of sympathy for America was treated like weeds growing through cracks in the sidewalk and promptly eradicated by the toxic new laws. Listening to the BBC or any other Western radio station was absolutely forbidden — one had to make sure that doors and windows were securely closed and hope that nosy neighbours would not denounce the listeners. Nightly searches were conducted on the pretext of finding imaginary documents and signs of spying. The dreaded midnight knock at the door kept everyone in a state of constant fear. Children were indoctrinated in school and in the youth movements and encouraged to denounce their own parents, landing many in prison or labour camps.

None of my family's friends were members of the Communist Party, most of them identifying with milder socialist ideas. Still, the pressure to join the Party became overwhelming. In the new order of things, not being a member of the Party made life difficult and dangerous. Many doors to success and even to employment were closed to non-Party individuals.

Disturbing analogies are evident in the free world of the 21st Century that takes so much pride in its hard-won freedom of expression. Political correctness has become eerily similar to the limitations on free speech under communism. Invited speakers are violently threatened and barred from appearing in universities or other public spaces if their views are opposed by those of certain groups. For those of us who experienced life in Communist Romania, a strong feeling of déjà vu emits warning signals. With the privilege of hindsight, we are foolish not to heed the lessons of the past.

Heavy propaganda invaded our lives. Posters of ugly, cigar-smoking American capitalists wearing Uncle Sam top hats perched precariously on grotesque and menacing heads, glared down at passers-by. Wearing fancy clothes stretched over obese bellies, they were portrayed squeezing the necks of poor workers and stepping on the backs of peasants. Chillingly, these posters were a mirror image of the rampant anti-Semitic propaganda of Nazi Germany, with Uncle Sam now replacing the rapacious Jew.

The flipside of communist propaganda consisted of social realism-style posters extolling the virtues of the peasants and the working classes. In this brave new world, young men and women brandished the various implements of their work, smiling happily and wearing clean work clothes. Everybody in these propaganda posters was young and handsome, muscular and healthy.

The resemblance to the Nazi propaganda posters showing the blond, blue-eyed young Aryans was uncanny. Sometimes these clean-cut workers were depicted crushing the ugly, greedy capitalists and triumphantly achieving victory over the enemies of the proletariat — sinister echoes of Nazi posters showing fat greedy Jews strangling innocent Germans. America and the West, the former Allies who fought alongside the Soviet Union against the Nazis, were now the capitalist enemies of the 'just' communist society of peasants and workers.

The Cold War was on.

Elections had become a cruel joke. The 'free' elections, conducted with great fanfare, featured prominent posters showing a large, yellow sun surrounded by the words "Vote for the Sun!" This blatant masquerade of democracy was just for show since no other party was running candidates. The Party of the Sun was the only one in the race. Voting was a duty and an obligation but also a travesty of freedom. There was only one party to vote for — the Communist Party of the Sun. And what a scorching sun that was!

Not voting was dangerous. The reluctant voter could be accused of covert resistance or of capitalist sympathies. The fear of being overheard saying something compromising was so strong that people preferred to talk mostly about the weather. One had to be careful, very careful . . .

To my surprise, I was offered an interview for a chance to join the 'Red Neckties', the popular name for the Pioneer Youth Organization. Its nickname derived from the uniform's most visible component: a small triangular red scarf tied around the young member's neck, a visible and distinguished badge of honour.

I was thirteen when my name was entered on the list of possible inductees to the Pioneer Organization. The offer itself was unusual. Being the granddaughter of a merchant and the daughter of an accountant, I was now part of a newly minted class: the class of people who had 'unhealthy social origins'. Merchants like my grandfather were labeled 'blood-sucking profiteering leeches' and the middle class was declared to be parasitic. We were deemed to suffer from an incurable disease associated with certain professions that made us less equal than peasants and workers. We became, in fact, inferior and unworthy of any rights, including higher education.

Due to my 'unhealthy' social origins, the committee had to ascertain whether this thirteen-year-old girl and her family were enemies of the state. Therefore, I had to submit to an Inquisition-like interrogation.

I was ushered into a small office with several stony-faced people seated around a table and the questioning began.

Who were my parents' friends and what were their names? What did they talk about when they met? Which radio station did they listen to? Was it the BBC or perhaps other imperialist/capitalist stations? What specifically did they talk about when they were alone? Did they ever mention the Soviet Union and in what terms? Did they ever talk about America? Did we have any relatives or friends in the West? If so, did they write to us? Did we read any Western literature? What did my parents say about the Romanian Communist Party? Why was my father not a member of the Party? Was there at any time any mention of leaving the Romanian Communist paradise?

It was a grilling that I would not easily forget. I had to be careful about each word I uttered, each sentence I answered and each silence I retreated into. I tried hard to be as evasive as possible, pleading ignorance to most of the questions. Stories I had heard about children who were trapped into denouncing their own parents due to their fervent wish to be part of the Communist Youth and wear the red neckerchief came to mind. I knew families where one or both parents had been deported or imprisoned, having been denounced by their own children. My inquisitors did not learn that my parents were indeed listening to forbidden broadcasts after making sure the doors were locked and the windows were tightly closed. I said nothing about our dreams of leaving Romania, nor did I whisper a word about our yearning for Israel. I simply pretended that I knew nothing and saw nothing.

This, of course, did not sit well with my inquisitors.

My interrogators must have been disgusted with this un-cooperative girl who was not enticed by the glory of becoming a member of the great workers' youth organization and was unwilling to deliver her family onto the altar of communism. I never made it.

I never received the privilege of joining the great social experiment that destroyed the bourgeoisie. Even so, at age thirteen, although frightened by this experience, I was also proud to think that I had actually won — by losing.

I left Romania two years after this unpleasant episode.

Years later, when I asked my parents about their life in Romania before and after the war, their answers were confused. In their minds, the fascist and the communist eras had blended into one painful period. There was one crucial difference however: the treatment of Jews was different under the new dictatorship. Under the fascists, the Jews were to be exterminated like vermin; under the Communists, they suffered as equals along with all other Romanians. That was, no doubt, a great improvement!

One constant aspect of life in Romania was the endemic corruption inherited from the Ottoman reign in the Balkans. The very word for bribe was *baksheesh*, an Arabic word introduced by the Turks and still very much in use. Everyone who could offer a *baksheesh* would do so as a normal part of business. In fact, it was this rampant corruption that helped us survive. Government inspectors often found fault with the way stores were run, threatening the 'parasitic capitalist' merchants with fines or even closure. A small gift could help, but since bribing was illegal, it could create problems. If the inspector felt that the bribe was insufficient, or if he happened to be a devoted communist, or worse, if he wanted to harm the business, there could be trouble. This is how my grandfather, whose store, La Moldoveanu, was still open, landed in the local jail together with a few other merchants.

My mother, the problem solver, went from one official to another, arguing, begging, explaining and, most surely, finding safer ways to bribe. She visited the prisoners daily, bringing them baskets of food as they spent their days dressed in pajamas and playing cards.

My grandfather was eventually released and life resumed as usual. Now he could play cards at home on Sunday afternoons, wearing, of course, his loose striped pajamas.

Chapter 19

An Unlikely Art Education

In the complex, invisible soft matter enclosed within our skulls, neurons quietly flash in the dark like bees, busily creating the honey of intelligence, feelings and memories. In mysterious ways, this brain of ours, this complex, astonishing soft mechanism of folds and crevices, electrical connections and computer-like perfection, directs our thoughts, our impulses, our longings and our will. We wonder at the rarity of genius and try to understand it by taking apart Einstein's brain but to no avail. We are in awe of the musical genius of Mozart, but we cannot understand it using rational thought. How does it happen, we wonder, that one becomes a scientist but not a painter, a painter but not a mathematician, a writer and not a musician? The mystery of creativity remains just that: a mystery.

It may not be surprising when a child born into a family of musicians becomes one as well, or when sons and daughters of actors yearn to follow their parents onto the stage. However, it is puzzling to have a painter, a mathematician or a writer emerge from a family that had no inclination towards any of these professions. No one in my family showed any interest in art although my father played the piano. His sister, Maria, would pass some of the time painting small, amateurish pictures that I never saw or heard anyone talk about.

In 1948 we went to see Aunt Frida and her family in Bucharest and visited the National Art Museum, located in what had been the Royal Palace before King Mihai was exiled to Switzerland. I can't say that this first encounter with a museum was an epiphany for me or that this visit changed my life, but it nevertheless was an experience I have not forgotten.

We climbed the wide stone staircase leading to the entrance of the imposing former palace and found ourselves in a huge hall with high ceilings heavily ornamented with gilded patterns. We walked through poorly lit halls, blinded at times by sunshine streaming through the tall windows. Large classical-style paintings depicting battle scenes, landscapes and peasants in the fields, portraits of workers, gypsies and more peasants hung on the walls. Nicolae Grigorescu, one of the founders of Romanian painting, was heavily represented.

Curiously, my art education did not come from exposure to real paintings. Today we might call it a 'virtual' experience since much of my knowledge of art was acquired by looking at reproductions.

The French-language *Larousse Encyclopedia* from my parents' library became a steady friend that brought me much delight during my early teens. I spent many happy hours reading definitions of words, life stories of famous inventors, kings and queens, artists and explorers; I enjoyed looking at the old-fashioned drawings of plants, machines and food; I pored over maps of various countries and portraits of great leaders, of writers and emperors, inventors and poets. The black-and-white reproductions of famous paintings on glossy pages were the crowning glory of those tomes for me. I would stare often at *Napoleon's Coronation* by David, Renoir's *Bal au Moulin de la Galette*, Ingres' beautiful nudes, Fragonard's saccharine paintings and Manet's *Olympia*. Géricault's dramatic *The Raft of the Medusa* and *La Liberté Guidant le People* by Delacroix captivated me, as did Gauguin's exotic Tahitian images. It was from these reproductions of poor quality that I received my basic education in the history of art. I never dared to think that one day I might see the real paintings hanging in all their glory on the walls of some of the great museums of Europe.

In 1948, after the closure of the Catholic schools, I transferred to a public high school for girls. The communist government had banned religion, considering it too dangerous for young minds. Even Christmas was abolished — the holiday became the 'Winter Holiday' and Santa Claus was renamed 'Father Winter'.

The new curriculum concentrated on studies concerning the Soviet Union and the Russian language. Most of us resented being forced to study Russian, but I secretly enjoyed learning the Cyrillic alphabet although I did not want to admit it. I can still read it today, albeit with difficulty. We had to study the geography of the Soviet Union in painstaking and excruciatingly minute detail. Each region, with its capital, its industry, its cooperative farms, or *kolkhoz*, and steel factories, had to be rigorously memorized. All the regions of the USSR, like Azerbaijan, Georgia, Kazakhstan, Kyrgyzstan, Latvia, Tajikistan, Turkmenistan, Ukraine and Uzbekistan were of no interest to us whatsoever but we had to study them. Maps had to be drawn and tests written. I can't remember any art classes included in this curriculum.

Since I had become adept at decorating the maps that we had to draw, adding small drawings and watercolours of villages, mountains and peasants, much as I used to do at the Sancta Maria Institute, and was also helping my schoolmates to design their maps, I developed somewhat of a reputation as the 'class artist'.

As a result of this reputation, I was given the 'important' task of producing a portrait of Stalin. The personality cult was now the cornerstone of the new order. Comrade Stalin was seen in large posters everywhere, a Cheshire Cat smile under his thick moustache, always dressed in his blue-grey uniform and wearing multiple decorations.

I clearly recall how terrified I was of making a mistake. Perhaps his moustache would come out too thick, perhaps his smile would not look so benign and the proportions of his body would be wrong. To play it safe, I enlarged the portrait by using a grid, much like drawing a map.

In my painting, the great leader, the adored, much-worshipped hero of the Soviet Union, the conqueror of fascism and the father of all the Russians, stood casually, wearing his blue-grey uniform and smiling his fatherly grin. The portrait was a success.

Two years later, before leaving for Israel, I had to take an oral examination of Soviet geography in order to get my ninth-grade diploma. By then, my mind was already set on the *Transylvania*, the ship that was to carry me away and I stumbled over some of the answers. In the nastiest voice she could muster, the teacher asked me, "Miss Savin, won't you feel embarrassed when you are asked questions about the Soviet Union in Israel and do not know the answers?"

Well, I was sure that nobody in Israel would be interested to know how many factories there were in Uzbekistan, but I swallowed my words.

Chapter 20

History Happens

I simply can't build my hopes on a foundation of confusion, misery and death . . . I think . . . peace and tranquillity will return once more.

Anne Frank
The Diary of a Young Girl

On November 29, 1947, following months of negotiations, political maneuvering, intense meetings and endless discussions, Resolution 181, approving the partition of Palestine, was read at the United Nations. Thirty-three nations approved, the United States being the very first, followed three days later by the USSR. Thirteen countries rejected the decision and ten abstained.

On May 14, 1948, the day that the British Mandate over Palestine expired, the Jewish People's Council in Tel-Aviv passed a proclamation declaring the creation of the state of Israel according to the partition plan. David Ben-Gurion, the first prime minister of Israel, read the Declaration of Independence at the Tel-Aviv Museum.

The state of Israel was born.

The newly created map, similar to many other maps concocted by committees of western politicians with no understanding of the facts on the ground, was absurd. It set boundaries for a minuscule country that was defenseless and vulnerable to attack, consisting of two small pieces of land joined by a narrow strip and a larger mass in the south that was mainly desert.

The Jews, living under the British Mandate of Palestine, accepted the partition immediately while the Arabs, living under the same British Mandate, rejected it out of hand, along with most of the Arab states, and threatened to smash and destroy any Jewish entity in the area.

There was great rejoicing in the new state of Israel. People danced in the streets, singing and celebrating until late at night, seeing it as an end to two thousand years of persecution and the beginning of a new legitimacy for the Jews as a free people in their own land. Jews all over the world sat glued to the radio listening to the historic news, crying and laughing with happiness.

The very next day, on May 15th, rejecting Israel's hand offered in peace, five Arab states — Egypt, Syria, Lebanon, Iraq and Jordan, with Saudi Arabian units fighting alongside Egypt — invaded the tiny new state.

During the difficult months of Israel's 1948 War of Independence, we teenage kids in Brăila were anxiously following the news, raising money and spending many hours in intense meetings where we discussed our fears and concern that, just as we found ourselves on the threshold of a new era of freedom, the fledgling new state may be lost. Beyond everything else, we desperately kept hoping.

Miraculously, despite heavy casualties, as well as poorly trained and sparsely armed Israeli forces, the fledging young country prevailed — the biblical victory of David over Goliath was repeated in the 20th Century. Unfortunately, this war was only the beginning of many more to follow. Israel would always win, but peace would never be achieved.

Now, in the second decade of the 21st Century, the vilification of Zionism and Israel has metastasized from the old anti-Semitic cancer. The world has forgotten the initial reason for Israel's conception: the very survival of the Jewish people whose roots were buried deep in that ancient soil. Had the state of Israel been created before the war, it could have served as a refuge for European Jews.

Chapter 21

My Father Flees Romania

Freedom from fear . . . could be said to sum up the whole philosophy of human rights.

Dag Hammarskjöld
from a speech at the celebration of the 180th anniversary
of the Virginia Declaration of Rights, May 16, 1956

"Arrested! They were all arrested! Everybody on the board has been arrested!"

The words tumbled out of my mother's mouth. The news was bad — very bad indeed!

Most of the people sitting on the Board of Directors of the cooperative store in Brăila, including my father, were members of the Social Democratic Party. Unfortunately for them, the Communists were gradually and systematically extending their grip over politics. The Social Democratic Party was literally swallowed up by the Communist Party, meaning the end of socialism in Romania. It did not take long for the Communist Party to put unbearable pressure on the Board of Directors to become Party members.

One day the axe fell. Not joining the Party was considered an act of treason and non-members, such as the non-affiliated Board of Directors, were declared unfit to serve the organization. They were duly rounded up and arrested.

Except for my father.

Being in the right place at the right time, as the old cliché says, was his saving grace. At the time of the arrests, he happened to be in Bucharest as merchandise buyer for the co-op. My mother warned him not to return home since doing so would ensure his arrest as well.

Unexpectedly, my father found himself at a crossroads with little time to make the crucial decision that would shape his and his family's future. Joining the Party would end his personal freedom and force him to live a lie but preserve his job. On the other hand, following his conscience would be fraught with danger, making him a fugitive and forcing him to flee Romania.

He opted for the latter and went into hiding in Bucharest, at a family member's apartment. There was no going back.

Although I was almost fourteen years old at the time, details of this emergency were kept from me. The old cloud of worry and uncertainty darkened our life anew. Comings and goings, meaningful eye contact and whispered conversations meant that important and dangerous things were about to happen. It was safer to keep me in the dark, as harsh interrogations of children whose families were on the authorities' blacklist were only too common.

Our lives changed drastically overnight. Living in our house became unsustainable, so we moved in with my grandfather, who was on his own after my grandmother's death. What anguish and worry must have been my mother's share, what fear and stress she must have experienced! This was the first time she had been separated from the husband whom she had known and loved since childhood. I have no idea how she managed the big move, how she disposed of all our things, the furniture, the books, the pots and pans, everything we had. The only memory I have of those days is a constant pervasive feeling of anxiety. But my mother was a fighter. That was the time when my belief in her ability to overcome any of life's ordeals became entrenched. She was the 'fixer' of the family as far as I was concerned.

My mother went into action. For her own safety, she had to express publicly her dismay at her husband's treacherous behaviour towards the communist paradise. Without losing any time, she filed for divorce. This was the only way of showing her loyalty to the new régime and to distance herself from her guilty husband. This being a civil divorce, the authorities never realized that the religious Jewish marriage was not undone and according to Jewish law, she was still Lascar's wife. According to Romanian civil law she was now a free woman, safe from suspicion of collaborating with a fugitive.

The efforts to smuggle my father out of the country went into high gear. Hurried trips to Bucharest and consultations with various friends and people with the right connections followed in quick succession. It all was eerily familiar to situations experienced during the war when the fascists ruled the country.

I don't recall how long it took and I don't know how much it cost, but finally, a deal was struck with the captain of a Yugoslav freighter active in the business of smuggling people out of the country. This was 1949, a time when the Communist Party was tightening the noose of oppression — for ridiculous reasons, or for no reason at all, people were disappearing and not heard from again. A growing number of Jews and of course, former fascists, were desperately trying to leave Romania by any means possible. A popular escape route was via freighters sailing on the Danube, whose captains smuggled refugees across the border into Yugoslavia where they were accepted by the régime of Joseph Broz Tito.

Fleeing Romania was not easy, nor was it safe. So much could go wrong! The captain might denounce his illegal cargo for yet another bribe, or once in Yugoslavia, the authorities might arrest the fugitives and return them to Romania.

One day, the good news arrived at last: my father had left Romania and was safe in Yugoslavia. He told me the story of his escape later although, I'm sorry to say, I never asked for enough details. I'll never know how he was taken from Bucharest back to Brăila, where he boarded the freighter in the dead of night and hid below deck, carrying in his coat lining some jewellery and a few *cocosei*, 'little roosters', the golden coins stamped with a rooster's image that had become the secret currency in Romania. After the radical fiscal reform that wrought havoc on the middle class, robbing it of its assets, owning any of these gold coins was strictly forbidden. Still, somehow, people managed to hide a few coins, hoping for some monetary security.

The trip to Yugoslavia was a short one. At nightfall, the captain dropped off my father and his companions on Yugoslav territory. One may easily imagine the fear gripping the hearts of these illegal passengers who found themselves in the dark, not knowing where they were and what they should do. Were they still in Romania? Or were they perhaps in Bulgaria? Or had the captain been honest and brought them to Yugoslavia as promised?

At daybreak, after a few hours of great anxiety, a group of armed Yugoslav soldiers appeared and arrested the small group. The fugitives were thoroughly searched and taken to a camp set up specifically for Romanian escapees. My father's money and jewellery were confiscated. Ironically, the camp's inmates were not only Jewish refugees but also Romanian former fascists fleeing the Communist régime. The tables had been turned on them by a quirk of fate: they had now joined their former victims and were fugitives themselves.

Lumping together these strange bedfellows was quite common after the war. Great Britain dealt with the flow of refugees from Germany and other countries by interning them all together as enemy aliens, later sending some to Canada and Australia. It did not matter to the British if these people had fled the Nazis or if they were Nazi themselves. As long as they were German aliens, they were interned. This led to some awkward situations as the oppressors and their former victims found themselves living in close proximity.

While Lascar awaited his fate in the Yugoslav refugee camp, important events were unfolding in post-war Europe.

Following Israel's Declaration of Independence, an intense rescue effort by The American Jewish Joint Distribution Committee, known as "The Joint," to bring as many surviving Jews as possible to Israel was underway. The memory of these post-war times has faded over the years — chaos reigned all over Europe with hundreds of thousands of refugees desperately trying to find lost families, searching for ways of returning to the homes they had left and finding them destroyed or occupied by others. Europe was teeming with the traumatized survivors of the inferno of the Holocaust, who had lost their entire families and had no home to return to. Abandoned children and survivors of scattered families were roaming the devastated land looking for parents, siblings, spouses. Eventually, many found themselves in displaced persons (DP) camps where they were nurtured back to life and helped to start anew.

It is frightening to behold the ugly wave of anti-Semitism sweeping Europe in the 21st Century, only seventy years after the war. We see again crowds of hooligans torching synagogues, attacking Jews on the street and Jewish children in the schools, shouting "Jews to the gas!" As unbelievable as it may seem, this is happening again in London, Amsterdam, Paris, Malmo and Berlin. The only difference is that now there is a place of refuge: Israel.

Young Jews from the British Mandate in Palestine were working hard to rescue as many refugees as they could and bring them to Palestine. Finding friendly ports to sail from and seaworthy boats that could brave the voyage was not easy.

One such friendly port was Trieste.

With the helping hand of the Jewish Agency, my father was able to leave the refugee camp in Yugoslavia. He became part of the great wave of immigration to Israel, the 'ingathering of exiles', or *kibbutz galuyot*. Before leaving the camp, he had an unexpected heartwarming experience: the Yugoslav guards returned all his personal belongings, including the jewellery and the gold coins.

A few days later, we received the much-awaited news: my father had arrived in Israel safe and sound.

The year was 1949 and he was thirty-nine years old.

Chapter 22

Deaths in The Family

The life of the dead is placed in the memory of the living.

Marcus Tullius Cicero
Philippica IX, 5

One night in 1949, shortly after my father had fled Romania and Freddy's old room in my grandfather's house had become mine, I was awoken from a deep sleep when my bedroom door opened. Startled, I stared into the darkness and saw Tzilly standing there, white as a sheet and shivering uncontrollably.

Half awake, I sat up and asked what happened.

"Dead," she whispered. "Tata Mare is dead!"

I could not believe it. Did she really mean it? Had I heard her properly, or was I dreaming? We had just had dinner together and I had seen grandfather before going to bed.

Leaning against the doorjamb for support, Tzilly related the shocking details in a hoarse whisper.

She had been sleeping with Leon that night, a regular habit that I had been completely unaware of although his bedroom was just across the hallway from mine. This time though, it was different. Fate had unleashed its mighty lightning rod and struck Leon in the chest just as he was performing Nature's most ancient pursuit. His heart stopped midway, his body crushing Tzilly under his considerable weight. I believe that his death was one that many men would wish for themselves. My grandfather had died while happily fulfilling his duty as the male of our species. A most pleasant death, indeed!

Not long after, Gabi's father died. Sammy was a jolly extroverted man, a *bon vivant* who loved to eat well, a modest swelling of his stomach just above his belt indicating that he had put on some unnecessary weight in his late thirties. During the war, he had been caught in the dragnet that sent Jews from Brăila to labour camps, where he'd fallen sick with a dangerous kidney condition and managed to return home only after a hefty bribe was paid. His condition required a stringent diet, but his philosophy of life did not allow it. Even though his doctor warned him that his kidneys would not withstand his eating habits, he refused to give up eating the foods he liked. "Better live life at its fullest the way I like and die young, than forego its pleasures and live in misery," was his maxim. Was he thinking at all about his adoring wife, Maria, or about Gabi, his young daughter?

Gabi's father was only forty-two years old when his kidneys finally gave out. Maria and Gabi, fourteen at the time, were devastated by his early death. In the Jewish tradition the burial takes place the day after death, with children not allowed in the cemetery. The safe edifice of a loving family crumbles as if destroyed by a sudden earthquake, leaving a gaping hole behind.

That night Gabi and I slept together in grandfather's house, sharing my bed in the temporary room upstairs. It is only this night that I remember. All other details of the day have been erased from my memory.

Here we were, having grown up together like sisters, now facing the harsh reality of life. We hugged one another in the darkened room and wept together.

Gabi cried for a very long time, shaking with grief, tears streaming down her cheeks. Her father had been her hero and her anchor and now he had abandoned her. I tried to comfort her, desperately racking my brain for the right words.

I hugged her tightly, but nothing I could say could comfort her. How could one console a child over the loss of her beloved father? At least, I thought, my father was still alive and one day I might see him again. But for Gabi there was no such hope.

Chapter 23

One Chapter Closes, Another Opens

A person's destiny is something you look back at afterwards, not something to be known in advance.

Haruki Murakami
The Wind-Up Bird Chronicle

Like most things in life under the Communists, our travel documents did not come easily and, fearing that the papers would never arrive, my mother went to Bucharest for a face-to-face meeting with the minister in charge of emigration. On her return, she told us how she had begged the stern official sitting like a god behind his desk to release the exit papers, finally breaking down in tears. It worked. The trip was a success and the long-awaited documents were approved. I think that her tears helped, but not as much as the *baksheesh* I'm sure she had to pay.

On May 8, 1950, my mother received the paper that would close the chapter of our lives in Romania. Printed at the top in large letters, it reads, "The Romanian Popular Republic: Certificate of Travel, valid for a trip in one direction only, to the State of Israel." I am mentioned as Paula, a child accompanying her mother.

There was so much to do! We found ourselves in the no-man's land between two stages of our lives. My mother, her Romanian roots torn asunder, was leaving behind her past, her family and friends and leaping unto the blank pages of a yet-unwritten script. Even so, the certainty of being reunited with her husband, the love of her life, filled her with happiness.

For me, at age fifteen, this was *it*! My dream of living in a country that I could call my own was about to come true. The great adventure of my life was about to begin.

One may think that this momentous change in our lives would have stayed clearly in my memory. However, I remember almost nothing about the preparations for the trip: the packing, the disposal of items to be left behind, the shipping and the leave-taking are all lost in a blur of excitement. We were fortunate to be the last group of emigrants allowed to take some of our possessions in a 'lift', a large crate loaded on the boat.

Although my memory is a blur, the small black-and-white photographs in my possession show without doubt that I did take leave of my friends. Most of them wrote hopeful words on the back of snapshots, expressing their wish to follow me soon to Israel. One photograph shows three girls hugging: my non-Jewish friends, Aurora and Cici, with myself between them. Their words of good wishes and friendship written on the back of the photograph warm my heart even now.

We left most of our photographs with Domnica, our former housekeeper, who promised that she would send them to us later. Alas, this never happened — those small mementoes with their serrated white borders documenting our lives are lost forever.

Three memories from our voyage stand out clearly. The first was a mild visual disappointment. I had never seen the sea before and always imagined an expanse of ultramarine blue reaching as far as the eye could see, meeting the sky on the horizon. When we arrived at the port of Constanza on the Black Sea, it happened to be a windy day. The blue expanse was not blue at all but rather a steely grey punctuated with whitecaps. My ideal of the wide blue sea was shattered by reality.

The second memory is an unpleasant one. The customs officials, sitting behind a long row of desks and disdainfully (if enviously) glaring at those treacherous Jews who were leaving behind the Communist Eden, were doing their best to make our departure as disagreeable as possible.

As I stood before the customs official, wearing small earrings and a little gold ring on my finger, he put out his hand and barked at me in a last spiteful farewell.

"Give me your ring and earrings. You won't be needing them where you're going!"

I did as I was told.

The third memory is very different. I may call it a coming of age. A young man whom I knew as the boyfriend of my older cousin Lily approached me on the ship. Five years my senior, his short stature did not seem to interfere in the least with his confident self-image. His curly brown hair was carefully combed back and oiled for better effect. A pair of large brown and very shiny eyes set close together like the lens of an inquisitive microscope made his face unusual. Sure of himself, he was strutting confidently on the deck, speaking with great authority and expressing strong opinions about everything. No wonder that I was so impressed by him! I was surprised and immensely flattered when he began flirting with me. I could not believe that he would even look at me after having dated Lily, my pretty older cousin from the capital. I was just a gawky, unattractive fifteen-year-old with little self-confidence and here he was, making passes at me!

I breathlessly waited to experience the great romantic feeling of falling in love with this unexpected suitor, but alas, nothing stirred within me. However, I did not allow this lack of infatuation to stand in the way of pretending that a great love affair was in the works and played along.

The stage was set. The script for my very first kiss on the deck of the *Transylvania*, on a romantic night with a full moon and stars shining on the waves, was written and I was chosen to perform the part of the star. What I was thinking? Was I dreaming of the passionate kisses of Bette Davis as Queen Elizabeth in the arms of Errol Flynn as Lord Essex that I saw at the local cinema in Brăila? I can only recall that my first kiss was not the wonderful experience I had dreamed about, particularly when my enterprising beau stuck his tongue inside my mouth. I did not dare show my disgust. I needed to show myself worldly and pretend that I was in heaven. Tzilly had never mentioned this type of kissing in any of her informative sessions. *Ugh!*

Finally, on June 11, 1950, the *Transylvania*, the sole vessel designated by Romania to carry emigrants to Israel, sailed into the port of Haifa with us on board. There, almost lost in the large crowd of people waving and shouting greetings from the quay below, was my father! More than a year had gone by since we had seen him.

Giddy with happiness at having finally succeeded in leaving Romania for Israel, we had been oblivious to the frenetic activity behind the scenes that had made our liberation possible. How true are the words of Haruki Murakami! I understood our destiny only much later, by researching Romania's sudden willingness to allow its Jews to emigrate. Even now in the 21st Century, this story is largely unknown. It had been kept secret for so many years that it had faded from the pages of history and languished, all but forgotten, in dusty archives.

The story of the Jewish emigration from Romania to Israel is complicated, but the basic fact is that it was considered as a business transaction: the Romanians sold their own citizens and were the first East European country to do so. The Jews had become a lucrative export, a good source of hard currency, as well as an exchange card for heavy equipment, for setting up poultry farms and other industries.

Israel was prepared to pay the price for bringing out the remaining Romanian Jews, who were the largest number of Holocaust survivors in Europe, excluding the Soviet Union. The Romanians, realizing that they had found a willing customer for their merchandise, kept increasing the price. From Radu Ioanid's book, *The Ransom of the Jews*, I learned that my mother and I had been worth $100 each. Over the years, under the Ceaușescu régime, this fee escalated to more than $5000. Despite the ugliness of the deal, we had been lucky. The corruption in Communist Romania helped us leave, just as it had saved lives under the fascists.

Between 1948 and 1951, Jewish emigration was an important source of hard currency for Romania, reaching about $2 million annually. By 1953, when the Communist Party closed the gates, about 100,000 Jews had left for Israel. Following intense negotiations during the next few years, emigration to Israel resumed in 1958. Due to the ongoing financial arrangements and in spite of rampant anti-Semitism, Romania was the only Eastern European country behind the Iron Curtain to maintain diplomatic relations with Israel. The Romanians' requirement for the continuation of emigration to Israel was to keep these business deals highly secret. The tens of thousands of Jews who applied for visas were ignorant of their importance as a revenue source for the Romanian government, which in addition to the per capita payments, made immigration a harrowing and traumatic experience. Applying for an exit visa automatically entailed losing one's job and often one's house, essentially condemning the applicant to live in limbo in the hope that approval would soon come. Sometimes the wait was short, but other times it could last years. In some cases, the travel papers never materialized.

Leaning against the rails on the deck of the *Transylvania* and seeing my father waving to us on the quay below in the hot June sun, we understood that the first act of our lives had ended. After a short intermission, the second act was about to begin.

ACT II
ISRAEL

Chapter 24

Israel

It is hot. Very hot.

A searing blanket of sheer light hangs down from the bleached sky and wraps itself tightly over white buildings, softened grey asphalt and the silky blond sand lining the turquoise Mediterranean Sea.

The heat weighs on the green hedges dotted by luscious red hibiscus flowers and the sunlight highlights the masses of bougainvillea hanging over walls like rich purple curtains. It bounces off the long narrow leaves of oleander shrubs lining the road to Haifa, bringing their white and pink perfumed flowers into sharp focus. The sun is everywhere: bright, hot and blinding.

August 1950. School begins very soon. I am able to read the phonetic Hebrew alphabet but do not understand the words and cannot speak the language. I sit for hours on my old bed/divan, now my parents' bed, memorizing words, words and more words. I should enter grade ten, but how? There is so little time to study and it is so very, very hot!

We arrived in the fledgling state of Israel just as the Knesset, or Parliament, had passed the Law of Return. This law gave all people of Jewish ancestry the right to come and settle as citizens in Israel. Following the United Nations vote to establish a state for the Jewish people, the gates opened wide. An unprecedented wave of immigrants poured in, more than doubling the new country's Jewish population of about 600,000 people.

We were the remnants of a bonfire of evil coming from all over Europe: Romania, Hungary, Poland, Germany, Ukraine, Austria, the Netherlands, France and many more. There were also hundreds of thousands who had fled persecution in the Arab world. They came from Iraq, Morocco, Yemen, Egypt, Syria and others, bringing with them different cultures and adding new sounds to this modern Babel.

The little-known but massive exodus of Jews fleeing Arab countries, chased from their homes, their citizenship revoked and their properties confiscated, began with the 1948 Arab-Israeli War. Their numbers outstripped the number of Palestinian refugees fleeing during the Arab attacks on Israel. Unlike their unfortunate counterparts, they were all resettled in only a few short years.

With the benefit of hindsight, I understand how fortunate my family was within the turmoil and upheaval of immigration. We arrived in a small country of few means that had just experienced a difficult war of survival. Within five years, from 1947 to 1952, the population doubled in size. The young Israeli pioneer wearing the trademark sun hat, the *kova tembel*, literally a 'silly hat', who had dried the swamps and prevailed against powerful foes, had suddenly grown up, his clothes bursting at the seams. We were but three of the thousands upon thousands of refugees arriving daily from the four corners of the earth, destitute and deeply traumatized from their war experience in Europe and persecution in the Arab countries. How does one house these people, how does one feed them, teach them the language, put them to work? One immediate solution was the establishment of the makeshift transit camps, or *ma'abarot*. At first, they consisted of tents and later *pahonim*, or tin huts.

Why was my family allotted a small one-bedroom flat instead of a tent? It was all due to my mother, a fervent Zionist who had been diligently raising money for Israel in Romania. As a reward for her efforts, we found ourselves among the privileged. We were allocated a *shikun*. What was a *shikun*? In the frantic rush to accommodate the multitude of new immigrants, the Israeli government came up with the idea of building cheap and easily constructed pre-fab housing, called *shikunim*, literally 'housing'.

Most of the Haifa suburbs were built along a narrow strip of sand, each called a *kirya*. Our *shikun* was in Kiryat Yam Ghimmel. Nicknamed Gav Yam Ghimmel, meaning 'the back of the sea', it was the newest and the very last in this row of settlements, *ghimmel*, the third letter of the Hebrew alphabet, standing for the number three. The new suburb was built directly on sand dunes on the shores of the Mediterranean Sea and consisted of uniformly white prefabricated two-storey cement blocks arranged in parallel rows. From the air, it might have looked as if children playing dominoes had placed these white rectangular blocks on a sandy table, ready for the game. The sand dunes, stretching all the way to the seashore, their shapes constantly altered by the shifting wind, surrounded the pre-fab blocks. We used to climb these dunes for fun, our feet sinking deep into the unstable sand. Amazingly, bits of vegetation sprouted on the sand like tufts of a teenager's beard.

In truth, I never liked the sand. It was everywhere; it coated our skin, entered our nostrils and invaded our clothes. The pleasant breeze constantly blowing from the sea brought sand inside the dwellings, depositing it in the corners of the room and covering the floor with a fine, gritty layer that had to be swept away at least once a day. It penetrated our sandals, settled between our toes, and was even found in our sandwiches. Over time, the sand became part of everyday life and I stopped thinking about it.

Our flat would now be called a studio apartment, which sounds more elegant than it really was. Located on the second floor, it consisted of one tiny room, a smaller kitchen and an even smaller toilet and shower. That was it. And we were lucky to live within solid walls rather than a tent!

My parents and I in
Kiryat Yam Ghimmel

My parents slept on my former bed, the divan we'd brought from Romania. Each morning, my mother removed the sheets and aired them on the windowsill, then folded and stored them inside the large box built at the head of the bed, just as she had done in Brăila. Stripped of the sheets and pillows, the bed reverted to a daybed/sofa for general use. I slept on a narrow green armchair that was opened each night into a stone-hard bed with no mattress. A similar ritual was performed with my sheets each morning: the 'bed' was folded back into an armchair and the sheets stored in the big box.

Sleeping in such narrow confines with my parents who were in their early forties and still very much in love, especially after a year-long separation, was not an experience I remember fondly. I wished I had some earplugs during those hot nights, but all I could do was stuff my fingers in my ears and try to ignore the moans coming from the bed across the room. I still wonder what my parents were thinking.

Two important items had been left behind in Brăila. The first were the family photographs that filled the ceramic pond of the little fisherman in our old dining room, which we had left with Domnica. The second item, the loss of which I regretted even more, was the journal I had kept from 1947 to 1950, which I had left with Gabi, asking her to mail it to me later. I had been afraid to take it along, worried that the customs officers would find this subversive document. But Gabi had panicked and burned it, fearing that it might fall into the wrong hands.

After my arrival in Israel, Gabi and I wrote regularly to one another. One day, I discovered that my curious father had been reading our letters. He, of course, saw nothing wrong and did not understand why I was upset at this breach of privacy. It was all in the family, right? He loved me very much, he said, and was interested in everything I thought, the friends I had, the things I did.

I did not see this intrusion of privacy his way and greatly resented it. We had to stop my well-meaning father from reading our 'secrets'. The solution was simple enough: we wrote to each other in Romanian, but instead of the Latin alphabet, we began using the Russian Cyrillic script that he could not read. At last we could put to good use the hours spent on learning a language we detested — this foreign script was now our 'secret code'.

My memories of the first months in Kiryat Yam are lost in a haze of excitement, with hours upon hours perched on the divan memorizing Hebrew words, full of anxiety about school. Arrangements were made for me to enroll in a school in the nearby suburb of Kiryat Motzkin, a small town on a sandy patch of land on the road to Haifa. This arid, empty land had been transformed into a green oasis of tree-lined streets and pretty bungalows with red tile roofs. The school was named Achdut (Unity) and is still in use.

Having finished grade nine in Romania, I should have been accepted in grade ten, but although familiar with most of the subjects, I could not yet speak Hebrew and could not write exams. Nor did I know enough English and my knowledge of the spoken Arabic taught in elementary school was non-existent. Taking all these factors into consideration, I was put a year back and found myself in grade nine again.

What a year that was! We studied chapters from the *Tanakh*, or the Hebrew Bible, which I could follow only with great effort, having had no previous instruction in ancient Hebrew. Doing homework and writing tests was as difficult as climbing Everest. I began mixing up the three new languages with Romanian, French and German. I felt like a top spinning wildly, just trying to stay upright. Even so, by the end of the year my hard work had paid off: I was fluent in Hebrew and even managed to bargain in Arabic at the Haifa market. The top had not toppled over!

Most of my schoolmates were native-born Israelis, or 'Sabras'. This nickname compares the Jews born in Israel to the fruit of a thorny desert plant known in English as prickly pear: tough and prickly on the outside but sweet and tender on the inside. These kids, wearing sandals and blue or khaki shorts, looked healthy and free. They seemed superior to me — sure of themselves, chattering away in Hebrew with an accent I thought was wonderful with its guttural 'kh's and French-sounding 'arrr's, proud and confident of their place in their own country. These youngsters were so very different from us, the immigrants. How I wished to be like them!

The *Sabras* looked upon the new arrivals with some measure of disdain. We were seen as the Diaspora Jews who went to their deaths 'as cattle to slaughter', while here in Israel, the Jews stood up and heroically fought for their freedom. The *Sabras'* sense of superiority made them see us through glasses tinted by dreary colours of persecution and submission which they disdained, but their youthful arrogance was unfortunate. Ignorant of the history of Diaspora Jews and poorly educated by their parents about the immigrants flooding the country, they had become an elite similar to the American Mayflower generation.

It was too soon after the Holocaust for all the stories of desperate bravery, such as the Ghetto Warsaw Uprising, to be known and appreciated. Most of the *Sabras* had no interest in or knowledge of Jewish life in Europe. I was amazed at the ignorance and lack of information when a girl in my class asked me whether there were sidewalks in Romania. Ah, the bliss of belonging to a generation of Jews born in freedom!

The basic yearning of human beings is to belong — to be part of a community, a culture, a place. Alas, as I was to discover repeatedly later in life, for the immigrant this yearning is a difficult one to satisfy. Once the break with one's place of birth occurs, the roots are severed. Learning a new language, adapting to a new culture and attempting to fit into new customs and new communities are difficult, if enriching, experiences. One may develop a certain sense of belonging, but these new roots will never be as deep as they are for people who never left their place of birth. The otherness of the immigrant follows like a shadow. A strange accent, a different childhood and different experiences are evident to the natives of the new country and create an invisible barrier between them and the newcomers. However, the chance to begin life anew away from danger, persecution and war is worth the price.

I was extremely happy to be in Israel. But then, why was I so unsure of myself? Why was I feeling ugly, clumsy and so much an outsider? Was this just the normal angst of adolescence? Or were these feelings the normal pangs of anxiety of growing roots in a new place? I felt more relaxed when I came home from school. In Kiryat Yam, all immigrants were like me. I could speak Romanian with young people who had a similar background to mine and later, after mastering Hebrew, I could converse with many others from all over Europe whose languages had been French, German, Polish, Hungarian or Czech. Here, there was a sense of belonging — and it felt good. This is the reason immigrants with a similar background tend to cluster together. In the midst of these momentous changes, we all felt that here and now, in this sparse and basic settlement hastily erected on sand dunes on the shore of the Mediterranean Sea, we had reached a place that connected us with our ancient past.

Chapter 25

All Is New, All Is Different

What matters in life is not what happens to you but what you remember and how you remember it.

Gabriel García Márquez
One Hundred Years of Solitude

I'm not a swimmer.

I never learned how to swim and always hated getting my face wet. I regretted not being able to jump into the blue water of the pool and swim like a fish, but I was clearly not made to be an amphibian and that was that.

Arriving in a new country and having to learn a new language, sharing a room with my parents and seeing my father unable to practice his profession as an accountant for his lack of Hebrew, made me feel as if I had been thrown into the water and had to swim for dear life. And swim I did. It helped that my face stayed dry.

Did I consider myself poor? No, I did not. Everybody else was just like us. In fact, we were better off than many others who lived in tent shanties. So what if my father could not be a white-collar accountant but was now driving a cement truck in partnership with another immigrant? When this partnership did not work, too bad! For me, this was the great adventure, but for my parents it must have been a time of worry, dislocation and uncertainty.

As Gabriel García Márquez said, "What matters in life is not what happens to you but what you remember and how you remember it." Yes, I do remember the anxiety of being a teenager torn between two worlds: the world of immigrants like me where I felt a sense of belonging and the world of the native-born *Sabras*. I felt bereft, an outsider who desperately wanted to be let in. But what I do remember most clearly is the sense of excitement and adventure in living a new life.

My father's interlude as truck driver did not end well. The business failed, the truck had to be sold and he was out of work for the first time in his life.

Food was scarce, since providing for the large number of immigrants arriving daily was no small matter and miracle workers, like Jesus, who fed the multitudes were not readily available. Instead, these were the days of the '*Tzenah*', of scarcity and rations, with food stamps and belt-tightening for everyone.

My mother took up sewing under the generous guidance of Reshka, our next-door Hungarian neighbour. People could not afford to buy new clothes, opting instead to alter their old ones and my mother, who had never worked before, was suddenly in big demand, an echo of her own efforts to help women make a living in Brăila. Reshka, the warm-hearted seamstress with a ready smile on her chubby face, was always there with advice and referrals for her Romanian friend. Ironically, German became the common language between them and many other European immigrants who had no time to study Hebrew, too busy trying to support their families. Being a seamstress benefitted my mother twice over: she was not only earning money, but also making new friends who needed alterations, almost always resulting in coffee and delightful gossip.

Despite the hardships and the uncertainties of everyday life, there was safety in the loving relationship of my parents and their love for me. There were the tender moments when my father would caress my mother's hand, put his arm around her waist or just hug her for no reason at all.

ART AS BUSINESS

My first goal was school. The next step could not be called a goal: it was the compulsory two years of service in the Israeli Army.

But then what? I would have loved to become an artist. An artist? Crazy thought! How could I make a living as an artist? These were difficult times. Food was still rationed, my family had no money and I wanted to be an artist? So what if I could draw and paint?

Nevertheless, these skills came in handy during the three years before I joined the army. For the second time after my short-lived business venture in grade two, I was earning money with my painting and happy to help my parents.

My first job was painting cuckoo clocks — an unlikely job in a new country running on food stamps, wouldn't you say? Even so, it was great for an enterprising sixteen-year-old.

A shop in Haifa selling watches and clocks of all kinds was keen to market Swiss-style clocks for children's rooms, featuring a cuckoo that jumped out on the hour chirping cheerfully. The owners made these clocks in the shop behind the counter and needed someone to paint the wooden front with colourful Disney characters. I got the job. The notion of appropriation or plagiarism was totally foreign to me then, so I happily painted cute Mickey and Minnie Mouse figures dancing and prancing on clock fronts among green vines cascading among the flowers. Snow White and the Seven Dwarfs were a favourite motif, as were Winnie the Pooh and other charming denizens of popular children's tales. One of my sources for plagiarism was the music book I had rescued from Romania, featuring music and images from Walt Disney films.

The store supplied the wood, cut into the right shapes and ready to be decorated. I would begin work by laying a waxed tablecloth on the table, on which I would arrange gouache paints, pencils and brushes. Painting these pieces of wood turned out to be an enjoyable occupation. How wonderful to earn money and have fun at the same time! However, after a few months, the demand stopped and the shop went out of business.

My second job came from a store selling lampshades. I suggested to the owner the idea of creating hanging lampshades for children's rooms and he readily agreed. Now I had to find a way to put my idea into practice.

I bought thick wires in circular shapes and traced them on thin Bristol cardboard — the lampshade would be the cutout cardboard that was then sewn to the wire with coloured raffia ribbon. The lampshade would hang from the ceiling by three thin metal chains attached to the wire. The best part of the job was decorating the cardboard with flowers, animals, figures of children dancing and whatever else came into my head.

Still, there was a problem. Since transparent parchment was unavailable, I had to use cardboard, which was not transparent. What kind of a lampshade would that be if the light could not shine through?

At last, someone gave me the idea of rubbing the cardboard with cooking oil. Presto! The white Bristol cardboard became exactly what I needed: a lovely, perfect ecru piece of transparent parchment. Eagerly, I set out to decorate my first lampshade when another unexpected snag arose.

My paints were fast-drying water-based gouache, while the surface I worked on was oily. Upon contact with the oily cardboard, the paint was immediately rejected, splitting into small particles like coloured bits of quicksilver. Disaster! Was this the end of my bold enterprise?

After a few days of frantic investigations, the answer was revealed. Simple and elegant like all best solutions, it resided in the innocuous bar of soap modestly resting on the sink. By dipping my brush into a soapy solution, the oil was instantly defeated, meekly accepting the water-based gouache paints. I was in business!

Just trying to stay afloat at school was an all-consuming experience. Investing all my energies into my studies was so important to my parents that when I offered to help my mother occasionally in the kitchen, she would send me back to my books saying that I would learn to cook later. My job for now was to concentrate on my studies.

One day we received a letter with the good news that Maria and Gabi, who were still in Brăila, had been allowed to make *aliyah*, which means "ascending" in Hebrew and is used to describe immigration to Israel. By then, the rules for emigrants had been tightened, allowing them to carry with them only a couple of suitcases. Jewellery was confiscated before boarding the ship and no valuables were allowed out of Romania. Desperate to salvage whatever they could, people resorted to unorthodox solutions. Ingenuity usually appears in dire circumstances — in this case, it was the invention of the diamond pill. Jewellery was dismantled, diamonds embedded in necklaces, rings and bracelets were removed and inserted into small capsules that were swallowed and retrieved later on the ship, once the Romanian shores had faded in the distance.

While waiting for Maria and Gabi's arrival, I realized that after only a few months in Israel, I had become the 'old-timer' who had (hopefully) learned the ropes of navigating this new place. It was up to us now to help our relatives deal with the trauma of finding their bearings in this unsettled sea of humanity. Due to arrive in January, Gabi would not be accepted in school. Her first priority would be to learn Hebrew, so I began looking for an *ulpan*, the Israeli version of an English as a second language school, where she could enroll.

Hiding behind my wish to help Gabi, Fate was preparing a fresh scenario that would define my life.

Chapter 26

Just By Chance

You can't control the wind, but you can adjust your sails.

Yiddish Proverb

Things just happen.

For no reason at all, I found myself in a place that would lead my life towards an unexpected direction. What made me take the bus to Haifa on that day, at that particular hour? And what made me sit next to the slight, black-haired boy wearing glasses and short khaki pants? His nose buried in a book, he seemed oblivious to his surroundings. Curious, I glanced sideways and saw that he was studying a Hebrew language manual. The boy was learning Hebrew! Here was a source of information about a Hebrew school for Gabi, who would be arriving soon.

As I tentatively began speaking to him, I was faced with a pair of green eyes adorned by the longest eyelashes I had ever seen. The conversation flowed easily when we found out that we both came from Romania. His name was Eddy. He was studying at an *ulpan*, one of the Hebrew schools for new immigrants, and was planning to enter grade eleven the next year.

"Oh," I said. "You have no chance! Look what happened to me! They'll set you one year back, as they did to me".

To my surprise, this information didn't seem to worry him at all.

"I have to get in," he said. "If not, too bad! I'll go away and be a sailor!"

I was mightily impressed by this daring statement. As a girl, my options were much less interesting, I thought. A secretary or a seamstress perhaps, or just a shop girl, but nothing as exciting as running away to the big blue sea. I liked this guy!

By the time the bus reached the station, we were friends. We discovered that we lived in the same settlement, but with a difference: his family had been able to buy a two-bedroom place in a larger building closer to the sea, making Eddy seem rich to me. He even had a room all to himself!

Our friendship continued throughout the year. We studied together. Eddy helped me with math and physics and I helped him with Hebrew, English and Tanakh. We studied in his room where it was quiet and we could concentrate, unlike in our one-room flat where there was no privacy. His parents were delighted with my friendship with their wild son who never listened to them.

The long-awaited day arrived; Maria and Gabi had landed. We took them home to our tiny one-room *shikun*, where they would stay for about four months while waiting for a shack in one of the *ma'abarot*, the transit camps for new immigrants. Gabi and I were overjoyed to be together again, but our parents had to struggle with the logistics and the hardships of everyday life.

This was the nightly sleep ritual: The table was moved tight against the wall. The new mattress was dragged to the middle of the room and my armchair/bed was pushed further back into the corner. The room became like a can of sardines, its five inhabitants packed tightly together.

Despite the overcrowding and the daily difficulties, I don't remember ever yearning for the comfortable house we had left behind. I never asked my parents if they had any regrets and if they did, they never mentioned them. Everyone was just too busy trying to get settled, make a living and adapt to the new conditions.

Eventually, Maria and Gabi received a shack and moved out. Their new abode was a far cry from what one could call a house or even a small apartment. Dark khaki tarpaulin walls enclosed the smallest space imaginable, covered with a corrugated tin roof that kept out the rain and protected its inhabitants from the fierce sun. Their former house in Brăila was now just a glowing memory of unattainable luxury. Mother and daughter had joined the ranks of immigrants arriving daily from the four corners of the Earth who transformed Israel almost overnight into a crowded refugee camp.

I was shocked seeing the *ma'abara* for the first time. The tarpaulin shacks stretched as far as the eye could see, row upon row of makeshift, drab, sad dwellings without enough shower and toilet facilities to serve the large numbers of people who lived in these shantytowns. This was a refugee camp in the real sense of the word! However, within three years, the *ma'abarot* were gone; small towns or villages sprouted like spring flowers in their stead.

The 'streets' between the rows of shanties were unpaved. During the winter, unrelenting rains reverberated like thunder on the tin roofs. One had to slog through deep mud, wade through puddles or teeter on slippery improvised boardwalks in order to move from one shack to another. During the summer, the sun blazed on the metal roof, transforming the little huts into hot ovens. I'm not sure which was worse.

Yet, amazingly, Gabi remembers the time she lived there as one of the happiest of her life. Young people from all over the world coalesced into groups and communities studying Hebrew and helping one another. Despite the difficult conditions, there was a sense of happiness and belonging created by deep bonds of community. Everyone was in the same boat. Everyone was poor, everyone had hope for a better life and everyone knew that they were home at last. And everyone had dreams.

It was exhilarating to be living during these emotional and exciting historic times. We were experiencing the prophetic moment of the 'ingathering of the exiles', or *kibbutz galuyot,* as promised by Moses.

That then the LORD thy God will turn thy
captivity, and have compassion upon thee, and will
return and gather thee from all the nations, whither
the LORD thy God hath scattered thee.

Deuteronomy 30:3

Even those of us who were not religious could sense the historical intensity of those times. We were living a two-thousand-year-old dream come true. The ancient *Haggadah* story of the liberation from Egypt read by Jews everywhere during Passover, that ended in the eternal sentence "Next year in Jerusalem!" was now a reality.

In our two-storey building alone, we had neighbours from Hungary, Poland and France. Some, like the woman who lived downstairs, had the ominous blue number tattooed on their arms. One day, she casually mentioned the reason she had no children: she was one of the Auschwitz twins experimented upon by the infamous Dr. Mengele. However, most people did not speak about their experiences, trying to forget the painful past and get on with the present.

My father, usually a dapper dresser, would return home tired, dirty and disheartened after a day of backbreaking labour in construction. The tiny new country had no work to offer the new immigrants in the professions they were trained for when they could not yet speak the language. Physicians were driving cabs, professors were sweeping the streets and women who had never worked in their lives, hired themselves out as housekeepers. Many of them eventually worked their way up to better and more suitable jobs but, in the beginning, they had to do whatever they could to support themselves and their families.

Chapter 27

Never A Boring Moment

Life is either a daring adventure or nothing at all.

Helen Keller
The Open Door

In the summer of 1951 Eddy and I both passed the exams. I skipped a grade and Eddy was accepted into grade eleven, just as he had planned. However, I realized to my dismay that high school was not free in Israel at that time. Although the fees were not high, they were out of reach for my parents. Not having managed to learn Hebrew, my father could not get work as an accountant and the construction job he had was poorly paid. Would my efforts to skip a grade have been in vain?

Unexpectedly and to my great joy, Eddy's parents came to the rescue. They generously offered to pay my school fees and life looked bright again. Maybe they were slyly planning for their son's future, making sure that our friendship would continue and who knows, perhaps, just perhaps, one day . . .

Eddy's parents, Kubi and Mina Granirer, were as different from one another as could be. Kubi, a short man with thick wavy greying hair and heavy glasses, was an intellectual, a gentle man who had been a teacher of French and Latin. Small, slim, with dark hair and ready wit, Mina was an intelligent woman with a good sense of humour and a great interest in money.

Like many other Romanian young men, Kubi had studied in Paris and then taught in Romanian high schools. During the war, after spending eight months in a labour camp, he was let go thanks to the intervention of Rudolf Donnermann, his German brother-in-law, who paid a hefty bribe for the freedom of Kubi, Mina and six-year-old Eddy. The family moved to Bucharest, where Kubi taught at the Jewish school, Cultura.

Unlike my parents, who married for love, Mina and Kubi were married through a matchmaker. Both came from religious families and were more observant than my own, although not orthodox. Living on a teacher's salary had never been Mina's idea of a good life and she constantly complained about her husband's low pay. In post-war Romania, her keen sense of business led to a brisk foray into the black market, substantially raising the family's living standards.

Kubi's sister Lola, who lived in Switzerland and had always generously helped her family, sent Mina aid packages with coffee and chocolate (a rarity in a time of austerity), as well as other staples that were in great demand. Mina sold these luxury items on the black market for a good price and at great risk.

Eddy had a difficult relationship with his parents, particularly with his mother. In response to her nagging, he acted the part of the rebel son, becoming an expert in the fine art of annoying his parents, particularly about such bourgeois values as buying clothes they thought were proper for him. His favourite wardrobe would not be considered unusual today, but to his more conservative parents, wearing only khaki shorts in summer and long khaki pants in winter was a constant irritant. At least he did not wear jeans, which were not yet in fashion. Mina was annoyed by these habits, paying less attention to her son's intelligence and love of learning than to his rebellious behaviour.

As for me, I was definitely in the good graces of Eddy's parents. Did they see me as the stereotypical female capable of exercising a civilizing influence on the male savage? Were they hoping that I would be able to achieve miracles and turn their son into the well-mannered and well-dressed person they had failed to raise? Whatever the reason, it was obvious that supporting and encouraging my friendship with Eddy was important to them. Their foray into the black market worked in my favour when they extended their generous offer. I could now continue my studies.

This is how things happen. 'Perhaps' became a reality. Who would have guessed that a chance encounter on a bus to Haifa would connect two lives forever? And who would have imagined that three years later, at the tender age of nineteen, we would be married?

Winding back the film, all this might have never happened had I not been looking for an *ulpan* for my cousin or had I not sat next to Eddy on that bus or had he not had spoken Romanian. Go figure! Would I have become a painter without that humdrum little meeting on the bus? I might have ended up as another frustrated architect and a closet artist. Or I might have never finished high school and become a secretary.

Yes, haphazard things happen. Some of those occurrences slip by unnoticed in their banality, but the repercussions of chance encounters spread slowly, like seeds sown by the wind, until they burst into full bloom and change the landscape of one's life. There are people who plan their lives meticulously, step by step — I have never been one of them. Of course, I had goals, but these were like signposts to be reached one by one, short-term endeavours without a specific plan for the faraway future. I rather liked the idea of floating along, steering my boat from time to time and hoping that I would reach my destination, whatever it was meant to be.

With friends in Gav Yam. Gabi, second from left, myself first on right. This photograph would become part of the third panel in my triptych *Out of the Flames*.

The summer of 1951 was a busy one with no time to get bored. I met many young immigrants, some even from my own town in Romania, with whom I began spending time, discussing ideas and sharing experiences. Many of us were keen on socialist ideas of justice and equality, which was not surprising, since the new Israeli society was founded on the successful socialist experiment of the cooperative farm, the *kibbutz*.

Interested in the idealistic ideas of equality and fairness, Eddy and I went to rallies, films and meetings and signed petitions for social justice. Socialism was the cornerstone of Israel's founders and we supported this dream. Some of our best friends were affiliated with the Israeli Communist Party, which organized many of the rallies.

However, since both Eddy and I were not joiners, we kept on the fringe of organizations and political parties, even while some of our friends became card-carrying members.

Chapter 28

Growing Up Fast

Somehow, we'll find it. The balance between whom we wish to be and whom we need to be. But for now, we simply have to be satisfied with who we are.

Brandon Sanderson
The Hero of Ages

The thought of finding myself had never occurred to me. How could I find something I had never lost?

Coming to Israel as an immigrant at age fifteen, I had crossed a real but intangible border from a place I knew well into an unfamiliar land, from a language in which I could write poetry to a language I could not speak. Life became like the towering sand dunes glistening in the glaring sun, on which our homes were built. Each and every step had to be watched carefully on this unstable ground. I never knew for sure if the sand would hold my weight or if it would suddenly give way as my feet sank into its shifting depths, the grains of sand rushing under my steps like a dry waterfall.

No, trying to find myself was not on my list. I knew exactly where and who I was. The important issue was to have a new roadmap and to create the person I would become. Meanwhile, just dealing with the usual teenage issues was enough to keep me busy. Four years went by quickly. Much happened.

TEENAGE WOES

Just when you think that life is such an interesting adventure — despite small bumps on the road, such as money shortages, no fancy food and no grand homes — boom! You discover that Mother Nature has decided to rein in those brash teens and their extravagant sense of uniqueness by inserting another, most inconsiderate woe in their lives: pimples.

While reading these words, I can see a condescending smile spreading across your face, dear reader. Pimply youth do not great literature make, you mutter to yourself. Perhaps only those who were so smitten by the unforgiving Fates could find an ounce of understanding for the plight of a young person whose face has erupted into a volcanic explosion of painful red sores. And this, no more nor less, at a time when said young person is acutely self-conscious of her looks and desperately tries to look as attractive as Vivien Leigh or Elizabeth Taylor.

Sorry, but since this affliction hit me hard and made me suffer much indignity and unhappiness, I just can't ignore it. Please turn the page if you find these revelations boring. Growing up is hard enough without having to worry about one's rebellious hormones, but having had to put up with this unfortunate process, I must mention it. I had the honour of being one of the chosen to bear this affliction. Most of my friends, including Gabi, never had to pass this humiliating test of coming of age. It is said that 'whatever hurts you makes you stronger'. I rather doubt the veracity of this hackneyed proverb — I am not convinced that my character got any stronger due to it.

It was hot during the day and not much cooler at night, but living on the seashore, we were blessed with a constant breeze that helped cool us off. Unfortunately, this pleasant breeze had a side effect: it blew the fine sand on which the settlement was built, everywhere. Sand stuck to my sweaty skin and fuelled the outburst of fiery red craters all over my face. Out of sheer desperation, I began acting the part of the mysterious veiled lady by covering my face with a thin veil while riding my bicycle to school.

I tried everything: ointments, pills, creams. The fight against pimples became an unending war of attrition. Finally, my mother heard about a certain dermatologist in Haifa and took me to him. His remedy worked wonders: he zapped my face with Roentgen rays, the newest invention of the eponymous Nobel Prize winner. These were simply X-rays that burnt the pimples to extinction. I found out much later from a dermatologist in the US that those miraculous rays did not only burn my pimples away, they also burnt the skin tissues beneath, leaving scars that deepened as I grew older.

ROMANCE

Amazingly, pimples or not, I did not lack in attention from young men. My hormones worked in more ways than activating the pimple explosion, when at age sixteen, I acquired my first serious boyfriend. Shmuel came from Austria and was older, in his mid-twenties. Without really loving him, I was greatly flattered by his interest in me and enjoyed his company. He was not handsome but had a lively sense of humour and an unending reservoir of interesting stories that more than made up for his hugely long nose. He was a policeman and a devoted son who shared a flat with his mother. Whenever we met, he kept me entertained with an infinite number of fascinating tales. I was puzzled by his romantic interest in a sixteen-year-old schoolgirl. I was still underage, but perhaps he thought that I was mature beyond my years. Nobody seemed to pay any attention to the age gap, including my parents, whom he visited from time to time, entertaining them in German with his exploits in the police force. However, my romance with Shmuel was a short-lived episode that died a natural death once my military service began.

SCHOOL

The Kiryat Motzkin school, Achdut, was located about half an hour's bike ride from home. This small town, older and more established than our own Kiryat Yam, had a population of old-timers and *Sabras*. Each day, Eddy and I rode our bikes down a road bordered with brilliant yellow forsythia shrubs. As we neared the town, neat little white houses with cheerful red tile roofs began appearing on either side of the road and green hedges and heavy curtains of purple-red bougainvillea flowers cascaded lavishly over walls and fences.

The school was small and so were the classes. There were twenty-two students in our class, five of them new immigrants. Some of the teachers, such as our Romanian English teacher, were Holocaust survivors from Europe. It is amusing to think that in Romania I learned French from a Greek teacher and in Israel I studied English with a Romanian one. Most of our teachers had come to Palestine in the 1930s when it was still under the British Mandate.

Our math teacher, Rafael Artzy, had come from Germany in the mid-1930s after earning a PhD in mathematics. He had a lasting impact on Eddy's life and, by implication, on mine. During Israel's War of Independence he worked for Israeli intelligence, but when the war ended and life returned to a semblance of normality, the new state was mired in overwhelming difficulties and jobs were scarce. The Hebrew University in Jerusalem was the only university in the country and much too small to employ the many academics who had arrived with degrees in various fields. The only choice open to Artzy was a position as a high school teacher. His loss was a tremendous gain for the students who were interested in mathematics; having a teacher of such calibre was a rare opportunity.

Artzy was a short black-haired man who talked with a German accent in rapid, clipped sentences, gesticulating with his hands to prove his point, his shoulders held back in a sharp angle. His thick eyebrows hovered over eyes that were always scrunched up, as if he were peering into the distance to discover something of great importance. There was a no-nonsense feeling when one talked with him and his method of teaching was, to say the least, unconventional. He focused on the students who showed a keen interest in mathematics, while the others, well, they just had to go through the motions and pass the exams.

Artzy began his class by talking, telling jokes and entertaining stories. And what about the math? This was delivered in rapid fashion during the last twenty minutes of the class, leaving it up to the students to grasp the concepts he so quickly presented. Four boys, Eddy among them, were his favourite students. Aware of their interest in math and understanding their potential, he would invite them to his house after school, giving them free private lessons — an act of pure love for mathematics. We nicknamed these boys the 'Big Four' and accepted the fact that they were the brightest math stars in our class.

Artzy's clairvoyance paid off. Amnon Pazi and Eddy Granirer became professors of mathematics and later Amnon rose to become president of the Hebrew University. Joel Adir, Amnon's cousin, became a very successful engineer and Pinchas Harris took up medicine and a few years later became the chief surgeon of the Israeli Defense Forces.

Those were the old-fashioned days when classes had a headmaster who actually cared about the general education of his students. Artzy's way of dealing with the headmaster's hour was to open for us the door to the world of classical music and push us through willy-nilly. We had to sit and listen to classical music for the entire hour. To this day, whenever I hear Mozart's *Eine Kleine Nachtmusik*, I am back in Kiryat Motzkin, sitting on the hard chair in our classroom and listening to the music pouring out of the black disk spinning on the turntable.

In grade eleven, students were divided into humanities and sciences. Although my natural inclination would have directed me towards the humanities, I was worried about the future, afraid that I would not be able to support myself as an artist. The closest profession to art was architecture, or so I thought. I understand now why so many of the architects I met later in life were 'closet' artists. But for my lucky star, I would be one of them today.

Believing that mathematics was needed for the study of architecture, I ended up in the science stream, taking also chemistry and physics. Eddy's friendship and help were invaluable during these last two years of high school.

Along with science courses, we studied English, literature and Tanakh. In grade twelve, our old Tanakh teacher retired. A religious man with a straggly white beard and the ubiquitous black *kippah* on his bald head, he taught from a traditional orthodox point of view. Very quickly, he succeeded in turning this fascinating book into a boringly dull subject. Luckily for us, he was replaced by a young teacher who was, surprise, surprise, a woman!

On her first day in class, the boys decided to test her wits. They asked us all to fix our gaze for as long as we could on her rather voluminous bosom and watch her reaction. To our admiration, she ignored the goofy teenagers who tried to humiliate her and went on with the lesson as if nothing happened. And what a lesson it was! Through her teaching, the formerly boring subject became a lively, exciting adventure of history and mythology. Her questioning mind, analyzing and dissecting the words and the meaning behind them, presented the ancient text almost like a thriller. She brought to life the actions and deeds of the prophets, the kings and the storytellers, the myths and the history. Due to her, the Hebrew Bible has become a life-long interest for me. My imagination soared through the windows she opened in that class of 1953, helping me

Class picture, 1952. I am sitting on the left, first in the front row, Eddy stands first in the left back row.

to embark thirty years later on the creation of a major work entitled *The Trials of Eve.*

Even though the science division was separate from the humanities, our school thought that even geeks and nerds (words unknown at the time) needed to have some general culture. Not only was our math teacher keen to introduce us to classical music, our curriculum also offered a course that gave us a glimpse into another precious legacy of civilization, the history of art.

Then, two short years later, school was over. Another chapter had ended. I was eighteen years old and the Israeli army was beckoning.

Chapter 29

A Soldier? Me?

Trust your own instinct. Your mistakes might as well be your own, instead of someone else's.

Billy Wilder
cited in *Know Your Limits — Then Ignore Them*
by John Mason

The small black-and-white photograph shows a unit of young girls in army uniform smartly walking in step, their arms swinging in rhythm, their legs treading in unison. Right, left, right, left, right, left — one can almost hear the sound of their black army shoes hitting the pavement, their legs like a forest of moving trees all pointing in the same direction.

But wait! Something is wrong! The diagonal pattern of marching legs is broken. One of the girls, the seventh from the end of the column, is out of step. Peering closer into the photograph, trying to identify the tiny faces of the girl-soldiers, I immediately recognize the culprit: it's me! It would not be far from the truth to say that I had literally started my army career on the wrong foot . . .

Young Israelis of both sexes were automatically drafted into the army at age eighteen. The draft was obligatory since the security of the fledgling state rested on their shoulders. The army was a true melting pot for the thousands of youngsters originating from different cultures, languages, countries and continents. Tzahal, the Israeli Defense Forces, was the great equalizer where one grew up and matured quickly. Boys spent two and a half years and girls two years in uniform. In addition to military training, the army had an extensive educational component, where the immigrants were taught Hebrew and courses were offered in various trades, preparing the young soldiers for civilian life. These activities forged a sense of pride and belonging so that at the end of the military service, everyone had a shared experience, spoke Hebrew and embraced the Israeli identity. Following a period of basic training, one was attached to a military unit such as the Air Force, Infantry, Navy, Intelligence and so on. I was drafted into the Engineering Corps, Kheil Handassah.

The basic training was intense for men and somewhat easier for women. Target shooting and marching were a staple, as were the strict rules of cleanliness, discipline and proper dress. Inspection was a nerve-wracking experience each day. The officer in charge would enter the barracks with her aide and walk slowly from bed to bed as we stood at attention. She then proceeded to check if the sheets and the blankets were folded exactly according to code, our shoes were clean and shiny and the brass insignia on our berets sparkled like a new silver coin. Woe to the soldier who had missed a small crease in the blanket, whose rifle had a speck of dust in the wrong place or whose insignia was not shiny enough! The punishment was swift and painful: no pass for the weekend. Instead she would be cleaning the toilets or performing another humiliating penalty devised by those who strived to turn us into obedient and disciplined soldiers.

After my basic training I was transferred to a military camp in the seaside town of Netanya. I particularly remember a tall sergeant with a huge drooping red moustache who was in charge of us, six high school graduates — the only girls in the camp. The mustachioed corporal had barely finished elementary school in his country of origin and regarded us as snobbish intellectuals who had to be taught a lesson. Here was his chance to show who was boss! Oh, the aphrodisiacal pleasure of power over those uppity educated girls under his command! He barked his orders at us and made us execute drills that would prove his superiority. His favourite display of power was lining us up for inspection. After checking our uniforms, our shoes and our insignia, he would march us from one end of the yard to the other shouting "Right, left, right, left! Keep your shoulders straight! Look straight in front of you! This is not high school. This is the army!" After this useless exercise, he would dismiss us with stern warnings about disobeying his future orders.

The Netanya camp was used primarily as a training camp for men. One of its more unusual features was a detainment centre for soldiers who had misbehaved and needed to be punished. It was not unusual to see the inmates of the small detention barracks running around in a circle, carrying their metal beds on their backs.

The camp was small and quite rudimentary. There were no special barracks for women, so the six of us were housed in a very large tent. During the day we worked in a small wooden telephone hut, manning the old-fashioned phone lines connected by thick rubber wires that had to be plugged in a particular hole for each call. It took some time before we learned to cope efficiently with the tangle of cables and managed not to mix up the various calls by connecting the right wire to the wrong outlet. Today's young would not even imagine that such an antiquated system could exist.

We did not mind sleeping in the big tent but as it turned out, this was not to last. One winter night we went to sleep as usual and were deep in dreamland when we were woken up by thunder and lightning. As the storm gathered force, the sound of rain on the canvas tent combined with the deafening blasts of thunder became more ominous than a Wagner symphony played at the highest volume. Then, in a grand finale, a powerful gust of wind lifted our tent up and crashed it down on its side a minute later. Still dressed in our pajamas, we were exposed to torrential rain pouring down on our heads in pitch darkness broken only by the occasional flash of lightning. Soaked to the bone, we wrapped ourselves in our coarse army blankets and ran to the only safe place we could think of — the telephone shack.

This temporary shelter became our regular abode for the remainder of our stay in the Netanya camp. Six narrow army cots covered with khaki blankets were crammed together with almost no space in between. The small wooden shack served now a dual purpose: workplace and sleeping quarters. It probably was the warmest place in the camp and kept us safely out of rain and cold weather. Still, as we soon discovered, we were not the only ones to seek shelter from the elements. The nights brought us unexpected furry guests: busy little mice, happily running up and down our blankets after the lights went out. I can't really say that we shared the pleasure of their company.

I met Shlomo at the Netanyah military base. An officer and a technical draftsman in civilian life, he offered a course in architectural design and perspective that I found much more interesting than working on the telephones. I immediately signed up and so did most of the other girls. Each day, we sat on high stools at wide tables spread with large sheets of finely lined paper. I loved using the Rapidograph pens with black India ink oozing out of their thin nibs. The perfume of the sharpened black pencils reminded me of my first box of Koh-i-noor coloured pencils and even the rustling sound of the paper being unrolled on the tabletop gave me a little shiver of happiness.

Was it my visible pleasure in discovering the principles of perspective drawing and my enthusiasm at learning that shadows have to be drawn according to clear and definite laws that made Shlomo pay more attention to me? Whatever the reasons, we began spending more and more time together, going on long walks after dinner, making elaborate drawings and discussing everything under the sun.

Shlomo, a Bulgarian immigrant, was in his late twenties, although he seemed much older and wiser to me. Tall with thick wavy black hair and pleasing symmetrical features in a long, narrow face outlined by two deep creases along his cheeks, he was kind and soft-spoken and made me feel special. I wondered why he, an officer, had chosen me when some of the other girls were prettier and taller and, I thought, much worthier of his attention. We were physically attracted to one another and spent many wonderful romantic nights under a starry sky high on the rocks above the beach outside the army base. Shlomo was the only person who ever chose to call me by my birth name, Paula, although I have never been fond of that name. Coming from him though, it made me feel loved and mature.

Did I love Shlomo as he loved me? Not really. It was more a case of 'reflected love'. I was living a true romance, but in the back of my mind, hidden deep under insecurity and guilt, I knew that this was not meant to last. Our worlds outside the army were too different; I could not envisage a future together.

On weekends, I went home on leave and I would meet Eddy and other friends who came home on leave as well. Away from Netanyah and Shlomo, this was a familiar world, safe and comfortable. Eddy belonged in this world. Our friendship had deepened over time — we had much in common and knew one another well. I loved and admired him for his intelligence, his humanity and his dreams for the future.

Playing Romeo and Juliet on the beach, 1952

Eddy was very outspoken about his love for me and of his hopes of building a life together. Here I was, caught in a real Shakespearian quandary, having to make a decision that would shape my life. It is surely easier to see such dilemmas on stage than to experience them in reality!

I created an imaginary balance to weigh my options. On the right was Eddy, my best friend, who loved me deeply and was the same age as me. I felt relaxed in his presence, comfortable and safe in the knowledge that he would always stand by me. With him, I would achieve my dream of studying art, I would share my life with someone who had the same values I had — joining him would mean a true partnership. Starting out as good friends, our relationship had a solid foundation in which we both felt secure in the knowledge that we understood one another and could share openly our experiences.

On the left was Shlomo. What did I know about him? We had had only a very short time together in unusual circumstances, far removed from real life. My attraction to him was mostly physical and that, even I knew, may not last forever. He already had a profession, which meant that there would be only a small chance for me to continue my studies. I would perhaps end up as a designer for architects instead of becoming an architect myself. I did not really know him well enough — our relationship was not built on the kind of deep and long friendship I had with Eddy.

Many years after this impasse, when I was taking a workshop in hypnosis, the instructor told me that I was a leftie, someone who thinks with the left side of the brain. I was too logical. Perhaps he was right, but I still value logic and common sense over decisions reached by unruly hormones, to be regretted later.

My decision was made. Eddy was my choice. In 2014, we celebrated our 60th wedding anniversary. I had made the right decision.

Nazareth

My next posting came soon enough. I was transferred to the biblical town of Nazareth in the Galilee, where the army base was located in one of the old British police stations scattered all over the country. These massive fortress-like buildings, usually set up on a hill with a sweeping view of the valley below, had been built during the British Mandate in Palestine.

By now, I knew only too well that if Israel had to rely on my soldierly skills for its safety, it would be in a rather sad state.

In Nazareth I was introduced to a profession for which I had no talent whatsoever: filing clerk. On my arrival, I was put in charge of the files in the main office, having to make sure that each one was returned to the exact spot assigned to it on the shelf or in filing cabinets. Did someone ever say that boredom was deadly? Could one actually fall ill from boredom? I can answer these questions with a definite and resounding "Yes!" After a few weeks in this office, I developed a fatigue as heavy as a ton of lead resting on my shoulders. I had trouble concentrating and was even more distraught when I began missing files or finding them in the wrong places. Going to work each day became an ordeal that I dreaded from the moment I woke up in the morning after nightmares in which I was pursued by files floating in the air, files falling out of cabinets and masses of files covering large tables.

One day with no warning, I found myself in a hospital bed with no recollection of how I got there. The nurse gently told me that I had had a nervous breakdown as a result of total mental exhaustion and needed rest. I was stunned. Exhaustion? What from? I had not been working all that hard! The work itself was the culprit: files, files and more files, day after day after day, boring, boooring, *booooooring*. No creativity, no job satisfaction. I began thinking of those who worked in factories where they became automatons repeating the same gestures again and again and again. Filing might be better, but not for me!

After a week in hospital, I returned to my base and was posted to the much more interesting job of drawing maps in a large well-lit room.

INCIDENT IN NAZARETH

It was Shabbat, a sunny Saturday morning. Although I was off duty, there was no transportation available to take me home and the day was mine to use in any way I wished. And what I wanted more than anything was to draw the beautiful Galilee landscape around the base.

It was spring and the sun was shining gently down on the hills and on the conical green cypresses dotting the landscape like proud sentinels. It was a perfect day for roaming outside the stone fortress.

I felt elated walking alone among the cream-coloured hills, seeing the spring flowers still in bud under the clear blue sky and hearing the birds chirping.

I packed a bottle of water, a drawing pad, pencils, watercolours and pens, then headed out to the hill overlooking Nazareth. After walking for a while along a narrow path, I found just the place I had been looking for. There, at the edge of the trail, was a large smooth stone that would be a comfortable seat on which to sit and gaze at the wonderful panorama in the valley below. A row of eucalyptus trees behind the stone provided shade against the sun. The Arab town of Nazareth, a jumble of houses with flat white roofs punctuated by the occasional church spires and minarets, was spread beneath me. I settled down on the smooth rock, took out the sketchpad and began drawing. The hills in the background, the cypresses in the foreground and the houses below slowly took shape on the white paper. I was in heaven. The wonderful aroma of pine needles and the shrill songs of the cicadas added up to a feeling of total bliss. The real world was far away. All was peace and beauty — wars, conflict, danger, injustice, these were forgotten now. My real world was only the one that came to life on my sketchpad and nothing else mattered.

The sound of footsteps on the rough trail broke the spell. Looking up, I saw a young Arab man about my own age approaching me. He was not very tall, had dark curly hair and was wearing a vest over a shirt and khaki pants. He approached me shyly and standing behind me, he gravely examined my drawing uttering small grunts of approval.

"Very nice," he said. "I like that! Are you an artist?"

He was obviously looking beyond the uniform I was wearing, which pleased me. He asked whether he could watch me working and when I agreed, he sat down for a while, critically checking whether the lines and shapes on the paper matched the landscape in the valley. When the work was done, he lavished much praise on the finished landscape.

Show me the artist who does not respond with pleasure when offered this kind of unsolicited interest! Naturally I was flattered, even though I was quite sure that this was probably the first drawing this young man had ever seen. And so, I could not refuse when he invited me to come to his house, meet his family and show them my masterpiece. My idealistic concept of the world made me see this visit as a unique opportunity of a friendly interaction between a young Israeli woman and an Arab family. It was all about peace and harmony, friendship and love in a world of fear and mistrust.

We descended into the valley. By then it was getting warmer. The sun had climbed in the sky, its rays now directly over our heads. I had to watch the time, but there was still no hurry to return to the base.

I did not understand the words he said to his mother, his brothers and sisters when he ushered me into a large room lined with carpets and comfortable sofas, but from their reaction I could tell that they were pleasantly surprised to see me. Arabs are well known for their hospitality and this family did not disappoint. I was invited to sit down and show my drawings. Then the ubiquitous, fragrant black coffee with cardamom seeds arrived in the usual shiny small brass coffeepot, the long-handled *finjan*, accompanied by delicious cookies and cake. They urged me to eat and drink, refilling my tiny cup again and again.

Finally it was time to go, but they would not let me leave empty-handed. Competing with the stereotype of the Jewish mother who keeps urging her children to eat, the Arab mother of my newfound friend filled my bag with the remaining sweets, just in case I got hungry on my way back. In exchange, I offered them my little drawing.

What a great day and what a wonderful unexpected adventure! I walked back, elated by the warm, friendly contact with people I would otherwise have never met — and all this was due to my art! I could not wait to tell everyone the story of my visit with the Arab family who had received me with such warmth.

Bursting with enthusiasm, I looked for my friends and proudly told them my story. My adventure showed that we could live in peace with our Arab neighbours — they were people like us. My experience had proved how hospitable they were.

What I read on my friends' faces as my story progressed was not the pleasure I expected. As I continued, their expressions grew darker and darker, shock and dismay visible in their eyes.

"How naïve you are!" they said. "You were a soldier in uniform and you allowed yourself to be alone in the midst of an Arab village! They could have killed you like they did to other trusting Israelis!"

I was back in the real world.

Chapter 30

A Peculiar Wedding

*So I think you have to marry for the right reasons,
and marry the right person.*

Anne Bancroft
on successful marriage
in an Associated Press interview

My first year of army service was coming to a close. It was time to think about the future.

How much wisdom does one have at the tender age of nineteen? Can one see clearly the road ahead and take the right decision about one's future? At this stage, everything seems simple and hope is plentiful. We feel immortal and see life as a thrilling adventure with a happy end writ large. One plunges headlong into the future with the confidence of a well-trained trapeze acrobat leaping into the air, sure of landing on one's feet.

And so, we did just that: we leaped. It was just the practical thing to do. Eddy and I were married on August 10, 1954.

Let me explain. We were still in uniform, penniless, with no profession and no expectations of financial support from our parents. Since the Israeli army does not conscript married women, the solution to our problem could not have been clearer: tying an early knot would free me from the important task of defending my country, giving me the opportunity to work and thus defend our personal interests. The money I would earn would help us start our lives as students in Jerusalem.

Being poor did not bother us much — everyone else we knew was poor as well. We were rather proud of it, flaunting our poverty like a badge of honour. Our achievements would be our very own.

Life was difficult in the young country. The economy began to recover only in 1953 when West Germany agreed to pay reparations to Israel as the heir to those who had died during the Holocaust and left no survivors.

By then, Eddy's father, a teacher of French who could not find work in Israel, had moved to Buenos Aires, Argentina, where his brother lived and Eddy's mother was to follow him soon. We were expected to join them at the end of Eddy's military service, the big lure being the tuition-free university system in Argentina.

Parents may plan their children's lives, but the children don't always agree. We certainly had no intention of leaving Israel.

Meanwhile there was a wedding to be planned. As ardent socialists, we wanted nothing to do with a large and showy bourgeois affair that would put our families in debt and would be attended by crowds of people we did not care for. We put our foot down. The wedding would be small — no more than thirty people could attend and no public space would be rented. The ceremony would take place in Haifa in the small apartment of Eddy's favourite aunt, Beca, mother to his dearest older cousin, Ehud. Money would not be wasted in buying an expensive dress: I would wear a short white dress that I had bought in a second-hand shop and worn already on several occasions. The veil would be rented.

Eddy informed our parents that he did not need any special clothes and would attend the wedding in his usual attire of khaki shorts. My mother declared that she would stay home if he did that. Tensions mounted. The parents were unhappy with their rebellious children and we were stubborn in our idealistic, anti-bourgeois stance. What kind of wedding, they asked, was this going to be for their only child? What would people say? Would not everybody be insulted at not being invited and their friends snicker behind their backs? How could they possibly pare down the list of invitations to less than thirty since just the close family numbered already more than ten? Feverish negotiations were held, angry words were spoken and the old art of blackmail was used to put additional pressure on the two crazy youngsters.

Under this mounting pressure, Eddy relented and agreed to wear a suit altered for him from an old suit of my father's. A few more people were added to the list. On all other issues we did not budge. Oh, yes, another problem arose on which, however, there was general agreement: the *mikvah* issue. The orthodox parties in Israel have total monopoly in all civil matters from birth to marriage to burial: all ceremonies had to be held according to religious law. Following *Halakhah*, the Jewish law, the prospective bride is required to purify herself before the wedding ceremony by immersion in the *mikvah*, the traditional bath. No such demand is made on the groom — he, of course, was considered as pure as a newborn babe.

This cleansing ritual might have been a lifesaver in the ancient past and in the Middle Ages, protecting people from rampant plagues by the simple act of washing, but now it had become just a ceremonial religious act, accepted by the observant Jews and imposed on the secular population.

I could not accept undergoing this religious ritual. With our families' support, an accommodating rabbi was found. In exchange for a generous donation, he made a deal with God and handed out the dispensation needed to avoid the unwanted bath. I never saw this important document and always wondered if he simply misled God about my watery immersion or invented some danger awaiting me if I descended into the sacred pool. Whatever the excuse, I was now pure enough to take part in the ceremony, without having dipped a toe in the traditional bath.

The small apartment on Pevsner Street filled quickly with close relatives and friends according to the quota we had asked for. Aunt Beca, a small plump woman with short curly hair who never managed to learn the Hebrew language, flitted like a butterfly among the guests, making sure everything was in the right order, chatting and smiling, her twinkling eyes shining with happiness.

Beca was the kindest and warmest person in the family and we loved her dearly. Her husband had died, leaving her alone to care for Ehud, their only son. And care she did. Ehud, five years older than Eddy, was the sun shining brightly in the centre of Beca's universe. She knew that his future could be assured only through education, but education was too expensive for her means. And so Beca became a housekeeper, hiring herself out to well-to-do families, cooking and cleaning to earn the needed money that allowed her son to attend the Technion School of Engineering in Haifa. Her efforts paid off: her son became a successful engineering professor who founded the department of mechanical engineering at the Technion and received many honours and important positions during his career.

Our wedding was on a hot August day and air conditioning was still in the realm of science fiction. It was much too hot to be wearing a jacket, so Eddy hung his new jacket on the back of a chair. In the general confusion, he conveniently 'forgot' to put it back on, proceeding to the *huppah*, the traditional wedding canopy set up in the middle of the room, in his shirtsleeves.

Ceremonies did not mean much to us. We were idealistic teenagers who regarded this as a necessary hurdle we had to put up with.

Finally, there we were, under the *huppah*: my parents, Eddy's mother, the rabbi and us, the bride and the (jacketless) groom. According to custom rich in symbolism we were ignorant of, the bride circles the groom seven times as the rabbi recites a prayer. So I, the bride, walked around my prospective husband counting to seven and barely able to stifle the giggles rising in my throat. Through my veil, I caught a glimpse of our mothers, tears glistening in their eyes. I sobered up, suddenly aware of the solemnity of the occasion.

The ceremony ended with the traditional breaking of the glass (carefully wrapped in a small towel) by the new husband, while everyone wished the young couple a loud "*Mazal tov* (good luck)!"

The most common explanation for the breaking of the glass is that it is a symbol of the destruction of the Temple in Jerusalem.

In keeping with this interpretation, some couples recite the line "If I forget thee, O Jerusalem, let my right hand forget her cunning."

Why does the bride circle the groom seven times? In keeping with the tradition of Jews having at least two different interpretations for everything under the sun, there are various views on this ritual as well. It may parallel the seven days of Creation, a symbol of the new couple creating their own new world. Others say that it symbolizes Joshua's circling of the walls of Jericho, resulting in the walls crumbling, so may the two people who enter the marriage break down the walls that exist between them. There is almost no end to these interpretations.

The ceremony was over. How strange that in just a few minutes I had transitioned from being a single young girl to being a married woman! Everyone who had a camera was snapping pictures. The bride and groom with their parents, the bride and groom with relatives, the parents alone, the two mothers standing, sitting, hugging. These black-and-white amateur snapshots still grace the pages of the old album on my shelf. Unlike the lavish, expensive wedding photos fashionable today, these reminders of our modest wedding are grey and informal, simple and inexpensive — just as we wanted them to be.

However, protocol expected us to produce a formal wedding photograph to be taken in a studio a few blocks down the street. Formal or not, we did it our way. I put my veil and the bouquet inside a large paper bag and we walked briskly to our appointment with the photographer.

The session was bearably brief. The smart photographer made sure that my short dress appeared like a long one in the photograph. All was well!

"Should I call for a taxi?" he asked.

We assured him that we lived downstairs and there was no need for transportation. We left, my veil and bouquet back in the bag, and walked merrily away to join the guests for the dinner that followed.

We spent our three-day honeymoon in Nahariya, courtesy of the Israeli army, where Eddy gave me my first swimming lesson in

Official wedding picture · Eddy's mother, my parents and us

With Auntie Beca

the hotel pool. To my regret, this experience only confirmed yet again that I would never be a swimmer.

As a married woman, I was discharged from the Israeli Defense Forces, leaving my poor new husband to defend the country single-handed for eighteen more months. I was free to set down the first stone in the foundation for our future.

I began looking for a job.

Chapter 31

Big Plans

Crossroads: A point at which a crucial decision must be made that will have far-reaching consequences.

Oxford English Dictionary

The year 1954 was an important crossroads in my life and a year of fateful decisions.

The first decision was to leave the army and get married.

The second was about language. Culture and identity are defined by one's language and immigrants tend to continue speaking the language of their country of birth, feeling more comfortable within a culture they know. Although Eddy and I spoke Romanian from the time we met, once married we desired to leave our old identity behind — we felt no allegiance to Romania and wished to become true Israelis. The decision was made: from now on, Hebrew would be our everyday language. This major cultural shift set us apart from our older relatives who still spoke Romanian, never having mastered Hebrew.

We had plans, big plans.

My best friend, who was now my husband, dreamt of becoming a mathematician while my dream was to be an artist. Financially, neither dream offered us bright futures since choosing a career in math was not too different from a career in art. Teaching positions at the Hebrew University in Jerusalem, the only university in the country, were nearly non-existent. And art? How many people could afford to buy paintings?

The Hebrew University was still young. In 1923, one of its founders, Albert Einstein, delivered the first scientific lecture and donated all his archives to it after his death. The teaching was excellent, but the best a graduate with a doctoral degree could hope for was a high school teaching job similar to that of Rafael Artzy, our math teacher who had inspired Eddy. Under normal circumstances, Rafael Artzy would have taught at a university rather than at a high school. Indeed, some years later when the space race began, he received a position at an American university where he stayed until he was invited to return to Israel as Head of the Faculty of Mathematics at the newly established University of Haifa.

Eddy's determination to study mathematics led to a new point of friction with his mother. Fierce arguments erupted in my in-laws' new flat in Tel-Aviv, with Mina bitterly reproaching her son for not investing his talents into something more practical, like engineering, instead of facing the prospect of becoming yet another low-paid teacher like his father.

I had never witnessed such fury in my own family and was appalled at the screaming and shouting. Her perennial anger towards her husband, who had chosen to be a teacher, a profession that would never fully satisfy her financial demands, was now directed towards her son.

Eddy, however, would not give up his plans. After completing his army service, he received a scholarship and began his studies at the Hebrew University in Jerusalem.

And art? How could I possibly believe that I could make a living as an artist? How realistic a dream was this? The best alternative, I thought, was to study at the Technion in Haifa and become an architect. Unlike Eddy's mother, my parents never interfered with my choice of career.

Still, the Fates had decided otherwise. My life was now bound to someone who considered mathematics his vocation, similar to my own passion for art. The best place to follow his dream was at the Hebrew University in Jerusalem. But if we went there, what would I do? There was no school of architecture in the Holy City, but wonder of wonders, there was an art school named after Bezalel, the first biblical craftsman, as it is written:

And the LORD spake unto Moses, saying, "See, I have called by name Bezalel the son of Uri, the son of Hur, of the tribe of Judah: And I have filled him with the spirit of God, in wisdom, and in understanding, and in knowledge, and in all manner of workmanship, To devise cunning works, to work in gold, and in silver, and in brass, And in cutting of stones, to set them, and in carving of timber, to work in all manner of workmanship."

Exodus 31: 1-5

Even the ancient Hebrew Bible was on my side: art was indeed a God-given gift! Later renamed the Bezalel Academy of Arts and Design, in 1955 the school was small, consisting of only three departments: Graphics, Weaving and Metalwork. Created after the European model, the graphics section included illustration, poster and book design, painting and printmaking. Graduating from Bezalel meant that I could earn my keep by working as an illustrator. What joy it would be to earn a living by doing what I loved best! I could barely believe my luck!

While waiting for Eddy to finish his military service, we rented a room in Kiryat Yam Ghimmel from the Anoushkas, a family of Russian immigrants who simply added us to their large family, feeding us copious breakfasts and lecturing us on the value of starting the day with a hearty meal. Unlike most people we knew, they looked like real Russian peasants. The husband, so tall that I had to crane my neck upwards when talking to him, had a ready smile and a twinkle in his pale blue eyes. It seemed that he almost never combed his light yellow hair, piled like straw thrown on top of his head. He drove a truck for a living and spoke in a heavily Russian-accented Hebrew. His wife barely reached her husband's shoulder and looked much older than him. Her face was heavily wrinkled and her grey hair gathered in a tight bun.

Once in a while, Eddy came on leave for the Sabbath, arriving Friday evening and leaving early Sunday. The two-day weekend, a luxury we could not have imagined, was unknown at the time.

Mrs. Anoushka would seat us down in her kitchen for a hearty breakfast and in no time at all, a bowl of fresh Israeli salad with tomatoes, cucumbers, onions and green peppers, all cut small and doused with olive oil and vinegar, would materialize on the table. Sunny-side-up eggs would follow, accompanied by fresh black bread. Sometimes she served us sardines, sometimes salami and always, always, orange juice and coffee. What a feast that was!

Chapter 32

Jobs

*Don't judge each day by the harvest you reap
but by the seeds that you plant.*

Robert Louis Stevenson and W.E. Henley
in *Admiral Guinea*

My first job was at Palceramic, a ceramic factory near Haifa. I went for an interview and was enchanted at the sight of people sitting on stools next to high tables, decorating plates, cups, saucers, bowls and teapots. I did not pay much attention to the big room across the hallway where other workers were bent over potters' wheels doing something that did not look very interesting. I brought along my first-ever portfolio in the hope that I would be hired when they saw the wonderful designs with which I could adorn the unpainted clay items. I got the job.

My very first salaried job! And not just any job, but one where I would be able to use my artistic skills! I could not wait to begin.

The next morning, the supervisor led me to the big room I had ignored the previous day and sat me down in front of a potter's wheel. She delegated an experienced worker to train me for the job I was expected to perform. What a bitter lesson in disappointment after such high expectations!

The job required me to sit very still on a stool facing the wheel on which my instructor placed a white unbaked clay plate. She showed me how to hold a thin brush dipped in paint in one spot above the plate so, as the wheel turned, the brush made contact with the plate, creating a blue line around the edge. This maneuver required skill and a steady grip since, at the slightest movement of the hand, the smooth line would become jagged or lose its circular form. I practiced the whole day, until my plates acquired a nice smooth line around the edge and my wrist was sore.

The next day work began in earnest. One plate followed another. Plate after plate after plate after plate, my hand clenched on the brush for eight long hours. My arm ached, my eyes watered, my back hurt. More of the same, day after day, plate after plate. The repetitive movement was like a drill slowly boring deep into my skin, etching round grooves into my brain. I felt like a factory worker on the unforgiving assembly line in a Charlie Chaplin film.

Whenever I could take my eyes off the spinning turntable, I would enviously steal a look at the other workers, who were happily painting flowers, leaves and decorations on clay dishes of all sorts. Perhaps one day soon I would be transferred to that room and paint with them? This hope kept me going for about three months. Nightmares of plates swirling under the merciless brush, of lines turning faster and faster in circles on never-ending numbers of round plates turning, turning, turning, invaded my sleep. Work became drudgery with the same turntable that never stopped and the same white plate on which I had to paint the same blue line, like an automaton.

I finally realized that without professional training in art, there was no chance of being promoted into the painting department. I also knew that I could not continue working in this repetitive job and retain my sanity. I was not meant to be a worker on the assembly line — and I handed in my resignation.

The next job could not have been more different.

Tuviah Friedman was a mild-looking balding man of medium height with piercing blue eyes. He was a Holocaust survivor and one of the first Nazi hunters. He spoke quickly in Polish-accented

Hebrew, using his hands to emphasize his point. Later, he played an important role in the capture of Adolf Eichmann, the notorious SS officer who had methodically implemented the murder of the Hungarian Jews during the last months of the war. In 1960, Eichmann was kidnapped from his refuge in Argentina and brought to justice in Jerusalem.

After his arrival in Israel in 1952, Friedman served as director of the Haifa branch of Yad Vashem, a modest office and a precursor to the imposing Yad Vashem Holocaust Museum in Jerusalem.

In 1954 I was hired by Friedman to help organize an archive from the flood of information pouring out of Europe. The office was a long narrow room with windows at one end, leaving half the space in semi-darkness. A heavy table surrounded with wooden chairs took up almost all the free space. Labelled files containing the worst nightmares of humanity were crammed on to shelves that covered the walls from floor to ceiling.

Papers, books and photographs in untidy piles were vying for space on the large table. Crumpled papers with frayed corners and cursive European handwriting and documents bearing faded photographs and blue stamps in foreign languages combined into a sad but powerful testimony of Nazi atrocities. They told the stories of the ones whose shadows hovered silently over these salvaged papers, begging the world to listen. For eight hours a day I sat at that table sorting out documents according to their provenance. Germany, Austria, Poland, Romania, the Ukraine, Hungary, France and other European countries were represented. There were personal papers documenting births, weddings, citizenship and most heartrending of all, desperate letters asking for help or crying out about the trauma of Jews trapped inside the Nazi iron grip.

Hitler's Germany was one of the best-organized and thoroughly documented dictatorships. The Nazis had kept detailed records of their activities in their official correspondence and in memos and papers documenting the administration of their well-oiled machinery of death. There were papers outlining the Nazi ideology and describing their successes in the extermination of the Jewish population and the inner workings of the Nazi régime.

And there were long neat lists of the murdered.

These were some of the documents I had to sift through. As days went by, details of these papers began haunting my dreams and accompanying me during each waking moment. Foreign voices whispered urgently in my ear. Images of concentration camps, skeletal figures and piles of corpses crowded my vision and filled me with anxiety, anger and fear. I knew I could have been one of those dead had I not been saved by pure chance. My own family could have been murdered during these nightmarish years of killing. What did I do to deserve the good fortune of escaping the horror that so many others went through? The number tattooed on the arm of our young neighbour in Kiryat Yam meant much more to me now. Hers was no longer a story casually told during a sunny afternoon — now I could actually see it all and feel the anguish. The reality of it weighed more heavily on me day by day until it became an obsession. I began imagining myself wearing the striped uniform over my emaciated body, standing up for hours during the roll call, starving, freezing, terrified. Would I have survived being there? Even when eating my lunch at noon on a bench in the nearby park, the terrible images didn't leave me.

This job, too, did not last long. I simply had to leave.

History has a way of repeating itself.

Following the unhappy experience of my first two attempts at finding suitable work, I enrolled in a typing and shorthand course. Armed with these practical skills, I took a job as secretary for an American import company dealing in tractors and heavy farm equipment. My boss was Mr. Shulman, a hefty, tall American with a southern accent so thick it threw me into a complete panic when I had to answer his telephone calls.

This time, I stayed in my job until Eddy finished his military service.

Chapter 33

Math, Art, Love and Spaghetti

Dreams are what guide us, art is what defines us, math is what makes it all possible, and love is what lights our way.

Mike Norton
from the afterword of *Fighting for Redemption*

We moved to Jerusalem and life was good. Who cared that our pockets were empty, that we lived in a small space and had to share the only table in the room, Eddy studying his math and myself working at my art? We had love and were doing what we wanted most — nothing else mattered. Math, art and the occasional spaghetti meal were all we needed. Money? We could do without as long as we had enough to eat and buy the essentials for everyday life.

Eddy had received a scholarship from the Hebrew University and took a part-time job as a bookbinder at the university library. My secretarial skills helped me get a part-time job at Hominer's, a large hardware store on Ben-Yehudah Street. And, to top it all off, my mother would send us a roasted chicken by special taxi service each Friday since my culinary skills at the time consisted mainly of spaghetti and eggs cooked in various forms. On Saturdays, we splurged. To live it up, we would go to Ben-Yehudah Street and buy ourselves a treat: a doughnut and a gazoz, an Israeli specialty of raspberry syrup with soda, sold in kiosks along the street. Then we would meet friends and solve the problems of the world together.

It was the happiest time of our life.

Our rented room was in a two-bedroom apartment owned by an eccentric retired engineer whom we nicknamed 'the little old man'. Built of beautiful, cream-coloured Jerusalem stone, the building was U-shaped around an inner courtyard and conveniently close to the Bezalel Art School and the centre of town.

Our friendly landlord was one of the messiest people we had ever met. Short and somewhat overweight, with wild curly unkempt white hair that stuck out like a halo of uncombed wool surrounding a shiny bald pate, he treated us like his own children, muttering under his breath whenever we displeased him — mainly when we tried to clean up.

We shared the kitchen, which meant that it was not easy to find a clean spot on the counter that we could use. Our untidy landlord left everything out: pots and dirty pans, greasy dishes, food and cutlery, filthy towels. Once in a while, when he was away visiting his family, we cleaned up the messy counters, washed the dirty dishes filling the sink and stored whatever we could in the kitchen cupboards. This activity caused our landlord great distress when he returned.

"What have you done?" he would complain. "I can't find anything anymore!"

His bedroom was an amazing place, a museum of unbridled disorder. So much so that we could not resist conducting an illicit museum tour when he was away. Watching our friends standing in the doorway and gasping in disbelief at the astounding sight was great fun. Today, in the second decade of the second millennium, I could have surely made a brilliant career as a conceptual artist had I recreated and exhibited the little old man's room as a work of art at the Tate Museum. I would have titled it The Room and it would undoubtedly have won me the Turner Prize!

As the sole artist in my family, I had never doubted my talent and happily basked in my parents' unlimited pride and admiration. Mine was a typical case of a large fish fed on endless praise, confidently swimming in a miniature pond.

Until I became a student at the Bezalel Art School.

A rude awakening was in store for me. After just a few weeks of classes, I realized that I was not all that special. I had to work hard to keep up with some of the students in my class who were, I thought, more talented than I. This was a humbling experience but also an exhilarating one. I found myself immersed in a stimulating and exciting artistic environment, working side by side with bright, gifted young people.

Years later, when I became a teacher myself, I always encouraged my students to walk around the class, look at each other's works and engage in conversation about shape and colour, technique and ideas, like bees flitting from flower to flower, gathering the precious golden pollen of creative ideas.

Many students were *Sabras*. Some were young *kibbutz* members sent to Bezalel by their communities who recognized their talent and paid for their education. Others were immigrants like myself. There was also one very gifted young Israeli Arab man. The school was a melting pot of different backgrounds, ages and experiences.

Most of our teachers were refugees trained in the European tradition. Some had arrived before the war in the early and mid-1930s, escaping the destruction that was engulfing that seemingly civilized continent. All were trained in the figurative tradition. In contrast to what was happening in North America in the 1950s, abstraction was not yet being taught at Bezalel.

The love for drawing and figuration acquired during my education at Bezalel would impact my future work as an artist and set me apart from the various trends in art during my career in Canada.

There is nothing more immediate than the swift movement of a pencil on a blank sheet of paper. The thrill of capturing an image in just a few rapid strokes is akin to a magician pulling a rabbit out of an empty hat. The artist creates a new reality out of thin air, bringing the subject to life more vividly than the camera can.

MY TEACHERS

Jakob Eisenscher who taught painting, was already in his late fifties when I became his student. Like my parents-in-law, he was born in

Czernowitz, a city in North Eastern Romania that had previously been a part of the Austro-Hungarian Empire. During time spent in Paris, he fell under the spell of the Cubist art movement and developed a great admiration for Paul Cézanne's work that greatly influenced his outlook on art. He imposed his views on the students, never losing an opportunity to show his particular disapproval for the insertion of lines in a painting. He taught that lines were optically created by the juxtaposition of colour areas, removing the need to physically include them in the work. But I dared to think otherwise.

There was no reason, I thought, to banish drawing in painting. His rules were too narrow and too confining. Would he have failed Picasso and Matisse had they been his students? Were these important painters on his blacklist because drawing was prominent in their paintings?

The time I spent in Eisenscher's class convinced me that arbitrary rules have no place in art — art would become stagnant, as mouldy as a piece of stale bread.

Ironically, the work selected by Eisenscher for inclusion in the graduation show was Ein Karem, one of my village landscapes in which there was liberal use of drawing. I could not bear the thought that this work would stay in the permanent collection of the school and would always be exposed to my teacher's disapproval. When the exhibition came down, I quietly removed the painting from the wall and took it home. It hangs now in the home of private collectors in Vancouver.

Woodblock printing was taught by Jacob Steinhardt, a kindly small man with a shock of wild, thinning white hair and a strong German accent. He had studied in Berlin and had met Henri Matisse while living in Paris. He served in WWI and came to Israel in 1933 after being harassed by the Nazis. His main interest lay in biblical subjects. I did not find his classes very inspiring, perhaps because by then, he was a tired old man who did not have much energy left for teaching.

After Steinhardt's retirement, a younger teacher took his place, Jacob Pins — another Jacob! — who had come from Germany in

1936. Like many other German Jews, his parents refused to believe that a people as cultured and civilized as the Germans would be capable of the horrors that followed and remained in Berlin, hoping that the disturbing events taking place in Germany were temporary. Both were murdered in the Riga Ghetto in Latvia.

Pins was not only an inspiring teacher, but also an avid collector of Japanese woodblock prints, which he later donated to the Israel Museum. Pins opened for us a door to a wonderful world of black-and-white, negative space and strong shadows. The contrast between light and darkness, the richness achieved with the simple means of grooves carved in a block of wood, were his gifts to us. Sometimes he would invite the class to his house for a viewing and, wearing white gloves, he would carefully open large drawers, pulling out one Japanese print after another. We truly felt that we had been given a glimpse of Heaven or at least that we had been transported into Aladdin's cave of treasures.

Jacob Pins was short and stocky with a mane of dark wavy hair, always carefully dressed in a sporty jacket and a silk scarf nattily wound around his neck. His trademark was the pipe that seemed like an extension of his lips.

He established the Jerusalem Artists' House, exhibiting Israeli artists. Unlike North America where students are encouraged to show their work early on, Pins felt that students should not be allowed to exhibit professionally. A print I had done out of class and entered in one of the group shows was returned to me, with "inadmissible — student's work!" scrawled on the back in Pins' handwriting.

Despite the rigorous teaching and emphasis on skills, we were taken aback by the possessiveness Pins showed regarding certain techniques. He had a special way of emphasizing the grain of the wood in his prints that he refused to teach us, saying that it had taken him a long time to develop this technique and now it had become a trademark of his work — we should discover it on our own!

Since woodblock printing became my favourite medium, I'd like to share this pleasure with the reader. The visual power of relief printing, so direct in its simplicity is greatly appealing. A printing press may be used, which I did only once, in Pierre Ayot's studio in

Montreal, but there is no real need for it. All one needs are an idea, a piece of wood, sharp carving tools, a table, a spoon, a smooth surface for rolling the ink on, a rubber roller, some printing inks and a sheet of good paper. What could be simpler than that?

Recipe for printing from a carved block of wood:

First comes the search for the image. Would it be a streetscape, a figure from the marketplace or the head of a Jerusalem beggar? Once chosen, the image is drawn on a sheet of paper the same size as the block of wood. There are changes to the original image — the lines are made stronger and the details simplified. This being a relief print, only the relief areas that are not gouged out of the block will be printed and the image will appear in reverse. I transfer the drawing to the block and open the box where my carving tools are lined up like soldiers on parade.

The white areas are the first to be carved away. Then, using a narrower gauge, I carefully carve around the lines in the drawing. The most difficult parts to cut out are the lines that run across the grain of the wood since it could splinter easily. I love the smell of the fresh wood wafting out of the sharp cuts and the neat raised surfaces that appear.

The carving completed, I move the roller back and forth, spreading the ink on a piece of thick glass or plexi, making sure the roller is well covered. All my senses are alive — my nostrils inhale the sharp smell of the ink and I delight in the splish-splash sound created by the roller. My hand moves rhythmically, spreading the sticky black substance from the glass onto the relief surfaces of the block. Once inked, the block is ready for printing. I carefully place a sheet of rice paper on the inked surface of the carved block and rub it on the back. Next, a sophisticated tool called a 'spoon' is applied on the waxed back of the paper in small circular movements until the ink is transferred from the block. Presto! I slowly peel the paper away and, as if by magic, the blank sheet has now become a woodblock print.

Wood engraving is different. It requires wood that has been cut across the grain, like sliced salami. Unlike the wood in a plank, here the absence of grain allows for fine detail in any direction of the cut.

Flower Women
1965 | woodblock print | 17 × 33 in | 43.2 × 83.8 cm

Soon after graduation, I met Moshe Ha'naami, a young poet who was about to publish his first poetry book, *Small Poems*. A publisher was willing to take it on and needed an illustrator. I was thrilled when I was offered this opportunity: my very first job as an illustrator. My suggestion of using wood engravings carved from blocks of olive wood was accepted and I set to work.

These small rounded blocks were smooth as silk and beautiful to behold. Instead of the larger tools used for carving planks, all I needed now was one tiny sharp etching tool designed to carve out the lines for the fine detail.

The publisher had a limited budget and, to save money, he decided to forego the production of the customary metal plates, printing the engravings directly from the blocks instead. This was to be done by students at the international Jewish trade school, ORT — the name is a Russian acronym meaning 'Association for the Promotion of Skilled Trades'. This school was run by a non-profit global Jewish organization that promotes education and training in over one hundred countries. Vocational training and technical skills are important aspects of these schools and the Jerusalem campus offered a training course for the printing business.

The decision to print directly from the blocks was taken to save money when in fact, we were producing an 'artist's book' with original prints. Being blissfully innocent of the conventions of the art world and the art market, we never realized the potential value of the book we were producing.

I was also unaware of the pitfalls of broken contracts between artist and publisher — getting paid took longer and was more laborious than producing the work.

It was not until much later that I fully understood how ignorant of art conventions we had been when we published *Small Poems*. In 1994, Barbarian Press in Mission, British Columbia, included one of the very prints from *Small Poems* in the expensive limited-edition book *Endgrain: Contemporary Wood Engraving in North America*. The small block,

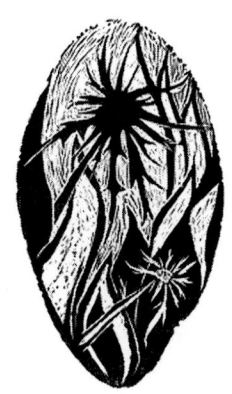

Thistle Fire
1958 | wood engraving
5 × 3 in | 12.7 × 7.6 cm
From *Small Poems* by
Moshe Ha'naami

still in my possession, was printed for this collector's book in the very same way it had been printed in 1958 in Jerusalem: directly from the block onto the page, resulting in an original print rather than a reproduction. *Endgrain*, a limited-edition book with engravings of artists from Canada and the United States, is a rare and expensive collector's item, while *Small Poems* lies forgotten and unappreciated.

Small Poems is now on a shelf in my studio, its light green jacket faded and the cardboard corners frayed. The poet died a long time ago, but his memory is alive in his poems. I kept some of the original blocks and took some blank ones with me to Canada. Their presence in the drawer in my studio is a solid link between past and present, giving me comfort and a sense of continuity.

We studied drawing with Isidor Ascheim. He was an established artist who, like Jacob Steinhardt, had served for Germany during WWI. Now in his late 60s, he was a tall, soft-spoken balding man whom I never saw without his trademark red bow tie.

The figure drawing class was my favourite. We experimented with various media, from graphite to watercolour to oils to pastels. We used the cheapest paper we could find, since none of us had any spare cash and we had never heard of acid-free paper — we even used newsprint for sketching. According to the high standards in art materials today, that paper should have disintegrated long ago. Amazingly, most of the drawings I kept from that time have the same freshness as they had in the 1950s!

Our models were sometimes the students themselves, but nude models and colourful beggars from the streets of Jerusalem were also hired. The latter were not always easy to get. The hiring procedure was quite primitive and not always successful since Jerusalem beggars were members of a well-defined profession.

Figure Drawing Class
1957 | ink drawing | 9.5 × 13.5 in | 24.2 × 34.3 cm

On one occasion, a student friend and I went in search of a beggar to hire. Having seen the pitiable figures dressed in rags that stood or crouched on the pavement on street corners close to the school, we thought that it would not take long to return with an interesting find. The first man we approached was sitting on a miserable little carpet, his hand held out towards the passers-by begging for alms, his thin frame covered by a pair of dirty pants and a bedraggled grey shirt. His haggard, unshaven face showed no emotion as his eyes stared blankly. We gently asked if he would like to make some money posing for a drawing class.

"How much do you pay?" he asked.

When we quoted a certain fee, he rejected our offer.

"Forget it," he said. "I make more than that in half an hour on the street!"

We walked on until we reached a woman standing against a wall holding a tiny cup in her hand. Her unkempt grey hair spilled out of the soiled rag that covered it. She wore a long skirt with a frayed hem that hung loose over thin legs encased in torn shoes. When we repeated our offer, she demurely refused, advising us that she needed her husband's permission for this kind of job. In desperation, we approached another miserable but picturesque man sitting on the next street corner, dressed in rags and feigning blindness. After a short bargaining session, we offered him a higher fee and he finally followed us to school.

My exposure to abstract art might have been sorely lacking but thanks to Isidor Ascheim, I acquired an everlasting love for drawing.

Mordecai Ardon, an internationally known artist, taught us Art History and introduced us to *Primitive Art* by anthropologist Franz Boaz, featuring a black, white and red design of a Kwakwaka'wakw sea monster on the cover. The chapter I loved most was the one on the art of the indigenous people of the Northwest Coast of British Columbia. The totem poles, elegant oval shapes and the symbolic significance of the abstract forms

Beggar With Basket
1957 | graphite on paper
13.5 × 9 in | 34.3 × 23 cm

fascinated me. These shapes conveyed meaning for a people with no written language, becoming signifiers for their history and the animal world surrounding them, creating a rich and varied mythology. I strongly admired the beauty and sophistication of this art. Little did I know at the time how meaningful this would prove in my future work as an artist.

During my fourth and last year at Bezalel, a new teacher appeared in the printmaking section, offering a course in etching. Yehuda Bacon, of Czech origin, was the youngest of the teachers and the survivor of several extermination camps and death marches. He was alone in the world, his whole family murdered by the Nazis. Barely alive, Bacon was liberated from Auschwitz by the US Army in May 1945, just four days before the end of the war.

Despite the hell he had been through, he never spoke to us about his experiences. We vaguely knew that he was a survivor and talked in whispers about it among ourselves, but never asked him questions about his past. Only many years later did I learn that immediately after liberation, at the age of seventeen and without any art training, Yehuda Bacon began to draw feverishly from memory, giving shape to the horrors he had witnessed during the time he was forced to work in the crematoria in Auschwitz. His drawings served as a living witness during the Eichmann Trial.

Illustration, taught by Yossi Stern, was the *raison d'être* of the Graphics Department at Bezalel. Graphics, or illustration, was the profession that would enable the students to support themselves in the future. Yossi, born in 1923 in Hungary, was tall, slim and graceful, with straight brown hair falling over half his brow. He had rosy cheeks and a heavy Hungarian accent. Everybody knew that he was gay, but no one cared. His sunny personality, despite his difficult past as a Holocaust child survivor, endeared him to all of us. Yossi created the ubiquitous little figure of the 'new Israeli', the young *kibbutznik* who wore sandals, a blue shirt over blue shorts and the iconic *kova tembel*.

Yossi was completely focused on his personal vision of the shape figures should be drawn. He not only advised us, he sometimes used tracing paper to correct the faces in our works, so that everyone ended up with exactly the same face. It was not difficult to identify students who had taken his courses — the identical faces in their works told the story quite clearly and became the trademark of Israeli illustration. It took me years of conscious effort to finally free myself of the round smiling face Yossi Stern had imposed on us. On the other hand, through his influence on the numerous students who became illustrators, he created an easily recognizable Israeli style.

I drew everything in sight. I drew our neighbours, our landlady washing her clothes, our friends and their children. I drew the streets of Jerusalem, the colourful Mahane Yehuda market, the small villages perched on the Judean hills and the people on the street. Interesting and colourful images were all around me. I simply had to record them on the drawing pad I always carried. The few drawings I have kept are a precious memory bank of my years in Jerusalem.

Lifta Village, Near Jerusalem
1959 | pen and ink | 4 x 6 in | 10.2 x 15.2 cm
Collection of Jona and Uri El-Hanani

The Mahane Yehuda Market in Jerusalem
1959 | pen and ink | 13.5 × 9 in | 34.3 × 22.8 cm

Chapter 34

Life in Jerusalem

It was time to move on. Our landlord wanted his room back and anyway, it had become too confining for us. We needed more space.

Our search for a new abode brought us to Mamilla, a border street ending in a threatening roll of barbed wire, on which hung the ubiquitous Jerusalem warning sign, reading "Border!" The room for rent was in a house located in a narrow lane off the very end of the street, accessible from an inner courtyard. Opening the door, we saw a spacious room featuring a high-vaulted ceiling. We rented the room on the spot. Like other border areas in the city, the run-down Mamilla neighbourhood was home to families of poor Jewish immigrants mostly from Arab countries, a friendly place with children running around and people chatting on the street. It was also picturesque with its decrepit houses, old walls and arched windows. I quickly became an attraction for the children who somehow seemed to have an invisible telephone line signaling my presence as soon as I set up my easel on the pavement. As if by magic, they materialized out of nowhere and gathered around, their eager eyes following the lines appearing on the paper, oohing and aahing with excitement as the familiar street became alive under my pen. This young audience was the most appreciative I had ever had!

After living on Mamilla Street for several months, we began our search for a more permanent place to live. We had managed to save some money and borrowed some more, hoping that we could buy our own home.

Painting on Mamilla Street

It was not long before we found what we wanted: a two-room apartment in a house on yet another border street. Living on the border carried its own risks, particularly if one wore a set of false teeth. It may seem strange to mention this, but life is sometimes stranger than fiction. While leaning on her window, a woman living on the border lost her loose dentures in the 'no-man's land' below. This was an incident of international proportions! UN officers arrived waving a white flag and the dentures were retrieved without further incident.

Border living seemed to have become our specialty and the only one we could afford.

Our status went up one notch. At last, we had our own apartment, bought with a small payment of 'key money' that we managed to put together. Key money was a kind of down payment, an antiquated real estate transaction dating from the British Mandate.

Beit Suleimanoff, or Suleimanoff House, was a two-storey stone building owned by Mrs. Suleimanoff, a Jewish woman of Iraqi extraction from whom we bought our apartment. The house was officially on Shmuel HaNavi (Samuel the Prophet) Street, but things were never simple in Jerusalem and the address was deceiving. This long street, ending at a border crossing known as the Mandelbaum Gate, was the physical border with Jordan and subject to frequent attacks by Arab snipers and the Fedayeen, a terrorist group established and supported by Egyptian President Gamal Abdul Nasser. A tall wall running the length of the street was built for protection against those snipers.

Our home was on the second floor. We had two rooms, a tiny balcony and a bathroom shared with a Hungarian family of three. The original kitchen had been split in two by a wall that did not reach the ceiling, so that privacy was at a minimum. In fact, I became an expert in exclaiming *rettenetes!*, the Hungarian word for 'terrible', used to convey frustration and uttered incessantly and with great gusto by our short, stocky neighbour on the other side of the wall. The kitchen was long and narrow — I could touch both walls at once just by spreading out my arms. There was only cold running water for washing dishes and I ended up with a painful rash on my hands. Luckily, my husband took over the dishwashing, claiming that physical work helped him relax when he needed a respite from his brainy math work. Of course, I was only too happy to pass him this job, which became a 'tenured' one over the years. We had an icebox, since refrigerators were a luxury we could not afford. The ice truck came by very early each morning, the frozen block carried to the kitchen with iron tongs and inserted in the icebox after emptying yesterday's melted ice.

Unlike cities with a neat grid-like pattern, Jerusalem's streets were a chaotic combination of wide roads and narrow alleys. Due to this haphazard geography a few houses had been left unprotected behind the wall. A thick roll of barbed wire, installed as a deterrent against terrorists trying to cross into Israel, was deployed behind our new home, adjacent to the open area of the 'no-man's-land' between Israel and Jordan, looking as if it had come directly from the trenches of World War I. We were well protected — we hoped!

Still, it was cheap (not many were willing to live right on the border) and the view of the Sheikh Jerrakh neighbourhood in Jordan, seen across the large no-man's-land was great! We were young and nothing could harm us. The first time my parents came to visit they were less thrilled — they were actually horrified.

"What?" they cried. "This is dangerous! You are completely exposed to snipers! And all this barbed wire, what if some terrorists cut through?"

To our amused relief, the only invader that managed to sneak through the barbed wire was an emaciated yellow stray dog that gave birth to a few puppies next to our house.

"Oh well," we joked. "No wonder she braved the barbed wire, our standard of living is higher than in Jordan . . ."

We fed this gentle canine mother and cared for her safety.

Border View Of Jordan From Our House
1959 | ink drawing | 8 × 12 in | 20.3 × 30.5 cm

The route home from Bezalel took me through Mea Shearim, the fanatically ultra-orthodox neighbourhood of the 'Neturei Karta', whose members lived in a time warp. They did not recognize the state of Israel, pointing out that the Messiah has yet to come. Their bizarre medieval dress set them apart from the rest of the population, arousing animosity and ill feelings.

The narrow streets of their enclave were plastered with prominent posters bearing detailed instructions for women's proper dress: precisely how many centimetres of bare flesh could be seen between the wrist and the elbow, how long the dress should be and what colour was allowed for stockings. There were rules about women shaving their hair, rules for the right kind of head covering and the strict injunction for women not to ever, ever, ever wear men's clothes, such as pants. We used to poke fun at these outrageous laws and the strange clothes worn by this sect.

Walking these streets, one felt transported a few centuries back to the time when Orthodox Jews lived in small settlements called *shtetls* in Eastern Europe and wore distinctive clothes. Rigid and unbending in their outdated beliefs, members of this fanatical sect scurried along in the Jerusalem heat, dressed in shiny black caftans, wide-brimmed black hats and tight black stockings. On special holidays they were seen in ridiculously tall fur hats better suited to cold Polish winters, curly sidelocks dangling down their ears and *tzitzit*, the fringes of the prayer shawl, hanging outside their pants. I felt sorry for the women dressed mostly in black, brown or grey, their shaven heads tightly covered with drab headkerchiefs and surrounded by their numerous offspring. I also felt sorry for the men sweating profusely in the hot Middle Eastern sun, dressed in inappropriate clothing. My sympathy, however, was totally misplaced, since this was done by choice. They considered secular Jews like us and women in particular, as degenerate sinners.

Orthodox Man
1956 | charcoal
9.5 × 6.5 in | 24.2 × 16.5 cm

One warm spring day, I dared to walk home through Mea Shearim dressed in light slacks and a sleeveless blouse, shamelessly exposing my naked arms to the world. A group of small boys not more than four or five years old, were sitting on the sidewalk, their young faces framed by long curling sidelocks. Suddenly, one of them stood up and pointed at me.

Pritze! Pritze! he shouted in a thin childish voice, the Yiddish word for 'whore'. He then threw an orange in my direction, but his aim was not very accurate and the orange fell at my feet, breaking apart. The bright orange rind splintered on the road and the sweet, sticky juice spilled in the gutter. These children had been taught that young women like me were *pritzes*, whores to be abused and despised since we wantonly showed our arms and wore trousers.

My sympathy vanished forever. Fanatics are not in my good books, even if they are Jewish.

The walk home from school in the afternoon heat was a long one. First I had to cross a small square planted with flowers where a tall bronze menorah, the ancient symbol of the candelabra from the first Temple, towered over the street and then I continued along King George Avenue. For a shortcut, I would walk through Mea Shearim, hurrying as fast as I could and hoping that I would emerge without incident, until finally arriving at Shmuel HaNavi Street. To reach our house, I had to leave the safety of the wall through a narrow opening that led me to a cluster of houses protected only by the barbed wire fence.

During the year that we lived in Beit Suleimanoff I found a new source of income painting Israeli and Japanese motifs on small wooden plates. Japanese, you ask? It was bizarre, but for some obscure reason, tourists found them attractive and bought them in the gift shops.

Our landlady, Mrs. Suleimanoff, who lived on the ground floor, became my model, albeit without her knowledge, while washing her laundry the Iraqi way. She would squat in front of a metal tub filled with water and energetically rub her clothes on a washboard. Then she would hang them to dry in the sun, unaware that her every movement was recorded by the nosy neighbour upstairs.

Mrs. Suleimanoff Doing Her Laundry
1958 | charcoal | 8 × 12 in | 20.3 × 30.5 cm

As far as we were concerned, we lived in the lap of luxury. Who cared that the bathroom was shared, that we had to get up at dawn to buy ice or that we had a kitchen the size of a matchbox with no hot water? We had two rooms now: one for sleeping and one for working. We often saw our friends, most of them students with grand leftist ideals, some even card-carrying Communists. We signed petitions for peace and for social justice and were convinced that our vision for a future of equality and fairness was the right one. We went to lectures and performances at the leftist Culture House where we heard The Weavers and Pete Seeger sing, watched inspiring films and spent long hours in animated discussions.

We talked about world issues, peace, the perceived injustice towards the Arab population and the problems facing the new immigrants. We upheld the model of Stalin and the Soviet Union as the solution for everything.

I cringe now with stinging embarrassment while writing these words — how could we have forgotten so quickly our Romanian past under the Communists?

And then came the great political earthquake.

On March 18, 1956, Soviet leader Nikita Khrushchev's speech to the 20th Congress of the Communist Party in February was made public, exploding like a bombshell that shattered long-held lies and deceptions. Khrushchev denounced Joseph Stalin, the Communist 'god' who had introduced the concept of the personality cult, as a brutal despot, a murderer, an anti-Semite and a ruthless ruler. To our horror, we learned that the man so many admired was in reality a monster hiding his crimes behind the fatherly smile. This discovery was nothing short of an earthquake that flattened and destroyed the illusions carefully built around the despicable deeds of the Communist régime. The gulags, the murders of faithful officers, doctors, artists and writers, the huge scheme to control countries and populations and to manipulate people's beliefs and ideals, all these were suddenly illuminated by the spotlight of the powerful and daring words of a man who had been part of the Big Lie himself.

We still believed in social justice, fairness and equality, but not through the soiled lens of communism. We immediately cancelled our subscription to the communist newspaper and stopped all activities connected with it. A blindfold had been removed from our eyes. This was the end of our involvement with anything on the far left.

We thought that our close friends who were Party members would also take off the blinders and see the truth, but to our disappointment, many of them reacted differently. Deep denial set in. They refused to believe the facts, pretending that Khrushchev was lying, trying to usurp Stalin's reputation. For them, nothing had changed — it was politics as usual. While they defensively manned the destroyed barricades of their beliefs, they considered us as traitors who collaborated with the greedy capitalists and the despised bourgeoisie.

Seeing our friends turning against us was a painful experience and we wondered if they were our friends only due to our shared ideas. Was there no friendship beyond politics? If we were prepared to preserve our relationship, why were they not? We had just learned a difficult lesson about the power of fanaticism over friendship and common sense.

In 1956, Egyptian President Abdul Gamal Nasser stepped up his campaign against Israel, violating the armistice signed between the two countries. Following the closing of the Suez Canal, he shut down the Straits of Tiran that linked the Israeli port of Eilat to the Red Sea, effectively cutting off Israel's trade to Asia. The media were constantly reporting infiltrations of Arab Fedayeen whose aim was to spread panic and fear among the Israeli civilian population by attacking innocent people at random. In 1955 alone, 260 Israelis were killed or wounded by these terrorists.

War broke out on October 29, 1956 and Eddy was called up to the reserves. From one day to the next, our house did not seem so idyllic anymore. The barbed wire fence and the no-man's-land became threatening, inspiring insecurity and fear. If some armed Fedayeen crossed the no-man's-land across from Beit Suleimanoff, what would I do, alone in the house?

I packed up and went to stay with my parents in Haifa until the Suez war ended on November 6 of that year.

Chapter 35

Another Move — a Noisy Actor Enters the Stage

Parenthood remains the greatest single preserve of the amateur.

Alvin Toffler
Future Shock

We were slowly but surely making our way up in the world. Could it be that since we parted ways with the utopian ideals and wonders of communism, we became closer to the formerly despised bourgeois way of life? We had left the bohemian two-room flat in Shmuel HaNavi and were now the proud owners of a small apartment in Yefe Nof (beautiful vista) in a large complex overlooking a deep valley.

The new homeowners, 1959

Our apartment was on the third floor (no elevator, of course!) in a building wrapped around a large inner courtyard. Typical of Israeli construction, all the floors and stairs were lined with *balatot*, stone tiles that kept us cool in the hot summers and were easily washed with soap and water. Winters were another story. Jerusalem is colder and drier than the rest of the country and insulation unknown. The small kerosene stove responsible for heating our apartment stank to the high heavens, but kept us relatively warm.

We had more space than ever before: two bedrooms, a living room, a small kitchen, a bathroom and a minute balcony. The living room became our office and the bedroom doubled as living room, involving the old routine of transforming our bed into a sofa during the day. I had a larger table to work on and enough commissions to keep me busy. I was doing freelance work and I had a regular, quality customer: the Government Information Centre, responsible for educational material.

Never a dull moment — the jobs coming my way were varied and interesting: information brochures for schools, posters for the Tourist Office and, most wonderful of all, a series of fairytale filmstrips for pre-schoolers.

These filmstrips were meant to introduce young children to the magical world of classic and Israeli tales. An ideal job made just for me! The text was divided into segments to be illustrated and then the finished work was photographed either in slide format or on a continuous filmstrip screened with a small projector. These static images were a long way from animation. No horses galloping, no Snow White wandering through the forest, no seven dwarves dancing and no sound. It was simply a slideshow with a live narrator telling the story. Producing new illustrations for the stories of my childhood, instead of the copies I used to make from the Brothers Grimm and Charles Perrault books in grade two, was an exciting opportunity. Now I created my very own, original version — and got paid for it!

The slide trays and the small tubular metal containers housing these illustrations are languishing now in an old shoebox in my closet, most probably never to be seen again. How could these still pictures compete with the sophisticated animation of today's technology? Would children spend time watching a slideshow when they have amazing special effects, movement and sound at their fingertips?

Commissions for book illustrations led to an unexpected dilemma concerning the name 'Granirer'. In Hebrew, the letters of the alphabet are all consonants, while the vowels are small dots and lines placed under, above and within the letters. These vowels are printed in the Tanakh and in poetry, but one has to be quite literate to read a book or a newspaper where only the consonants appear. When printed without the vowels in the credits of a book, it was difficult to read my last name correctly. I was faced with a perplexing dilemma: what to do about my last name. I decided to use a pen name for my professional work, choosing an easy to read Hebrew name: Goren. From then on, all my illustrations were published under this new alias.

Shortly after moving into our new apartment, our lives changed drastically when a new actor appeared on stage, quickly and noisily making his entrance and taking possession of the second bedroom: Eran, our first son, was born.

Mercifully, Eran was in a great hurry to enter the world. It took him only one short hour to make the transition from his cozy, bumpy existence in my body to the status of an independent person to be reckoned with. I have wondered ever since about the suffering of women whose inconsiderate babies take many hours to be born.

As prescribed by the Jewish faith, Eran had to be circumcised on the seventh day after birth. This ritual would be performed in the hospital by a *mohel*, a specialist in this delicate operation.

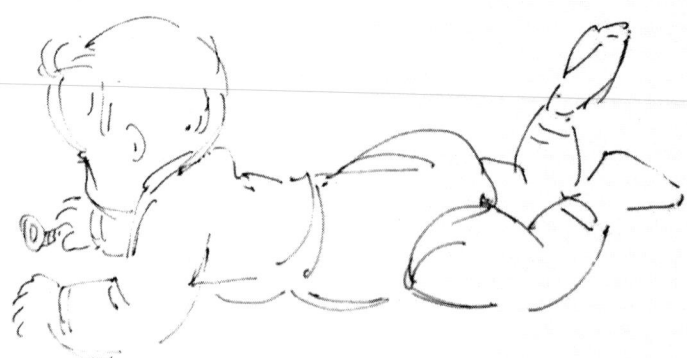

Baby Eran
1960 | ink drawing | 6 × 8 in | 15.2 × 20.3 cm

My mother prepared a large array of goodies for the invited guests. Dainty sandwiches, elegant pastries and fresh fruit were laid upon a table covered with a white tablecloth, set up in the hall downstairs, visible through a glass wall from the second floor where I was standing. The hospital was run in accordance with religious rules, so mothers were not allowed to be present during the circumcision. I could only watch the ceremony unfold from behind the upstairs windows. The baby was carried into the hall on a cushion covered with a long white lacy coverlet, like a sacrificial offering, I thought. I was surprised at the anxiety I felt about the ordeal in store for this fragile newborn. Perhaps it was better that I was not allowed to witness the actual performance.

In no time at all, the usual prayers were sung and the traditional surgery was over. The doors to the hall were opened to allow the guests in. To my horror, I watched helplessly as a horde of beggars invaded the room, descending like a murder of crows upon my mother's beautiful culinary creations, frenetically filling their pockets with food. There was little remaining on the table by the time they left.

The next day we took the baby home. A new chapter in our lives was beginning: parenthood.

Oh, the sleepless nights, the crying, the ear infections, the exhaustion wrapping around us like a straightjacket! The feedings, the cloth diapers that had to be rinsed and boiled for reuse, the short blessed quiet when the baby napped in the afternoons, and then that tired feeling again . . .

However, there was also the sheer bliss at the sight of the angelic smile of the same baby who was screaming at the top of his lungs just moments before. Every day brought its sorrows and its rewards, every day the little actor surprised us with a new skill and made us discover the world anew through his wide-open eyes. A flower, a pebble, a spoon, a book — I had forgotten how wonderful everything around us was, how nothing was taken for granted. As I helped him discover his world, this small child taught me to see again.

As we had no telephone and no television, we listened constantly to the radio for the latest news. We were living on

Eran learns to walk

the brink of unseen but imminent dangers like terrorism and the threat of yet another war that might engulf us at any moment and shatter our peace. Just a few months before the birth of our son, in May 1960, the spectacular news of the capture of Adolf Eichmann, the evil architect of the destruction of the Hungarian Jews, exploded over the country. We avidly read the newspapers, followed the sensational trial on the radio and engaged in heated discussions with friends. We were proud of the Israeli intelligence agents who captured Eichmann — almost all were survivors, such as my former boss Tuviah Friedman, who had lost their families due to this mass murderer. They had prevailed, bringing him to justice to face his victims in Jerusalem.

Months went by. I had the ideal job for a young mother — what can be better than reading stories and making pictures in your own home? I also drew the baby lying on the carpet, sleeping, playing. When he stood up in his crib, I drew him again and again. And, miracle of miracles, words appeared from the small mouth, lovely words. We took delight in each word and thought that our baby was the smartest child on Earth.

Eran and Yifat

Across the large inner courtyard of our complex lived another young family with a small girl about Eran's age named Yifat. The children played often when we met in the garden and a sweet romance developed between them. They would hold hands, kiss one another and Eran would call out to her at the top of his lungs: "*Taaati, Taaati!*" A true story of romantic love for these two toddlers, who had been in the world not more than fourteen or fifteen months!

Chapter 36

Big Changes

The secret of change is to focus all of your energy,
not on fighting the old, but on building the new.

Dan Millman
Way of the Peaceful Warrior: A Book That Changes Lives

Finished! All done!

Eddy had completed his PhD in Mathematics, becoming Dr. Edmond Granirer. Despite this impressive achievement, he would never present himself as 'Dr.' — he was far too modest and felt that flaunting his degree was showing off.

But a true professorial life cannot begin without an academic position and reality proved Eddy's mother right: there were no such positions available in Israel. There were too many PhDs and too few universities to accommodate them all. However, Lady Luck was waiting in the wings, ready to help us anew.

Eddy giving a math lecture, 1961

An unexpected event of spectacular proportions that changed the world and our own lives occurred in 1957.

On October 4, 1957, the Soviet Union launched Sputnik, the first artificial satellite ever to orbit the Earth. I remember well our excitement and awe. How did the Russians achieve the amazing feat of escaping the power of gravity? This was science fiction come true, an unimaginable feat. The idea of space travel brought to mind Jules Verne, one of the first science fiction writers, who dared imagine this epic journey in his book *From Earth to the Moon*, written before the end of the 19th Century, at a time when space exploration was unthinkable. I was familiar with his books, which had kept me in their thrall during my teenage years with predictions of spectacular inventions that seemed possible only in the author's fertile imagination. Jules Verne's *20,000 Leagues under the Sea*, telling the amazing story of the Nautilus submarine, at a time when any ship under water could only be a shipwreck, still has a place of honour in my bookcase and Captain Nemo's name appears often in crossword puzzles. Jules Verne was at least one hundred years ahead of his time and no one seriously believed that space travel could ever become reality.

Now the Soviets had sent Sputnik up! The first man-made satellite had escaped the pull of gravity and humanity was on its way towards space exploration.

We stood outside in the dark night and stared at the sky to catch a glimpse of the small object that had catapulted the world into the space age. Blinking faintly above our heads, the tiny man-made object moved confidently in the blackness of the firmament. It was clearly visible, a new star within a multitude of stars.

The space race was on.

A month later Sputnik 2 followed, carrying Laika, the space dog. On April 12, 1961, after an unfortunate fatality in the first attempt to put a man in orbit, the Russians succeeded in launching Vostok 1, carrying Yuri Gagarin, the first human to escape the Earth's gravity and return. These spectacular successes came as a total surprise to the United States and a mad scramble ensued to catch up with the Soviet Union. The Americans began pouring money and resources into research hoping to be the first to put a man on the moon. Universities clamoured for scientists. Mathematics, the cornerstone and essential building block of scientific research, was suddenly in high demand all over North America.

The old hackneyed sayings are true, after all. Being 'in the right place at the right time' or being 'born under a lucky star' reflect old folk wisdom. Events beyond our control do change the course of our lives. In challenging the United States for the conquest of space, Sputnik opened new vistas of opportunities for us. In 1962, when Eddy completed his PhD at the Hebrew University, jobs opened everywhere in the United States and Canada. Eddy was offered a position as assistant professor at the University of Illinois in Urbana-Champaign. A momentous change was about to take place in our lives.

We began preparing for this adventure. We got passports, rented our apartment for the three years that we would be away and began packing. Reluctantly, having heard that in the US university professors had to wear a tie while lecturing, Eddy bought one. I chose some of my drawings and a few paintings and packed them as well. I am happy to have these early works now in my studio in Vancouver. Without their presence, there would be a large gap in my life as an artist.

On May 31, 1962, three months before we left, Adolf Eichmann was sentenced and executed by hanging. Since there was no death penalty in Israel, a special law had to be introduced for this occasion. Justice was done.

Our very first plane trip! We were twenty-five years old and had never flown before. How disappointing then to be ushered into a small propeller plane and crammed together in tight seats with barely enough room to move. With a deafening noise, the plane took off. Did it really? How could air be so bumpy? We felt as if we were travelling in an antiquated noisy truck, over a road full of potholes.

Mercifully, it was a short haul to Athens, which looked surprisingly similar to Tel-Aviv — the same hot sun shining on white buildings, the same slender conical pine trees lining the roads, the same loud and lively interaction between storekeepers and their clients. Nobody spoke anything but Greek. We sat down in a restaurant for breakfast and tried to order an egg for Eran. How does one say 'egg' in Greek? We clucked like a chicken and I waved my arms with my elbows bent like chicken wings and mimed the shape of an egg with my fingers. Eureka! We got our egg!

We had only one full day in Athens and visiting the Parthenon was a must. Even so, seeing this famous monument in the company of a toddler was less exciting than we had thought. Eddy carried Eran on his shoulders while we slowly climbed the steep hill of the Acropolis. The heat was searing, just like in Israel. The hill, crowned by the famous ancient building was steep, much too steep. We felt as if we were moving through an oven set on broil — sweat was pouring down, trickling from our foreheads to our necks and creating dark wet stains under our armpits. I shall always remember the heat and the sweat, but I have only a vague memory of the Parthenon itself. One sees the world differently when a baby rules the roost.

From Athens, we flew to Zurich to visit Eddy's aunt and uncle. I had never met them but was familiar with the important part they had played during the war when Rudolf Donnermann, the Gentile husband of Eddy's aunt Lola, had generously paid large bribes to rescue the family from detention camps.

Zurich was a beautiful city where the streets were clean, the shop windows were laden with abundant merchandise, the trams ran on time and where, wonder of wonders, we encountered our very first vending machine, which rewarded us with chocolate when we simply inserted the right coin in the slot. The Israel we came from was a poor country with no such luxuries as televisions or slot machines. We were like two yokels entering the civilized West. Lola and Rudolf owned a television store and we gaped in wonder at the heavy wooden sets displayed in the window.

We went for dinner in a small restaurant and I ordered my favourite dish: chicken livers and mashed potatoes.

"*Ach, nein,*" said the waiter, all decked up with a bow tie and a white apron. "Livers are thrown to the dogs. We don't serve *that*!"

Lola and Rudolf welcomed us with great warmth, treated us lavishly and brought us up to date on family gossip. Lola was an elegant woman dressed in expensive clothes, chic suits and high-heeled shoes. Her blonde hair was neatly coiffed in a conservative style and she strode confidently ahead, clutching her fashionable leather purse. She and Rudolf have shown unstinting kindness to Lola's family whenever the need arose.

Rudolf was not very talkative; he wore a buttoned-down suit and a little hat perched on his thinning hair. Once in a while, he came alive when he felt the need to berate an incompetent waiter who displeased him in some obscure way.

Our departure day arrived. We boarded the plane to Chicago and from there to the twin towns of Urbana-Champaign, where Eddy would take up his first teaching position at the University of Illinois.

This time we flew in the luxury of a large jet with elegant stewardesses. We were about to turn the page unto a new chapter in our story.

Ein Karem
1959 | oil on card | 19 x 27 in | 48 x 69 cm
Collection of Dan and Daphne Gelbart

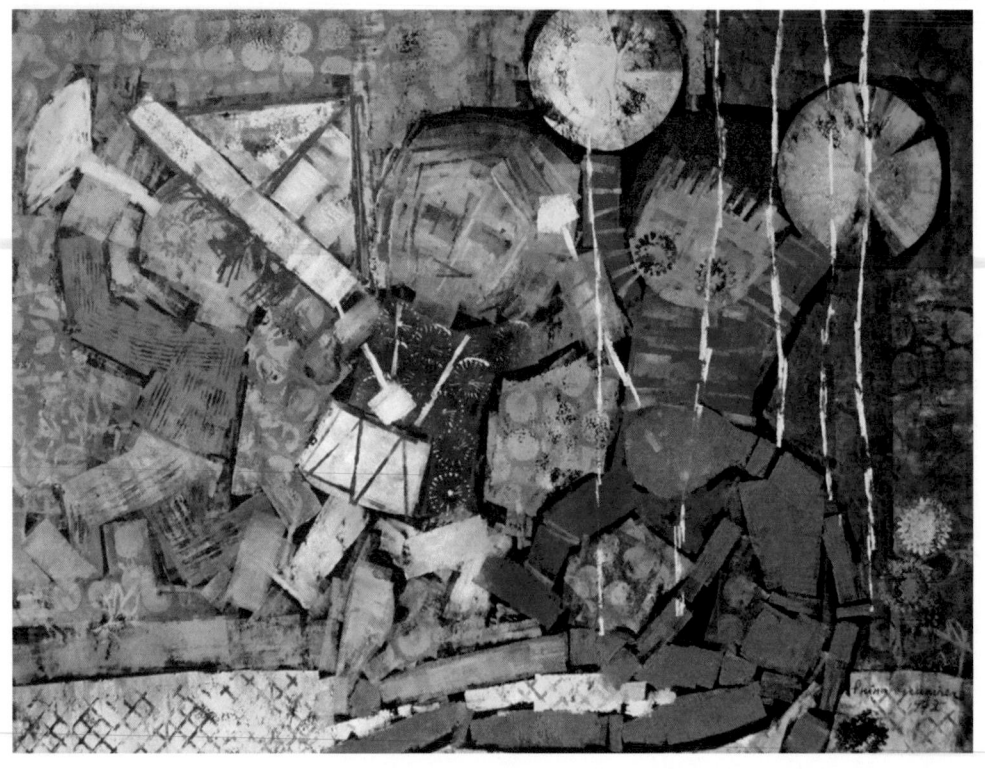

Parade
1964 | printing inks on card | 22 x 30 in | 51 x 76 cm
Collection of Don and Phyllis Lamont

Child's Journey
1975 | diptych | mixed media on paper | 2× 30 x 22 in | 2× 76 x 56 cm

Legend of Forbidden Plateau
1978 | triptych | mixed media on Fabriano paper | 3× 39 x 27 in | 99 x 69 cm
Private Collection

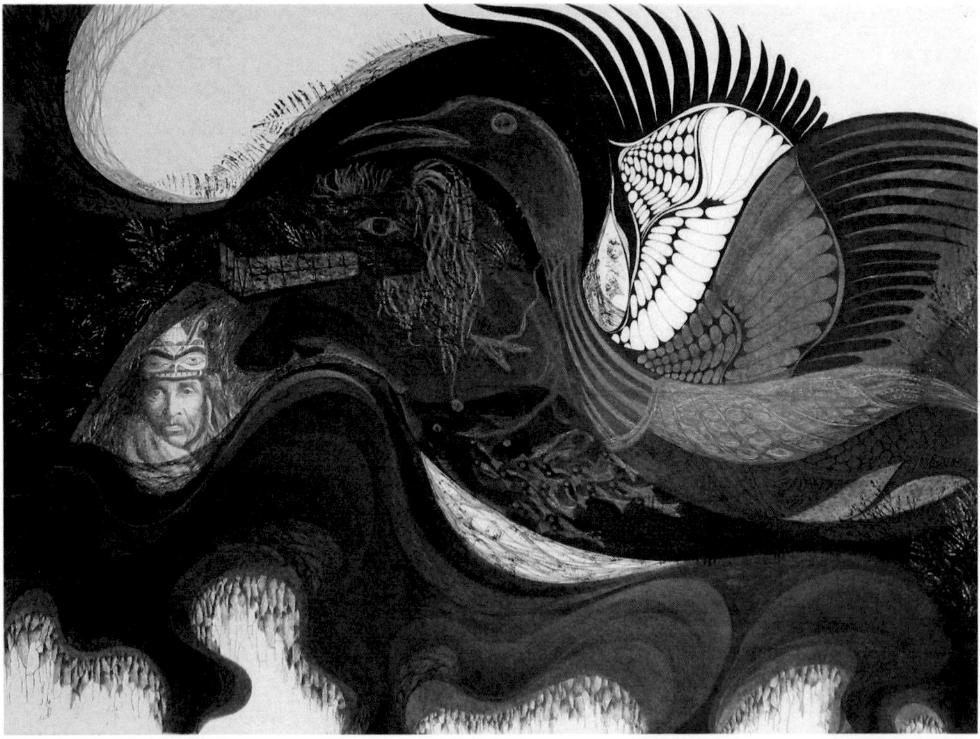

Portrait of a Kwakiutl Man
1978 | mixed media on Fabriano paper | 22 x 30 in | 56 x 76 cm

Out of the Flames
1988 | triptych | mixed media on paper | 3× 40 x 30 in | 101.8 x 76 cm
Collection of Yad Vashem Museum, Jerusalem

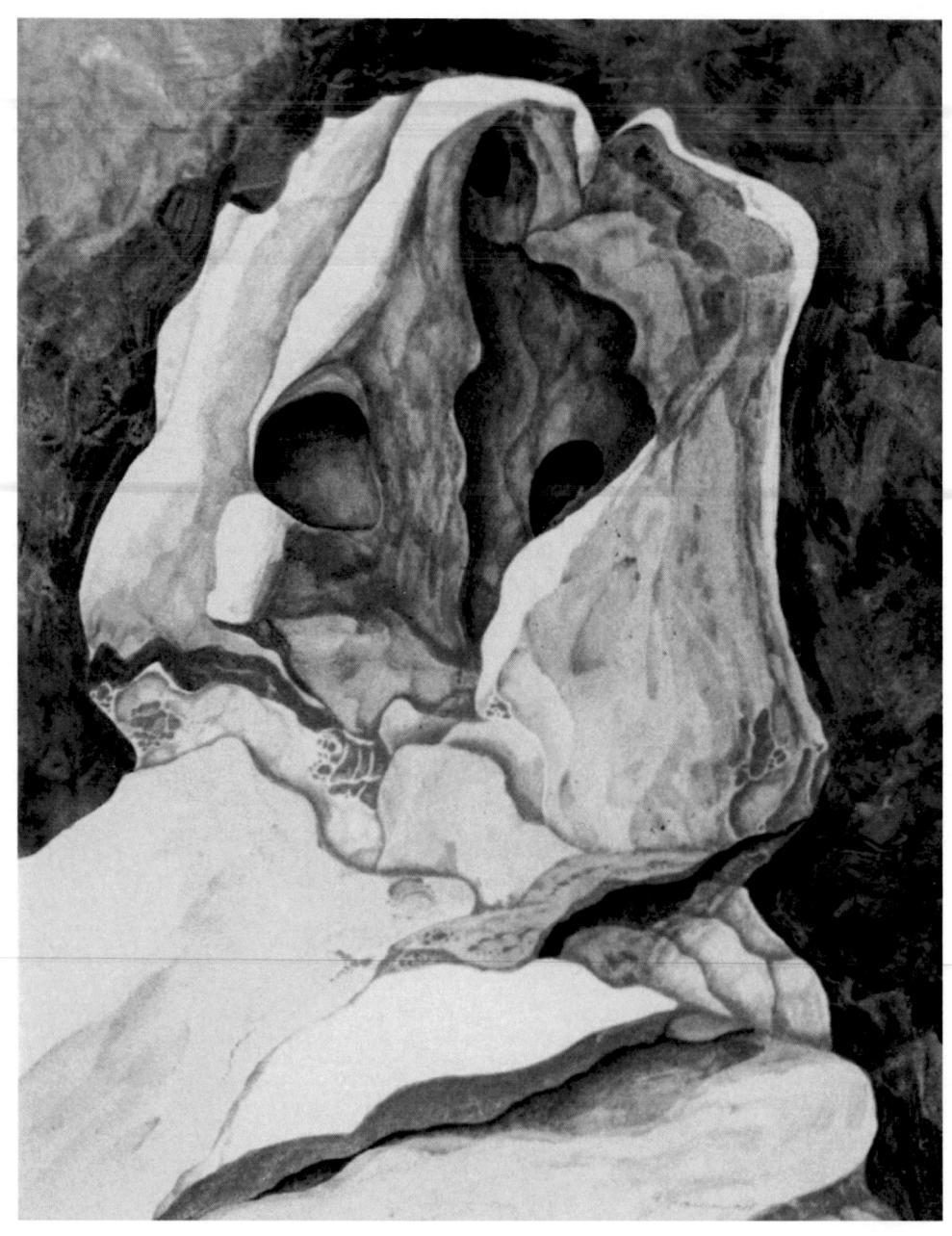

Stonehead blue
1988 | mixed media on paper | 30 x 22 in | 76 x 56 cm
Collection of Two Rivers Gallery, Prince George, BC

Stone Birth
1989 | mixed media on paper | 30 x 40 in | 76 x 101.5 cm
Collection Earth, Oceans & Atmospheric Sciences, University of British Columbia

Carved Stones
1988 | diptych | mixed media on paper | 2× 40 x 60 in | 101.5 x 152.5 cm
Collection of Two Rivers Gallery, Prince George, BC

Fantasy in the Old Quarry
1989 | mixed media on paper | 22 x 30 in | 56 x 76 cm
Collection of Fundación Museo Eugenio Granell | Santiago de Compostela, Spain

Three Kings
1989 | mixed media on card | 10 x 12 in | 27 x 23.5 cm
Collection of Museo Nacional de Bellas Artes | Santiago, Chile

ACT III
AMERICA/CANADA

Chapter 37

America

*We know what we are now, but know
not what we may become.*

William Shakespeare
Hamlet

It is 1962. Urbana, Illinois, a small town with a large university in
its midst, will be our home for the next two years. Professor Mahlon
Day, Head of the Math Department, and his wife Frankie, receive
us graciously, pick us up from the airport and drive us to a house
where they have leased an apartment for us. The lease mentions
that the place had been rented to Dr. and Mrs. Edmond Granirer
and their child Eran, *"who are of the white race."* We are shocked.

Our new abode was a two-bedroom apartment on the first
floor of a small white clapboard house at 1011 S. Oak Street.

Contrary to my expectations based on the lavish, sparkling
home interiors seen in Hollywood movies, this place was dirty
beyond belief. I spent a few days scrubbing the floors, the windows
and the walls. We didn't order a telephone before Eddy's first salary
came in, worried about the expense, not realizing that we now lived
in the US and not in Israel, where we had never even attempted to
own a telephone due to the high cost and the long waiting time.
When we explained this to our host, Frankie Day, who couldn't

Our new home in Urbana, Illinois
1962 | ink drawing | 7 × 5 in | 17.8 × 12.7 cm

understand why we didn't have a phone, she laughed and told us that this is America: we could order now and pay later. We followed her advice and got our first telephone in no time. Amazing! It wouldn't be too difficult to get used to the comfortable life in this country.

We were overwhelmed by the friendliness of everyone we met and pondered life in Israel where people were tense, always on edge. Was this living proof of the famous rat experiment showing that when under stress, individuals are less friendly? I asked Mrs. Day what makes people so welcoming in this small town.

"We live here in an ocean of corn," she answered. "There is nothing else. The only other thing we have is people. If not for friendliness, we would be left only with the corn."

We went for a walk in the neighbourhood, enchanted by the neat, ticky-tacky little houses and green lawns that Pete Seeger so aptly sang about. Even so, I could not shake off the feeling of walking through an empty stage. Where were the people? Was no one using the sidewalks? What sidewalks? There weren't any, only lawns stretching right up to the road! The only visible sign of life was the odd squirrel jumping on the grass, its tail twitching nervously in short bursts of energy. With time, we came to understand the vacant streets: instead of using their legs, people drove everywhere, even for very short distances.

Toys were scattered on the lush green lawns, but no children were in sight. A small red pedal car beginning to rust, was left by the front steps of a neat white bungalow. I was amazed at this casual waste. Owning such a fancy toy would be an unheard-of luxury for my small son and here was one, carelessly abandoned to decay in the rain!

How eerily peaceful was this place! It was almost dull — no Fedayeen crossing borders with murderous intent, no bombs, no war. However, it might get livelier if one happened to have black skin, as indicated by the cross burning brightly on the manicured lawn of the art professor who was married to a black woman.

Happy in Urbana, Illinois

Not having a car in a town where public transportation was almost non-existent condemned me to virtual house arrest. Eddy bought a second-hand bike and happily rode away to the university, while I was left at home with Eran, who was only 22 months old. Even though his Hebrew vocabulary was astonishing and much admired by the new Israeli friends we met, I felt that my own vocabulary was shrinking to baby-talk level. Days would go by without my speaking to an adult and my frustration reached limits I did not think I was capable of. Being only in a baby's company all day long, I was desperately lonely. I needed to get out, but there were no buses. There was only one solution: we had to buy a car and I had to learn to drive. So, we bought our first car, a huge blue and white used Mercury. Would I be able to conquer this monster?

Help came from unexpected quarters. Our new friends Nahum and Jane introduced us to the intricacies of life in Urbana-Champaign. Nahum was Israeli and a former *Kibbutznik*, Jane was as American as you can get. Their little daughter Yardena was Eran's age and we developed a warm and long-lasting friendship. Happiness! We had friends and Eran had a playmate.

Nahum was not a tall man, but one could almost see sparks of energy pouring out of his thin frame. He sported huge ash-blond bushy whiskers that gave him the stereotypical image of a Yankee capitalist and he spoke in fast, clipped sentences, trying to sound American, despite an accent that was neither Israeli nor American. He marvelled at Eran's large Hebrew vocabulary and long sentences. Jane was a social worker of pleasant demeanour, whose kind relaxed smile made one feel immediately at ease. They lived in a small house with a backyard where our children often played together and became our advisors in all matters. Hearing about our new car, they made me an offer I could not refuse: Jane would take Eran to their house, where he would play with Yardena, while Nahum would introduce me to the mysteries of driving.

We began right away. Nahum was a patient instructor and helped me overcome my insecurities. A few weeks later I was ready to take the test, but was too nervous and failed to convince the instructor that it would be safe to let me loose behind the wheel and I had to repeat the experience. A few more lessons and *voilà*!

Our first car

I got my driver's licence — my passport to freedom. Nahum, I shall be grateful to you forever!

The morning after the small document that would improve my life was in my possession, I looked out the window and gasped in horror. It was snowing! It must have been snowing all night and not just a few flurries, but heavy flakes that had changed the street into a gleaming white — and slippery — wonderland. I'd had plans for this day. I was going to sit proudly behind the wheel with Eran in the back seat (no baby seats in those days and no seat belts in the back) and drive to the mall. Having never seen a shopping mall before landing in Urbana-Champaign, we had been overwhelmed by the lavishness, the abundance and the diversity displayed in those places. Visiting the mall had become our weekend entertainment and a pleasant classroom in which to study the intricacies of the affluent American society. Anyway, where else could one go in this small town?

I bundled Eran up in his little blue snowsuit with white rabbit ears, put on my coat and boots and headed out the door, clutching the car keys in my gloved hand. I was excited — freedom, here I came! It was very cold and the car was an icebox, its windows covered with a heavy layer of white sparkling ice. *No problem*, I thought, as I vigorously scraped off the opaque layer of frost. I sat down in the driver's seat and turned the key in the lock while pushing down the gas pedal, as I had been taught.

What? What was this? Instead of the expected and reassuring purr of the engine, I heard a sickly cough and splatter and then silence. I tried again. Hoarsely, the engine loudly protested. I panicked. The battery was dead! What was going on?

Back in the house, I called the trusty American Automobile Association.

"Can you help me"? I asked the polite voice on the line.

"We'll be right over," he said, reassuringly. "The engine must have frozen overnight."

I'm not used to this kind of cold. Even during the rare times when snow fell in Jerusalem, nothing froze quite like this.

Soon, though, there they were! My rescue had arrived. This was my first experience of starting a car with jumper cables and I was relieved to hear the healthy sound of the engine purring again. Still, the car wouldn't budge, despite the rumble of the engine. The wheels spun noisily on the icy road with a shrill, hysterical whine, without moving an inch.

"You're stuck, lady," says my gallant knight in AAA armour. "We'll give you a push!"

And so he did.

Alas, winter driving had not been a part of my training with Nahum and was ignorant of the art of steering the car on ice. My lovely new/old Mercury, pushed from behind by the AAA truck, plowed straight into a car parked across the street, accompanied by the sickening sound of metal scraping on metal. My heart beat crazily. I left the engine running and stepped out to check the damage. To my great relief, it was just a small scratch, nothing major! Should I take this as an omen that I should stay home today instead of braving the elements and risking more damage? Omen or no omen, my mind was made up. I left a polite note on the neighbour's car, sat back in the driver's seat and took off to the mall.

Chapter 38

Champaign, Urbana and Lulu Belle

We don't see just with our eyes; we see with our mind and heart.

Dennis Merritt Jones
The Huffington Post blog

My arrival in Urbana-Champaign marks the second time I have come to live in a foreign country, speak a new language and adapt to a new culture. This time though, it will be a short-lived adventure lasting only three years, I tell myself. We plan to return home to Jerusalem and resume our life there once a position for Eddy opens at the university. Here I can simply relax and enjoy a hiatus in my life with no pressure to 'integrate' or to 'belong'. I am just a visiting Israeli accompanying my professor husband.

My English is not very fluent; the new words are like small pebbles rolling awkwardly over the tongue. My ears strain to understand the midwestern drawl that swallows the vowels like slippery watermelon seeds. When the telephone rings, I freeze; will I be able to understand the words coming out of the black earpiece?

I read Agatha Christie detective stories voraciously, hoping that my English will improve. Hercule Poirot, the famous French detective, is now my best friend — he has an accent just like me. I am puzzled seeing billboards with words spelled in strange ways:

why 'Tonite's movie' or '4 sale'? Had I had a crystal ball, I might have glimpsed the future of the English language. Reading this bizarre spelling, I lacked the foresight to recognize it as an early herald of the dumbing-down of language through texting and tweeting that would become ubiquitous in the next millennium.

Americans seemed to have a passion for shortening words and names. 'Wizard' was 'wiz', 'sister' was 'sis' and 'brother' was 'bro'. And names? 'Anthony' was 'Tony', 'Robert' was 'Bob' — I didn't see the connection here. And how did 'John' become 'Jack'? I thought that these were two separate names.

The otherness of a new place stands out in sharp relief and details that are seen as normal by the locals are strange and curious to the newcomer. One of the first things that I noticed was the rampant waste. With the first drop in temperature, the thermostat went up and up until the house was as warm as a hot summer day. Our neighbours walked around the house in shorts and T-shirts in the dead of winter instead of turning down the heat and wearing sweaters. Their TV was on from morning 'til night.

I saved the empty mayonnaise, mustard and pickle jars, old newspapers and milk bottles, and brought them back to the corner grocery store for recycling, as I used to do in Jerusalem. This was 1962, a long time before the recycling obsession would spread over North America. The grocer stared at me in disbelief.

"Why did you bring this garbage back? Just throw it out, lady!"

I felt stupid, unsophisticated and embarrassed, but also shocked at the waste. However, he may have been right about the local paper as garbage. The most exciting news items were details of local weddings, descriptions of the bride's dress, lists of the attending guests and the menu served at the reception. And, oh yes, the salary of the fire chief and other city employees. International news? Who needs that? Later, there was perhaps a line or two about the Cuban crisis that brought the world to the brink of nuclear war. Most of the important news came to us via the small screen of our television set.

Soon after arrival we were invited to our very first picnic, a new and pleasant experience. I was stunned at the sight of the gigantic steak offered to me by the cheery professor who cooked the huge slabs of beef on the grill. How could I possibly eat such an enormous piece of meat? This would have been more than enough for our whole family! No wonder people are so tall here!

A friendly faculty wife took me shopping. I looked for bread, but all I could find were white loaves as soft as foam, wrapped in plastic. My friend checked to see which was the softest one, while I searched for real bread. Where was the crust? Loaves of dark rye, baguettes and what I thought was real bread were nowhere to be seen. Eventually I got used to this happy-go-lucky way of life, where people were kind to each other, where items we considered luxuries were easily attainable and the principles of 'buy-now-pay-later' or the ubiquitous 'guaranteed or your money back' were the way business was conducted. We met a couple of foreign students who had enthusiastically embraced American entrepreneurship. They bought objects such as television sets and even clothes, each time at a different store. After using them for a while, they brought the goods back within the allotted period of time, making up some excuse for the return. They continued this game from store to store until it was time for them to return to their country, having enjoyed full television service without ever paying for even one set and wearing clothes that cost them nothing!

We discovered the culture of large parties where people stood around nonchalantly holding their cocktails, known to us only from Hollywood movies and novels from the western world. I was innocent of sophisticated alcoholic drinks, so I stuck to juice and white wine. I was unhappy at the tasteless coffee, which seemed to be just warm brown water, compared to the strong Turkish brew made in the Israeli *finjan*.

Still, the most shocking of all for me was this: I was not Pnina Granirer anymore. I had become 'Mrs. Edmond Granirer'. My identity disappeared the moment I arrived in the land of the free. I also discovered that as a woman, I was of very little interest to the polite (overwhelmingly male) professors we met at the various parties. Otherwise, why would the eyes of the tall man I'm talking to roam the room in search of someone else with whom to carry on a more interesting conversation?

Not having a work visa, I could not earn money. In hindsight, the door that closed on my career as a commercial artist and illustrator opened a new door for me: the practice of art for its own sake. Now I could draw, paint or make prints to my heart's content, without having to satisfy the customer or the publisher who commissioned the work. Of course, that also meant that I could not earn money and could not contribute financially to the family. My real contribution was more valuable, I hoped: making a home for my husband and child was a full-time job in itself.

I bought inks, rollers and paper. I bought pencils, pens and paints. I was ready to embark on my life as an artist and I began to search for subjects that would inspire me, but found nothing — no picturesque people like the multitude of characters in the Jerusalem marketplace, no interesting buildings like the ones lining the narrow lanes in the Old City, only neat little houses, neat little lawns, empty streets. It was a visual desert, albeit a peaceful and pleasant one to live in. I had no choice but to use the drawings I had brought with me from Jerusalem.

One day, I struck gold. Walking around Urbana's small downtown, I saw a second-hand store that appeared interesting, with a sign reading 'Swap Shop' on the door. When I opened it, I found myself transported into a world of semi-darkness, full of bizarre objects.

A red pillow, the word 'STOP' sewn on it in large black letters, greeted me ominously at the entrance. When I entered the store, a wild array of objects hit my field of vision: stuffed birds, old clocks, candlesticks, glassware, ornate tables and vases of all kinds, dresses carelessly hung on metal hangers, lampshades and weird sculptures filled every inch of the space. Mirrors in frames decorated in Rococo style reflected the objects hung on the walls, multiplying their presence.

Was anyone here? I saw nothing but inanimate things. When my eyes got used to the dim light, I noticed something moving behind a counter in the back of the store. What I first thought was a mask came to life. Perched on a high stool in half-shadow, I saw a black woman wearing a yellow bandana. She was staring at me,

Antiques

1963 | conté on paper | 30 × 40 in | 76 × 101.6 cm

the white of her eyes shining brightly. I greeted her and we began talking.

This was my first encounter with Vera, who grandly introduced herself as Lulu Belle and only later whispered in my ear her real name. I never found out if she was the owner of the store, but when she pointed to a sign above the door reading 'Antiques', it was clear that she was proud of it. No second-hand stuff here, no sir, these were real, valuable antiques!

Lulu Belle became my inspiration and model for numerous drawings and paintings. She reigned like a queen among the lifeless objects, exuding an aura of mystery and richness far beyond her humble surroundings. Her dress hung loosely on her tall, thin body like on a hanger in the closet. She was addicted to thin cigars that she smoked constantly, filling the shop with a bittersweet smell.

Flattered by the attention I paid her, Lulu Belle became friendlier as time passed. "I'll do something special today — just for you!" she said one day, coyly smiling.

She quickly removed the yellow bandana covering her hair, flashing a big smile.

"See? Nobody has ever seen me like this!"

Her tightly-crinkled greying hair was plaited into short thin braids, sticking out away from her scalp, making her look young and old at the same time.

While living in Urbana-Champaign, I was introduced to the popular art fairs. During the summer, artists organized outdoor exhibitions where they displayed their works in makeshift booths. It was great fun to walk around during this festive event, see other artists' works, talk to the many visitors and hear their comments. The first time I took part in such a fair I showed a few drawings of Lulu Belle, one of which had her name boldly written over her image. That evening, the local news featured the event on television and the camera happened to linger on her portrait. As I returned home that evening, the phone rang.

"I was on TV!" Lulu Belle's voice gushed excitedly into my ear. "I was on TV! I'm famous!"

This was the best reward I could offer my wonderful model who had become a local celebrity overnight.

Alfred Hitchcock was right when he so aptly said, "Ideas come from everything." A new idea came to me one day by pure happenstance. Producing woodblock prints was one of my favourite ways of making art and I loved everything about it, but not so much the cleaning up at the end. Once, as I was rolling the roller still loaded with ink on some newsprint so as to minimize the amount to be washed off, I noticed for the first time the textures left on the paper — beautiful transparent swaths of colour that became richer as they overlapped, allowing the paper to peer through.

Here was my 'aha!' moment: the roller could serve a new purpose by replacing the brush, flattening the colours and making them translucent. This kind of experience brings the artist a high more exciting than any drug.

I got to work, starting with a sheet of black cardboard. I squeezed some water-based inks of different colours on a large piece of glass and set a number of rollers of various sizes nearby —

Lulu Belle Smoking
1963 | conté on paper
7.5 × 4.5 in | 19 × 11.4 cm

Vera's Braids
1963 | conté on paper
8.5 × 5 in | 21.6 × 12.7 cm

the smallest was about one inch wide, the largest about ten inches. I discovered very quickly that making marks with a roller had to be spontaneous, clean and final, with very little room for correction. These works were different from anything I had ever done.

I drew everything and everywhere I could. I drew my little son and the children at his daycare. I drew streets, houses, trees and friends. I also began a series of woodblock prints based on older drawings and on Lulu Belle. The works were piling up.

My very first exhibition took place in the gallery of the Student Union Building of the University of Illinois. Unfortunately, the greatest success related to this exhibition was the disappearance of one of my works. Was this an auspicious beginning for my future career? Everyone told me how flattering that was and how happy I should be. What better proof that some poor student loved my work so much — unaffordable to him even at a very low price — that he could not resist taking it home for free? I should be pleased, they said. But I definitely was not. I would have been even less thrilled had I known that my work would exert its irresistible power on other needy art lovers in the future as well. This temptation to collect art for free was repeated four times during my career. My friends' response was always the same: they saw these thefts as the purest compliment paid to an artist. I suggested they compare it to someone liking their new Jaguar and simply deciding to take it home since they could not afford to buy it. Would they be flattered?

Oh, the irony of the art world! Stealing my low-priced art was thought of as a compliment paid by an art-loving thief. Had I been as famous and as pricey as Picasso, stealing my work would have clearly been treated as a crime.

A year later we were on the move again, this time not very far — to Champaign, Urbana's sister city. We rented a small house where a spare room would become my very first studio. What luxury! I was thrilled.

Our new home was a typical white slat-board house on a tree-lined street set on a green lawn in a quiet neighbourhood. Unlike the concrete or stone buildings in Israel, here everything was made of wood, conveying a sense of fragility and impermanence.

A Whole House to Ourselves in Champaign, Illinois
1963 | conté on paper | 5.5 × 8 in | 14 × 20.3 cm

In the fall, the majestic maple trees lining the sidewalk turned into flaming red and gold torches that lit up the streets in spectacular displays. Soon after, the bright dead leaves floated down lazily in thick layers of pure colour, covering the green grass below in a multicoloured quilt. The children ran through the growing piles of dry leaves, tossing them about and jumping up and down in sheer delight.

In October, Jane and Nahum initiated us into the joys of Halloween. This was a new experience for us, particularly so for Eran. Dressed in a white rabbit costume and clutching his little bag, he ran frantically from house to house, amazed at this free bonanza of candies and goodies showered upon the children.

Soon after turning three years old, Eran developed a passion for playing his little banjo and singing at the top of his lungs. Little did we know that he would become an aspiring jazz musician in his late teens.

Mary-Jo, a neighbour's daughter a year or so older than Eran, took him under her wing and introduced him to the other children. She came often to play and loved to watch me drawing. We didn't lock our doors, so she just knocked.

"Will you draw me today?'" she would ask.

How could one refuse such an angelic, willing model? With her blue eyes staring from an innocent round face framed by blonde, shoulder-length hair and a small, perfectly formed pink mouth, Mary-Jo featured in many of my drawings and woodblock prints. One of the prints showing Eran sitting close to Mary-Jo, became a UNICEF poster in 1967.

Eran as budding musician

Togetherness

1971 | woodblock print | 21 × 16.5 in | 53.3 × 42 cm

Featured on local poster for UNICEF

Chapter 39

Of Sorrows and Pleasures

Do not grieve. Anything you lose comes round in another form.

Rumi
Unmarked boxes / Ode#1937
The Essential Rumi

Two years have passed since we arrived in Urbana-Champaign. It is time to return to Jerusalem, but as there are still no open positions at the Hebrew University, we have to linger on.

Our friend Nahum had finished his studies and landed a job in San Francisco, while Eddy had applied at several universities, University of Southern California, Berkeley among them. We hoped that Berkeley would come through so that our friendship with Nahum and Jane could continue, but unfortunately, the reply was late in coming and we couldn't wait any longer. Eddy accepted a position at Cornell University in Ithaca, NY, where his PhD advisor was teaching. Being an Ivy League school, Cornell was an excellent professional move.

Having chosen Ithaca meant parting from close friends, a painful experience and a feeling of deep loss. The dreaded day came when Jane, Nahum and Yardena drove by our house to say goodbye. It was a beautiful summer day — the world was unchanged, the sun shone as usual and a breeze ruffled the leaves of the maple trees lining our street. For us though, the world had suddenly darkened. We hugged our friends, promising each other never to lose our friendship. A moment later, they were gone.

I sat down on the sidewalk and cried.

• • •

Ithaca was a small university town with a very different geographical setting from Urbana-Champaign. Instead of cornfields surrounding the city, here the landscape was green and hilly. The town had been built at the southern end of Cayuga Lake, with beautiful streams, forests and parks. Was it the lack of cornfields, replaced by the beautiful landscape of this place that defined the character of its inhabitants? Unlike the friendly people in Illinois, we encountered a coldness that kept the newcomers at arm's length, making them seek each other's company. Perhaps enjoying the great outdoors was better than spending time with others? Hikes, picnics and walks along gurgling forest streams are time-consuming, so who has time for hospitality?

Our flat was in a complex of low-rise apartment buildings set around an inner courtyard, populated mainly by students or young faculty. Most of them were visiting faculty like us, who found it difficult to forge relationships with the locals and quickly became a close community of outsiders, visiting often and always ready to help out one another.

Very soon I noticed our neighbours' frequent visits to the local dump — and not always for disposing of their garbage. They were often picking up discarded objects left behind by people who had moved out. At first I was disgusted that anyone would pick up things from the garbage. How could that be? Only destitute people would do this! But our American friends assured me that this was a great bartering and recycling system, based on the philosophy of 'your junk is my treasure'. When moving away, many of the itinerant tenants placed objects they did not need near the garbage, knowing that newcomers might find them useful. Once we overcame our inhibitions, we became enthusiastic converts to this practical system. One could take home beautiful lamps, chairs and tables, sometimes even sofas, all in perfectly good shape, use them as long as needed and put them back by the garbage when moving away for others to pick up. Whenever someone from this transient neighbourhood left town, new items sprouted behind the bins, to be freely shared by anyone in need. A true treasure hunt that made perfect sense!

In addition to these weekly forays, we discovered the entrepreneurial spirit of garage sales. Was this activity possible only in an affluent society? In Israel, buying used objects was considered a sign of poverty, while here in America, it was just a common-sense activity.

I was expecting a new baby. Being an only child, I missed having siblings and wished to enrich Eran's life and ours as well, by having a larger family. This time however, the pregnancy was not going well. My doctor assured me that everything was just fine, despite the occasional bleeding and the numbing fatigue and back pain. But he was wrong.

One cold spring morning in the fifth month of my pregnancy, I was alone at home. Eddy was at the university and Eran at playschool. I wasn't feeling well. Suddenly, I experienced tremendous pressure and an overwhelming need to use the bathroom. Like a nightmare beyond my control, the toilet became a birthing stool and, to my horror, I felt the baby falling into the water below. The sense of reality left me.

This cannot be happening! It cannot be. What shall I do, what shall I do?

I reached down and lifted the small human being that had just left my body and noticed that we were still connected by the umbilical cord. Shaken to the core, I automatically searched for scissors, cut the cord, wrapped the baby in a towel and reached for the telephone to call Eddy. I was shaking, my head in a fog, This could not be me, alone in this room, holding the tiniest human being I'd ever seen! Fortunately Eddy was not teaching and told me that he was on the way. Time felt endless while I was frantically waiting for him, until he returned riding his bicycle.

At the hospital, the first thing the doctor told Eddy shocked us.

"The baby was alive for a couple of hours," the doctor said. "You may now claim him as a tax deduction."

We were both speechless at the lack of empathy and the crassness of this physician. We were also ignorant of the possibility of suing for negligence. All we wanted was to return home and grieve.

It was April and still cold outside. Immersed in our sorrow, we forgot that it was Passover, when we should have been celebrating with friends around the table. Instead, I was in bed, numb with pain, incapable of thinking about such practicalities as food, when the doorbell rang.

We were not expecting anyone. Who could it be? Eddy opened the door and there in the doorway, to our amazement, stood Ollie and Paul Staneslow, our downstairs Gentile neighbours, carrying a full, traditional Passover meal in a large basket: roasted chicken with potatoes, matzah, green salad and even a special Passover dessert, all carefully packed and covered with a white napkin. To top it all off, we found a bottle of red Manischewitz wine resting against the edge of the basket. We were moved to tears by this act of human kindness that we would never forget. Our friendship would last for many years to come.

Later, after recovering somewhat from this painful ordeal, I was commissioned to illustrate an educational project developed by the Department of Home Economics for parents of teenage children. The illustrations would become a slideshow accompanying the talk. This work was similar to the filmstrips for children stories I did in Jerusalem and the small problem of not having a work permit was resolved by a one-time honorarium. This is how the images for *Striving for Independence* came into being.

The problems encountered by parents dealing with teenage children described in the text were foreign to me and quite different from my own adolescence. The concept of a 'teen' was absent in the vocabulary of my youth — despite the usual angst that is part and parcel of growing up, the prevalent issues were not so much about resisting parental authority as about survival and planning for a secure future. Here, in America's affluent society, the worry of survival had disappeared and teenage rebellion, accompanied by a lack of parent-child communication, seemed to be common.

Time went swiftly by. Our US visas was about to expire and we had to think of the future. Despite Eddy's outstanding publications in his field of research, there were still no openings for positions at the Hebrew University and thus no chance for us to return home. We had to leave the US and go elsewhere.

Naturally, we set our sights on the closest and easiest alternative: Canada. Unlike the situation in Israel, all of Eddy's applications to Canadian universities brought back job offers. Being totally ignorant of Canada, we consulted with a Canadian couple visiting at Cornell University and asked them what was the best place in Canada.

"If you go to Canada," they said, "Vancouver is the place!"

Chapter 40

Vancouver

Toto, I've a feeling we're not in Kansas anymore.

The Wizard of Oz (film)

Coming from a tiny country the size of a pocket handkerchief, we have difficulties in grasping the visual feast of the immense Canadian landscape, where endless prairies stretch to meet the sky and rivers roar in a mighty symphony along the train tracks. And then, oh wonder: we enter the majestic kingdom of the Rocky Mountains. The train is like a small toy lost in this realm of dense forests and stone cathedrals piercing the sky. The spectacular nature of this vast country makes us feel small and insignificant.

The year was 1965. After a three-day journey from Toronto we arrived in Vancouver, where our new landlady met us at the train station. Still giddy after experiencing the vast, dramatic vistas stitched together by the shiny steel ribbon of the Canadian Pacific Railway, we were taken by her on a sightseeing tour of the city, while she pointed out the highlights on the way. We crossed the Burrard Bridge and drove west on Cornwall Street along Kitsilano Beach, named after Khatsalano, a Squamish First Nations Chief. The well-kept expanse of grass abutting the street ended in a sandy beach meeting the ocean and dotted by massive logs for people to sit on. What a waste of precious wood, I thought, comparing those thick tree trunks to the thin precious pines, lovingly and painstakingly planted one-by-one in Israel.

It was a warm summer weekday. People lounged on the grass and on the sand and splashed about in the water. Didn't they have to be at work? The city looked much like a vacation resort, with the downtown core built on a peninsula ending in a forested tip called Stanley Park, providing a dramatic sight against the mountains.

Our kind and welcoming landlady drove on. We entered the university campus following a road lined by majestic maples and divided by a grassy median adorned by rhododendron bushes and colourful flowerbeds, ending in a roundabout adjacent to the rose gardens. At the lookout, we saw the waters of the Pacific Ocean below, shimmering in the sun and on the horizon, a wall of snowcapped mountains rose under a cloudless blue sky. We were gazing at a postcard landscape of astounding beauty.

The city of Vancouver was built around village-like neighbour-hoods, each bearing its own name. Our rented house was in Kitsilano, not too far from the beach and only one block from a shopping area on Fourth Avenue, known at the time as 'Hippie Town'. These were the sixties, the time of the 'flower children', who had sprouted all along the street like pretty weeds after the rain. Young men, with long beards and even longer hair braided or gathered in a ponytail, sat on the pavement smoking or offering bead necklaces for sale. The girls wore colourful skirts that reminded me of the Gypsy girls in Brăila. Tie-dyed shirts, beads, bandanas and bare feet were the fashion for these young people who seemed to have a lot of free time on their hands.

A wide flight of stairs brought us to the heavy front door of our rented house. Inside, we found a spacious living room, a dining room and three bedrooms on the second floor. One of those bedrooms would become my studio. A pleasant surprise awaited us in the living room: a large bouquet of flowers and a basket loaded with fruit were laid on the table as a welcome gift from our gracious landlady. This gesture was yet another jewel in our treasure box of human kindness, joining the Passover gift of the Staneslow family in Ithaca.

A pattern was established as the days went by. Each morning I drove Eddy to the university and Eran to kindergarten and then I was free to work in my studio for a few hours. I worked mostly on paper or thin card that did not require too much storage space. I didn't have a plan or a definite goal in mind. I was simply happy to snatch a few precious minutes to put pencil or charcoal to paper and watch the drawings emerge.

From the very onset of my professional career as an artist, my priorities were clear and would remain so: family comes first. I was sure that I could do it all and be both a housewife and a professional artist. Only later would I discover the hidden maze of art politics, marketing and connections that one needs to navigate in order to become successful. Naïvely, I thought that all that was needed for success and recognition was talent and hard work. I had a lot to learn.

Chapter 41

Art

Soon after my arrival in Vancouver, I became aware of the lavish rhododendron and azalea bushes with their resplendent masses of red, deep pink, yellow and white flowers. Clumps of smaller brightly coloured flowers hung in thick clusters cascading over walls and rock gardens. A sense of déjà vu and a shock of recognition flashed through my mind. I was ten years old again, longingly staring at the garden on the old chocolate box cover in my room in Brăila. Now I had found that garden. It *did* exist. It was real and it was here in Vancouver.

Driving my husband to the university, I noticed the Danish Art Gallery on 10th Avenue just off Alma Street and one day I stopped and walked in to have a look. Peder Bertelsen, a tall, friendly man of Danish origin with sandy blond hair and a thick accent, greeted me with a big smile. His gallery consisted of two large rooms crammed with paintings, drawings and prints. Some of the works were excellent while others, in stark contrast, were of the commercial kind one sees in a Woolworth store. After a few visits, I became comfortable enough to ask him the question that had been on my mind: why did he lower the quality of his gallery by showing works that were so poor? Peder's honest answer was my first lesson about art dealership.

"This is what sells," he said. "This is what most people like to hang on their walls. Most people know very little about art and have no taste. In order to make a living, I have to give them what they want."

Peder began his career as an art dealer by peddling paintings door to door until he had saved enough money to open his own gallery. Being a salesman had taught him the realities of survival in the art business. As an immigrant with no connections, he had only his basic commercial instinct and common sense to rely on. By holding his nose and offering his clients the kind of commercial art they liked, he eventually could afford to exhibit better artists and develop a market for higher-quality art.

One day Peder asked me whether I would like to exhibit my work in his gallery. Would I? This offer was something I had only dreamed about, without daring to think that it could happen. Trying to control my excitement and the beating of my heart that was surely reverberating loudly against the gallery walls, I responded as nonchalantly as I could. Yes, I would like this very much! This was the very first opportunity for me to show in a commercial art gallery.

In 1965 Vancouver was far from being a centre for the visual arts. Save for the small public Vancouver Art Gallery, there was only one good commercial gallery in the city representing serious artists: the New Design Gallery.

Here I was, thirty years old, my self-confidence wavering like a newly-minted trapeze artist, precariously perched on the thin line between doubting that I was a true painter and the occasional flashes of absolute belief in my vocation. If my first priority was my family, how could I pretend to be a professional? On the other hand, how could I ever stop making art? Being an illustrator meant doing 'real' work, earning money. But art? Was I too self-indulgent?

The works dozing away in my drawers were now ready for their wake-up call, their coming-out celebration. They would be decked out in their best attire of smooth mattes and metal frames and hung on the white walls of the gallery, ready for the viewer's critical eye. The time had come to allow my other children, the images I gave life to during many hours of work, to enter the world.

One important element distinguishes the visual arts from all other art forms: the element of time. A definite timespan is needed to engage the spectator with words, emotion and action for any performance such as theatre, music or dance. Time is needed to enjoy the cycle of a symphony, the length of a song, the reading of a book or the duration of a play. The visual arts on the other hand, are silent — no time constraints are imposed on the viewer facing a painting. One is free to spend a mere second or a whole eternity gazing at a work of art. Engaging the viewer becomes the responsibility of the painter. Akin to shining a beam of light upon familiar matters, emotions, feelings and thoughts, the image on the wall has to interpret the world rather than imitate it, capturing the viewers' interest by presenting a new point of view.

These thoughts were not on my mind while I prepared for my first exhibition in a real gallery. My life consisted of getting things done instead of philosophizing: meals had to be cooked, my son had to be cared for and the house had to be cleaned. In addition, we had just acquired a small black Cocker Spaniel mongrel baptized 'Peter Puppy' by Eran. He had to be trained, washed and fed, and the mail had to be rescued from his sharp little teeth.

Each day after dropping my son off to kindergarten, I would rush to my studio and work until it was time to pick him up. I had an exhibition to get ready for.

Many of the works featured children, who were an integral part of my world at the time. A second group consisted of drawings and paintings of Lulu Belle and works based on older sketches, including ones I had brought with me from Israel. The third was a group of woodblock prints. I worked mostly on paper at the time, not only because I loved its texture and the way it accepted colour, ink and charcoal, but also as a practical choice. Our future was unclear — we lived in the moment from year-to-year and I had to think about storage and possibly new moves.

I was happy, excited and terrified at the same time. Suddenly, my work would be out in public, vulnerable to criticism. I felt naked, exposed to strangers' eyes. Exposure is essential for any artist, but it is also a tremendous risk, much as a sailboat is at the mercy of the elements. The harshest critic was myself, assailed again by serious doubts: showing these pieces was madness! I wasn't ready! The work was not good enough to be shown! Outwardly I put on a brave front, presenting myself as a confident young artist and hiding my doubts as well as I could.

Amazingly and beyond my expectations, the *Vancouver Sun* published a review of the exhibition by the well-known (but not to me!) writer and journalist, David Watmough. The opening sentence ended with these words, "(Pnina Granirer) is an artist of broad, catholic sympathies." Catholic? Sympathies? What did this mean? I was confused, since my English had only one meaning for 'catholic', the religious one. How had I, a Jewish woman, suddenly become a Catholic sympathizer? I went to the dictionary and read: "catholic: including a wide variety of things; all-embracing". *Aaah!* I had just learned a new meaning for this word. The review went on to criticize some of the works as sentimental and advised a more restrained approach. It was the first time that I was presented with a balanced, intelligent critique on my work and I was grateful. What is more, some works sold, boosting my confidence.

The highest compliment came from an unexpected place: my own five-year-old son. *The Leader*, a large mixed-media and collage work, featured a group of children led by a boy brandishing a wooden sword, wearing a paper hat and flowing cape and confidently marching parade-style towards the future. Deep in the grass, hidden from the youthful warriors, danger lurked in the shape of a lion hidden among the leaves. *The Leader* stood on my easel for a while, until a visitor expressed the wish to buy it and took it home to show her family. When Eran returned from school, he went upstairs and peeked into my studio. I heard a shriek and ran to the door, expecting some dire accident.

"Where is it?" an agitated little boy shouted. "Where is it"?

"Where is what?" I asked.

"The picture! Where is my picture?"

When I explained that someone might want to buy it, he burst into tears.

"No, no, no! It's mine! You can't sell it!" he sobbed.

I'm sorry to say that this was the first and last time Eran showed such keen interest in my art. I had no idea that he was so fond of *The Leader* and of course, I cancelled the sale. Family comes first! Fifty years later, *The Leader* proudly hangs now in the entrance hall of my son's house.

Life in Vancouver was good, but despite the gorgeous landscape of mountains, sea and city skyline, my heart was heavy with longing. I was homesick. This place, this city, despite its natural beauty, had placed me at the end of the world, far from my home in Jerusalem and from the life I was familiar with. The future was uncertain — where would it take us next?

1966 was a busy year. A second exhibition was scheduled, this time in Victoria, British Columbia's sleepy capital on Vancouver Island. My show at Bente Rehm's Pandora's Box Gallery was to take place in July, just one month before we were leaving for Montreal where Eddy had been offered a teaching position at the Université de Montréal. Victoria was home to the future 'Limners', a lively group of artists including Maxwell Bates, Pat Martin Bates (no relation), Herbert Siebner and Myfawny Pavelic among others, who were all exhibiting at Pandora's Box Gallery.

The day of the opening arrived. As the ferry made its way through the deep waters strewn with an uneven necklace of small islands, I worried about the looming evening. Would anyone come? No one knew me in Victoria and I had no friends there. Would anyone want to support me by coming to see my work or would I have to face an empty gallery like the vernissage of the American artist at a gallery in Vancouver's Gastown where we were the only guests? The sad memory of forlorn wine glasses lined up on trays, waiting for guests who never came, surfaced in my mind.

Arriving at the gallery on Pandora Street, we were met by Bente Rehm, who greeted us warmly. I saw my works on the walls looking back at me — they seemed different, like grown-up children independent now from their parent-artist. While these images were still living in the studio, it was difficult to let them go. The gallery walls created a degree of separation, helping me understand that like children, my works had found their wings and were ready to fly the nest.

People began to trickle in. I felt a surge of relief — there wouldn't be any orphaned wine glasses tonight after all! A small group entered the gallery and was greeted effusively by Bente, who brought me over and introduced me. These were the artists who would become the well-known Limners group in 1971. I was overwhelmed with joy. I did not expect such an honour! I was, after all, an inexperienced painter still trying to find my bearings and these established artists were all here to see my work. Moreover, Bente whispered in my ear that Maxwell Bates, an important and influential artist and writer, has just bought one of my woodblock prints.

I was unaware at the time that Maxwell Bates was considered Canada's most important Expressionist artist. Most of his work was figurative, powerful and often disturbing. His experience as a prisoner of war, forced to work for five years as a slave in the salt mines, marked his work forever.

His presence at my opening was a generous and unexpected gift.

The short, unassuming painter, now in his mid-sixties, casually approached me. We talked and he invited us to visit him the following day.

The next morning, Maxwell Bates received us in his small bungalow and ushered us into his living room. He talked about his life, his experience as a prisoner of war and later, as an established Canadian artist. I heard the anger welling up in his voice as he described the professional difficulties he had experienced. At one point in the conversation, he walked over to a large closet along the wall and opened the sliding doors, revealing a treasure trove of paintings crammed tightly together within the narrow space. Maxwell gestured wearily towards the canvasses.

"See these?" he said, his voice shaking with bitterness. "Nobody wants them! No one is interested!"

Despite numerous exhibitions, his work did not sell well. The Expressionist imagery in his work was too powerful, too difficult and too figurative for a country that worshipped the landscape and considered the group of Seven as the only true artists.

Maxwell Bates suffered a stroke in 1978 and died in 1980. An exhibition of his works was taking place at the Bau-Xi Gallery, as he was lying in hospital unable to speak. At the time, I was exhibiting there myself and was told the sad story of how all the paintings in his exhibition had been bought by one buyer for speculative purposes. When Maxwell found out, he became agitated realizing that now, as he was dying, his work had suddenly become a good investment.

Chapter 42

Montreal

In order to make progress, one must leave the door to the unknown ajar.

Richard P. Feynman
The Pleasure of Finding Things Out

We are on the move again. Eddy has been offered a position at the Université de Montréal and after a quick family conference, the decision is made: we are going to Montreal!

Our life unfolds like film shorts without a script, the recurring ending writ large on the screen: 'To be continued'. How? What next? This is our fifth move in less than five years. True to the proverb that says 'there is nothing certain, but the uncertain', we move through one open door after another, without knowing what lies behind.

Although ignorant of the script for the new play, I am firmly convinced it will be exciting.

I fell in love with Montreal at first sight. The city's strong European flavour felt familiar and its *je ne sais quoi* of a delicious mélange of language, culture, interesting shops, cafés and Schwartz's Deli made me feel immediately at home. The sense of alienation and distance I had experienced in Vancouver, despite its natural beauty, was gone. Montreal was a metropolis with wide avenues, tall buildings, imposing European-style stone mansions and a multitude of small shops, restaurants and theatres. Driving up to Mont Royal on the poetically-named Chemin du Côte-de-Neiges, gave me a frisson of delight. The city exuded a perfume of sophistication, energy and vibrant culture. This was the largest city I had ever lived in — and I loved it.

The cultural stimulation and the wealth of art, starting with the Musée de Montréal and spreading out in a multitude of galleries all through the city, attracted me like a magnet. In contrast to Vancouver, Montreal was a busy art centre. I loved walking along *rue* Sherbrooke and going in and out of galleries. Some lay hidden below street level, enticing the visitor to descend a few steps and discover untold riches of paintings, drawings, sculptures and prints. Other galleries boldly announced themselves as elegant storefronts displaying colourful canvasses or featuring large sculptures right on the sidewalk for the passers-by to admire.

The first time I came face-to-face with the full-size silvery medieval armour solemnly guarding the entrance to Le Petit Musée I stopped, amazed at the sight. If this was their *carte de visite*, how many more wonders would be hidden inside? Upon entering the gallery, I was immersed in a surreal world of tribal masks, sculptures, swords and instruments from the Dark Ages, old ceramics, headdresses, tapestries, banners and other mysterious and beautiful objects. Unlike Lulu Belle's second-hand antiques store in Champaign, this was the real thing. Established in 1890, the gallery's three floors held a rich collection of *antiquités* from all over the world, overwhelming the visitor with an endless visual feast. It was there, in Le Petit Musée, that I was introduced for the first time to African and tribal masks, which were to become a lifelong passion. We began our collection of tribal art in this cave of wonders: a large fish-pattern head mask from the Belgian Congo.

In 1967 Montreal was bursting at the seams with cultural activities and interesting things to do, culminating in the Expo '67 world's fair. Being parents of a young child, it was difficult to attend as many events as we would have liked to and babysitters were expensive. We lived frugally, not knowing what our future

215

held. As it is said in Ecclesiastes, "To every thing, there is a season." This was our time to experience the children's world. Playgrounds, parks and children's shows filled our days and images of children filled my work.

We settled into an apartment on *rue* Plymouth off *rue* Lucerne, facing the elevated freeway of the boulevard Métropolitain. In September Eran began grade one, which allowed me more time to work.

Soon enough the harsh Montreal winter engulfed the city. A heavy blanket of snow almost blinding in the reflecting sun, became a reality that was to last until late spring. The evocative and now-famous song written by Gilles Vigneault, said it all, "*Mon pays, ce n'est pas un pays, c'est l'hiver.*" ("My country is not a country, it's winter.")

I had experienced cold winters in the US Midwest, but had never seen such a gargantuan amount of snow. It buried streets, cars, roads and trees, distorting familiar objects into unearthly shapes. The city was used to these winters and knew how to dig itself out. Early morning, we would wake up to the deafening noise of snow-removal monsters that appeared out of nowhere, followed by a seemingly never-ending row of large empty trucks crawling along like giant metal caterpillars. A huge vacuum cleaner with a long, wide hose attacked the snow hungrily — with a mighty roar, it sucked it in and then, turning around, spat it into the waiting truck behind, filling it to the brim. As on a conveyor belt, the heavily loaded truck would move away and the next one would take its place. In no time at all, the snow was gone and cars could use the road again. We were not as efficient freeing our own car from its icy cover as the snow removal device at our service was only a shovel and sheer muscle power. It was hard work digging our car out of the heavy mountain of white stuff.

I don't remember how I discovered l'Atelier Libre, a print workshop founded and run by Pierre Ayot, a young Montreal printmaker and painter. This workshop had opened just one year earlier in 1966 (in 1972, it would become the artist-run Galerie Graff). Blissfully ignorant of the Montreal art scene, I knew very little about Pierre Ayot, who eventually became a well-known artist. Sadly, he died in a traffic accident in 1995 at the age of fifty-two.

The atelier was located on *rue* Rachel Est in the old city of Montreal. I would arrive most mornings around 9:30 eager to begin a good day's work while my son was at school. The studio, a large space filled with printing presses for the production of lithographs, etchings and woodblock prints, was down a few dingy steps in a nondescript old stone building. Prints by Pierre and other artists adorned the walls, while new ones were drying on racks set up in a corner. I was usually the first to arrive. Sometimes the lights were off and I had to fumble in the darkness for the light switch. An unusual sight greeted me most mornings: cuddled together on a makeshift mattress, Pierre and his partner, a young French-Canadian woman, sound asleep under one of the larger printing presses. Here was the real *vie bohème*, a way of life I was not accustomed to.

How bourgeois my own life was compared to theirs! There was order in my life, a child to care for, meals at regular hours and a real bed to sleep in. Of course, as life went on, I learned that there was a price to pay for this orderly pattern. I would never gallivant from one café to another or go bar hopping, networking and exchanging radical ideas with long-haired impoverished artists who slept under printing presses. I would, in short, never be a part of the scene — there would always be a certain distance between these two worlds, setting not only myself apart, but my art as well.

I began experimenting with various techniques. Oil paintings, drawings, collages, etchings and woodblock prints piled up. Most of Pierre Ayot's works were erotic lithographs that I found embarrassingly self-descriptive, clearly modelled after himself and his lover. The pop style he used never appealed to me, being too similar to commercial posters. So, I followed my own way, having no interest in the new fashions — pop, op or abstraction.

Pierre did not speak one word of English and I had never spoken French, although I read and wrote the language with no difficulty. Since leaving Romania in 1950, I had not had any contact with French and now, sixteen years later, I needed it to communicate.

Minor miracles do happen sometimes — when Pierre addressed me in French, the language returned fluently to my lips as if I had always spoken it.

Serendipity brought me one day to the Art Den Gallery on *rue* de la Montagne, a street lined by small boutiques, galleries, restaurants and cafés, running perpendicular to *rue* Sherbrooke. The Art Den was on the second floor, up a short flight of stairs. I felt immediately at ease with the gallery owner, Adele Dresdner, a short, friendly woman with blonde, too obviously dyed, hair. I visited her often following this first encounter. We had long talks about art, Montreal, family and more. I showed her some of my work, wanting to hear her opinion and was thrilled when one day, mirroring my Vancouver experience with Peder Bertelsen, she offered to exhibit my work. How wonderful! Having an exhibition in the very centre of this cosmopolitan and vibrant city so soon after my arrival and so early in my career was beyond my dreams.

Time was short. The exhibition was due to take place in early December. Feverishly, I began preparing for the show.

The exhibition opened on December 4, 1966. In retrospect, I realize how uneven my work was at the time and how typical it was of a young artist who had not yet found her own voice. The exhibition was a medley of styles, media and sizes: oil paintings, collages, drawings and prints. In her review in the *Montreal Gazette*, Rea Montbizon noted that these works reflected my background as an illustrator. One of the visitors was so bewildered by the great variety of the art on display that he thought it was a group show! With the advantage of hindsight, I cringe to think how unfocused were the pieces I showed and how clearly they demonstrated my inexperience. Even so, I was literally floating on clouds and, when Adele Dresdner bought one of the paintings, my happiness was complete.

RETURN TO ISRAEL

In May 1967 we returned to Israel for the first time since 1962, in the hope that a position would become available for Eddy at the

Hebrew University. We looked forward to this trip, eager to see our family and friends again.

It was wonderful to be back in Haifa. I had almost forgotten the soft, warm spring air and the strong light that painted deep shadows and sharpened the shapes of buildings, trees and flowers. We rented a small apartment on Mount Carmel and enrolled Eran, now seven years old, in a day camp. At the time he had a keen interest in insects, which were not as plentiful in Canada as in Haifa's warm, humid climate. His priorities were certainly different from ours in this respect. The first morning, a sight worthy of a Hitchcock horror film greeted us as we entered the kitchen: the floor, the counters and the sink were black with crawling cockroaches! I was horrified, but Eran was delighted. What a great start for the insect collection he had been dreaming of!

Preoccupied with our own life, we were unaware of the political drama that was unfolding behind a screen painted in the cheerful colours of normality. People were trying to live their lives as usual without paying attention to the imminent dangers facing the country and no one seemed to be worried. Still, the storm of yet another war was silently gathering strength behind the scenes.

It was good to see my parents, our cousins and friends and walk the familiar streets again. Despite the pleasure of living on beautiful Mount Carmel with its stunning views of the Haifa harbour and the turquoise Mediterranean Sea glimmering below, I experienced a feeling that had not been there in the past: a sense of an invisible barrier that separated me from almost everyone around me. There was a palpable dent in my perception of belonging. My connection with the land, the history and the physical surroundings was just as strong as ever, but the five years away had changed me. I realized at that moment that I would never belong deeply anywhere.

There was no position open in Eddy's field. In that respect, nothing had changed, so we had no choice but to return to Canada. It was a heart-rending decision.

On June 5, 1967, three weeks after returning to Montreal, the war between Israel and its Arab neighbours began. The drama that had been unfolding behind the scenes had burst out in the open.

Chapter 43

Last Move

*Home is a notion that only nations of the homeless
fully appreciate and only the uprooted comprehend.*

Wallace Stegner
Angle of Repose

After a second train journey across the continent, we were back in Vancouver hoping to settle down for good. This was to be our last major move.

In the fall of 1967, limited by our modest savings over the years, we began searching for a house. This was not a trifling matter — the wrong decision would have a negative impact on our life, while the right decision would most probably bring us happiness. Mrs. Roedde, our feisty realtor, was a tiny middle-aged woman with a striking blonde braid wrapped around her head like a crown. She showed us one house after another, but the choices fitting our budget were dark, small houses in need of repair. One day Mrs. Roedde suggested visiting a house that was quite above our means, located on 4th Avenue, the busy street leading to the university.

"Just to give you an idea of what is available," she craftily told us.

We were familiar with that street and recalled visiting a colleague of Eddy's who lived across the road from the house she wanted to show us. We also remembered thinking that we would never want to live on such a busy street. But she insisted. So, on a beautiful sunny day, we arrived at the house on West 4th Avenue and walked through a large, rather neglected garden. Overhung by a beautiful wisteria, the entrance was through a small porch opening onto a narrow, awkward hallway. As we walked on into the living room, a spectacular view of the North Shore mountains, English Bay and downtown Vancouver appeared through the old-fashioned windows, like a postcard designed to attract tourists from far away.

Showing us the rest of the house, our entrepreneurial realtor admitted to a major shortcoming the house had.

"There is a small problem you should know about," she said. "This house has only one bathroom and it's on the second floor."

How could this be possible? The owners had nine children. Did they use potties or give numbers for line-ups in the morning? Did this really matter? Oh, how quickly we succumbed to temptation! It was love at first sight.

"We must have it!" said Eddy.

"We don't have the money," said I.

Eddy was more daring in money matters than I — and more decisive. The next day we put down a counter-offer — and it was accepted!

We realized that the lack of bathrooms had been a real obstacle in selling the property. We could not have cared less — bathrooms can be built, but such a view was unique. The icing on the cake was one of the upstairs bedrooms that had been a mother-in-law suite and featured a sink. This room was to become my studio until 1990 when we built a bigger one in the backyard.

A few years after the historical moon landing in 1969, we met Mrs. Roedde on the street.

"I have just bought a ticket for the first tourist spaceship to the moon!" she said, smiling broadly.

Sadly, she has since travelled to meet St. Peter at the pearly gates, her ticket to the moon still unredeemed.

We moved into our new house, unpacked for the last time and folded the cardboard containers up for disposal. Seeing the pile of discarded boxes, Eran became worried.

"Why are you throwing them out?" he asked. "What are we going to do when we move again next year?"

For him, our constant moves had become a pattern, a way of life to be repeated year after year. But no, this time we were staying — this new home would become our anchor.

At this point I have to fast-forward some ten years into the future when a dramatic change occurred in Eran's life. The teenage years are difficult ones, but he had an added problem that we had been unaware of: his name. Born in Jerusalem, we had called him 'Eran', meaning 'lively' and pronounced in Hebrew with the emphasis on the last syllable. In English, the emphasis rested on the first syllable, sounding more like 'Aaron' and forcing our son to spell out his name constantly. One day, he had had enough.

"I hate my name," he shouted.

We were stunned, understanding only now the anxiety caused by his name.

"No problem. Just choose another name that you feel comfortable with," we said.

As a teenager, I had changed my name from Paula to Pnina and understood him perfectly. So, after going through the official procedures, 'Eran' became 'David' and he never had to spell out his name again. It took us only three months to get used to the change.

Baby Dan

Now we had the luxury of gazing day after day at the spectacular view from our window, but not enough money to pay the mortgage. We built a small bathroom in the basement and began renting rooms to students, an arrangement that lasted for ten years. Confident that we could do everything ourselves, except plumbing, we built some of the furniture we needed, such as seats covered with black fabric and a buffet made from old shelves painted and decorated with Mactac paper and glass, and that is still a conversation piece.

We bought used appliances and a second-hand car. I discovered the pleasure of working in the garden, the satisfaction of learning about plants and watching them grow, feeling the joy of getting my fingers dirty in the black soil that generously offered its gifts of snowdrops, crocuses, tulips and daffodils each spring. I could do it all: clean house, cook, garden, take care of our son and make art.

As a final precious gift, on July 15, 1968, at 3:30 am, our second son, Dan, arrived in great haste. I barely made it to the hospital on time.

Chapter 44

Leave Traces, Make Marks, Feel the Beauty

The aim of art is to represent not the outward appearance of things, but their inward significance.

Aristotle
350 BC

I found my voice as an artist in the early 1970s, after years of wandering through the jungle of artistic styles created by others. Without planning, consumed by constant doubts about my ability, pressured by the obligation of daily chores and childcare, I returned to my first love: drawing.

Lines flowed from my pen with a life of their own. The drawings had nothing to do with reality — they just materialized on the paper. The hours spent on intricate and textured patterns became a hypnotic, meditative process. For no reason at all, as if guided by an unseen master, shapes would appear on the white sheet. Most of these images related to nature, to the flora and fauna that give us life and sustenance. My pen drew them close to one another, filling the space: fish and birds, bears, plants and leaves. Life. I began collecting delicate skeleton leaves and feathers that I inked and then printed on the paper, real objects among imaginary shapes. The rich textures of simple objects, such as gears from a broken toy telephone, plastic doilies, lace, old wine corks, strawberry baskets and many more, enchanted me. The box filled with this large collection of printable things is still sitting in my studio, a reminder of the time when I incorporated found objects in my drawings.

I never knew what brought up these images — they just kept coming.

Fantasmagoria with Eagle
1974 | mixed media on paper | 22 × 30 in | 56 × 76 cm
Collection Legacy Art Gallery, University of Victoria, BC

My working table overlooked the water and the mountains; despite this inspiring view, I was not drawn to paint the landscape as it was. Interpreting and redefining it by the addition of symbolic elements and printed textures interested me more. I needed to find the inward significance of what I saw, as Aristotle so aptly said.

Since most of my work at the time was on paper, my handy husband built me a set of large drawers for storing drawings and prints. Only much later, in 1990, when we built a new studio behind the house, did I have enough space to store larger works on canvas.

I had little contact with the visual arts community in general and its avant-garde segment in particular. I didn't have much time for forging professional ties, as my world consisted of my husband and my sons, who were a great source of joy and a well of inspiration for my art. Our friends were mostly academics and newcomers to the city as we were. They were friendly and warm and quickly became our extended family.

Even so, the level of frustration and anxiety caused by constantly having to choose between my role as a wife and mother and my need to make art reached its peak. Should I put my career on the back burner until Dan was a bit older? Or should I just continue to draw at a slower pace? I was developing the stressful syndrome of the 'superwoman' who tries to keep too many balls in the air.

Each morning when my older son went to school and my younger son to a neighbour's daycare, I would rush to my studio and begin drawing. Each minute was precious.

Despite my frustration at the time, I am astounded at the amount of work I managed to produce. Oh, the stamina of youth! I am envious now of my own young self and of the energy I had during those years. I stare in disbelief at my own curriculum vitae, seeing that my work had been included in group and solo shows only two years after the birth of my younger son. I was even rewarded with positive reviews from a few art critics. Eerily, in a 1977 review in *Artmagazine* for my exhibition at the Bau-Xi Gallery, Deanna Levis made a prescient observation. She wrote:

The studio on the second floor, 1967–1990

Listening to her poetic manner of speaking,
one wonders if she might also have
made her mark as a writer.

This remark would hit home many years later when I began writing this memoir, but in the 1970s I was only interested in visual art. I was soon to discover that painting, much like writing, has a unique feature: solitude. Unlike printmaking in a studio workshop where creative people meet one another, a painter's work is solitary and soon the isolation began weighing on me.

Thinking that teaching might be the solution to this problem, I began offering courses in printmaking and batik through the UBC Women's Faculty Club. The following years, I taught mixed media painting for Continuing Studies at the University of British Columbia and at the Vancouver Art Academy. I realized that I loved teaching and enjoyed sharing my techniques and partaking in the enthusiasm of my students. It was a happy and fulfilling time.

Marvelous view of the city from my studio

227

Chapter 45

Childhood Magic

The year is 1974. My six-year-old son Dan has learned a few magic tricks and pretends to be a magician. According to him, magic exists only in the realm of childhood but disappears in a puff of smoke as soon as we reach adulthood. This worldview of the miraculous expressed in passing by my young magician-cum-philosopher, was the seed for the *Childhood Magic* series.

This is how it happened:

"When I grow up, I won't be able to do magic anymore," announced my little son. "Grown-ups know nothing about magic!"

Dan had mastered a few impressive tricks that he performed at his friends' birthday parties. I made him a magician's costume to fit the part: a flowing black cape worn over an elegant two-piece suit and a moustache with swashbuckling curled ends, cut out of black construction paper and precariously attached on his upper lip. The last, but most important items of this dashing costume were a top hat bought at the dime store and a magic wand. Before each trick, the diminutive magician would theatrically wave his wand and utter, "Abracadabra!" His favourite routine was a surprisingly well-done levitation act that required special props, including a large sheet and a willing volunteer.

What kind of magic was he thinking of? Was he aware of the profound meaning of his childish words? This was surely more about the world seen through a child's eye than about sleight of hand. Was he referring to the wonder I remembered from my own childhood when banal events acquired mysterious powers, when fairy tales were

Dan the magician

real and imagination ran wild? When a solemn burial procession for a dead bird covered with a fragrant blanket of brightly-coloured nasturtiums became a sacred ritual enacted in my cousin's garden?

"Some people, such as artists," I told him, "can still make magic, even when they grow up. They look at the world with children's eyes and see things that adults have stopped noticing."

How could I prove this to my son? First, I had to revisit my own childhood and listen to the echoes of my own magical moments. Where would I find objects to remind me of those days? I had none of the usual mementos children carry into adulthood. No worn teddy bears, no toys, no books or other items that could trigger memories — all that stayed behind when we left Romania.

However, one day as I was rummaging through my jewellery box, hidden under some bead necklaces, I spied a small golden charm in the shape of a tiny devil standing on one leg and still bearing the indentation of my teeth on his little bottom. This charm was one of the few personal items salvaged from my childhood. Finding it after all those years, I saw myself again as a ten-year-old girl staring at the glittery display of golden charms in the store window of the jewellery shop on Strada Regală.

During an old pagan spring celebration lasting for the whole month of March, gifts of a *mărțișor*, literally a 'little March', were exchanged as amulets of good luck. In early spring, the jewellery stores on Brăila's main street were loaded with glittering charms

229

 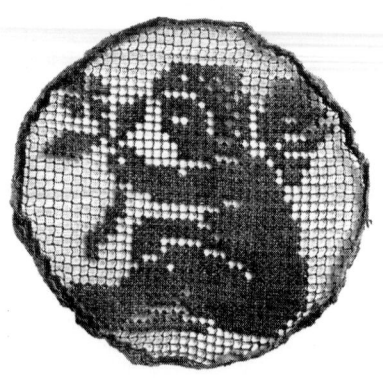

Golden Imp	Lace Cherub
0.75 x 0.25 in., 2 x 0.5cm	4 x 4 in, 20 x 10 cm

of gold and silver. Lavish displays of hearts, flowers, tiny anchors, small angels, little shoes and boots, animals of all sorts — bunnies and puppies, cats, dogs and ponies — all exquisitely and lovingly fashioned out of precious metal and hanging on delicate silver and gold chains were alluringly displayed in store windows.

I was probably not more than ten years old when my parents bought me one of those charms. Opening the small box, I found a tiny golden devil nonchalantly lying on the black velvet and grinning fiercely at me, his minuscule horns daintily erect over two large ears. How could I have guessed that one day this small imp would appear in my drawings not as an ornament, but as a symbol of evil?

Soon after the discovery of the imp I remembered another object. It was a remnant from an old sheet from my mother's dowry that had somehow survived the years. In the old days when there were no department stores selling ready-made clothes and bedding, these items were handmade to order by a seamstress. This particular duvet cover that had endured well over fifty years of wear and tear, had been lovingly and beautifully embroidered with inserts of crocheted lace cherubs. The sheet had fallen apart, ending its journey as fancy bedding.

What of the lace cherubs, though? I remembered carefully cutting them out for safekeeping and storing them in a drawer.

Finding these two items, I knew the answer to my quest. Their message was clear: the symbolism of the devil and the angel would anchor my explorations. They were the signifiers for the profound forces fighting for supremacy in the human soul: heaven and hell, the good and the bad, the yin and the yang. I could now embark on the search for the magic my son referred to.

Across two sheets of Fabriano paper, my son's footprints climb over a gentle hill in an imaginary space of wonders visible only to children's eyes, where intricate fine lines cover the paper with rich designs and fantastic shapes. The adults who have lost the ability to understand the magic ignore the marvels below their feet and the jaded art critic, who considers the rabbit crunched into a corner of the drawing to be sentimental, join the ranks of the unseeing, but for the child, it is a miracle of shape, movement and grace. Owl, fish, beetle, swan and bird — all co-exist within this enchanted place.

Time off for our magician

Barely visible, the angel and the devil are a haunting presence, deeply embedded in this tapestry of life. Grinning wickedly, the little golden imp lurks in his dark cave at the bottom of the drawing. He is just a whisper, a small echo of the great evil that engulfed the world and reverberated through my childhood. I hope and wish that my son would never have to face the imp's handiwork.

Below the footprints, hidden among the flowing black-and-sepia drawings that sing of a world teeming with life, sits the lace cherub. The rose he offers in his out-stretched hand is a fragile symbol of hope and goodness.

This drawing was the first in the *Childhood Magic* series.

My answer to my son.

Chapter 46

The 'Gift' and the Trials

Did I have the 'gift'? Some days I had no doubts, but there were times when I was not so sure. So why did I feel the overwhelming need to make marks on paper, to conjure shapes that did not exist and create imaginary worlds like a crafty magician pulling white doves out of his sleeve, even when there was no audience to applaud?

Descartes' famous words, *cogito ergo sum* (I think, therefore I am), matched my own thoughts, albeit with a minor change. For me it was "I make art, therefore I am." The *Encyclopaedia Britannica* goes on to quote his beautifully phrased argument on doubt:

"The statement is indubitable, Descartes argued, because even if an all-powerful demon were to try to deceive me into thinking that I exist when I do not, I would have to exist for the demon to deceive me. Therefore, whenever I think, I exist."

The thought that 'whenever I paint, I exist' had not occurred to me during those early years. All I knew was that in order to feel alive, I simply had to continue making art.

The year 1974 was an eventful one for my career as an artist. Not only was my work shown in six group exhibitions in Vancouver, Calgary and Toronto, but Werner True, who showed my works at his Mido Gallery on Main Street, gave me the best advice I have ever received from an art dealer. I shall never forget his words.

"Your works are too disparate, too scattered," he said. "It is as if a stone is thrown into a lake — and there are no ripples. Try working in series, allowing an idea to grow and mature like ripples spreading on the water."

I have worked in series ever since.

In 1975, I joined the prestigious Bau-Xi Gallery and began showing my work regularly. The years spent at this gallery were both successful and exhilarating. I worked hard, giving shape to a constant flow of new ideas that led to yearly exhibitions, reaching a large number of art collectors. These were the good old days when two thirds of the works sold on the opening night of the show.

During the same year, I was invited to participate in *Dawn*, an exhibition of women artists of British Columbia held in the Student Union Gallery at the University of British Columbia. The participants were honoured by a reception at the Faculty Club, where Pat Martin Bates, a printmaker and an art teacher at the University of Victoria, as well as a member of the famous Limners Group, and P.K. Page, a well-known poet and artist, sat on the panel. I shall never forget Pat Martin Bates' words: "Whenever I talk professionally about my art or find myself among other artists, I never mention my family, since I would be labelled as a 'housewife who paints' instead of being considered a serious artist."

In the future, I would experience the bitter truth of her words myself. Having children was definitely a liability for a woman artist.

In early 1980, I attended a workshop with Judy Chicago, the very first feminist American artist. The topic of the workshop was *The Dinner Party*, her major collaborative work that had made news all over the art world. I hoped that she would provide some answers to my frustration concerning the obstacles faced by female artists. *The Dinner Party* was inspiring because of its huge size, aesthetics and statement about the women artists ignored by history.

However, I felt a shadow hovering over her words and a sense of discomfort that I was able to identify only later: the overbearing, egocentric personality of the artist and the scant credit given to the many women without whose help *The Dinner Party* would never have been achieved. I realized that my own insecurities and the abhorrence of egotism (the 'don't blow your own horn' philosophy touted by my mother) that kept me from wholly sympathizing with the artist also showed me that in the real world, a large ego was an asset on the road to success. Being nice and self-effacing may relegate an artist to obscurity.

At the end of the workshop, Chicago ended her talk by echoing the words of Pat Martin Bates: "No woman artist," she said, "can ever make it big if she has a family!"

I went home that day and examined the lives of the few women who had had made it in the visual arts: Mary Cassat, Georgia O'Keeffe, Frida Kahlo, Agnes Martin, Louise Nevelson, Lee Krasner, Emily Carr. Judy Chicago was right — none of these women had children. Had I looked deeper, I would have discovered that despite the odds, there were a few women with children, such as Käthe Kollwitz, Louise Bourgeois and Barbara Hepworth, who had succeeded in building important careers. These women, however, were the exception.

That day I made a decision that had a profound impact on me. I remembered the words of Dietrich Bonhoeffer, the German pastor who gave his life in the fight against Nazism: "Not to speak is to speak. Not to act is to act."

I realized that ignoring the long and painful history of women ceased to be an option for me. I would speak through my art and act against the prejudices and discrimination that kept women from being full members of the human race. Immediately after attending Judy Chicago's workshop, I began working on a project that would continue for a whole year and would speak for the half of the human race that I belonged to, that had not been given a voice in history.

I called it *The Trials of Eve*.

Chapter 47

The Trials of Eve

My journey in the creation of *The Trials of Eve* began with a formless idea. The work that resulted after much soul-searching and research has had a strong impact on my life as an artist and as a woman. Wanting to make a visual statement about women's place in the world, I spent weeks agonizing over how to best express my thoughts, considering many possible scenarios. Would it be a painting depicting women full of sorrow, rage, despair? Perhaps a diptych, two panels in which female figures struggle to break through the invisible barriers society had erected around them? Figurative paintings? How many? What aspect of women's oppression should I address? I didn't want to be too literal and create propaganda posters, but on the other hand, the meaning of the work should be clear.

Looking for answers, I searched for the roots of the first known discriminatory act against women and a light went on in my head: Eve! In Western civilization based on Christianity, Eve was the first sinner; Paradise was supposedly lost due to her and she was made to bear the guilt for the world's misfortunes. Yes, Eve's action was indeed original, but it was not at all the sin it had been portrayed as.

Ideas began flowing. The excitement of having found a structure on which to build my ideas rose like quicksilver in a thermometer. What I wanted to say was based on an ancient tale — a myth some three thousand years old that still held us in its power. Eve and Adam have been forever caught in an ancient web of fabricated stories.

Contrary to the feminist art of the 1980s, I had no interest in violent images and depictions of misogynist practices. Painting aspects of discrimination was too similar to journalistic reportage, in my view. My goal was to examine difficult issues through a universal lens that would not address just one particular case, but rather invoke millennia of subjugation and discrimination, going back to the very source, hence the use of the creation myth. Reading the first two chapters of the Old Testament, I was reminded that there were, in fact, two different stories of creation. In chapter one, Adam and Eve are created equal:

"So God created man in His own image, in the image of God He created him; male and female He created them." (Genesis 1:27)

In chapter two, woman is created from Adam's rib:

"And the rib, which the Lord God had taken from man, made He a woman, and brought her unto the man." (Genesis 2:22)

This second version was the one chosen by St. Paul as the cornerstone for the relationship between the sexes, with unfortunate results for women. After a great deal of research I learned that this version was the older one, from before the destruction of the first Temple, when the Israelites were attempting to erase the gods, the goddesses and the snake worship of the pagan cultures, to be replaced by one God.

The story in the first chapter on the other hand, was written later, after the return from the Babylonian exile (438 BC), where the Israelites had been exposed to the concept of the goddess as an equal partner to the god.

During the year I worked on *The Trials*, I learned much about ancient mythology, monotheism, Judaism and Christianity. Layer after layer, book after book, new revelations lifted the veil cast over mistaken or false beliefs. It was a true voyage of discovery. For the first time in my artistic career, I decided to jump into the murky waters of controversy and take a political stand as an artist and as a woman. The new knowledge was rich in disturbing details. How was I to do it justice? I realized that I could not convey this complicated message in only one or two paintings. Perhaps the tale should rise on a scaffold, like a building to be explored room by room? Eve's tribulations have put her on a trial that has lasted for millennia. The work would be a narrative, or better yet, a play in three acts: *The Trials of Eve*.

Now that I had decided upon the format of the work, the next problem was one of representation. My goal being universality, how would Adam and Eve be portrayed?

Were they to be white or black? Were they Asian, African, Native American or Maori? My eyes fell upon the wooden marionette standing on a shelf in my studio. This was the answer to my dilemma! This puppet was the right symbol for both Adam and Eve: its face blank and its body sexless, its race undefined, its sex ambiguous, its limbs easily manipulated.

Just a human being.

Chapter 48

The Work

Knowledge is power.

Francis Bacon
Meditationes Sacrae and Human Philosophy

The first act opens with the basic premise of the work: it was all a set-up. Eve, the first human to reach for knowledge, did so against dire threats of a jealous God. The injunction of harsh punishment should God's children dare to partake of the Tree of Knowledge, was meant to keep humanity in ignorance — powerless.

Act One — "*The Set-Up*", sets the tone:

> *The curtain rises*
> *On centre stage*
> *its branches laden/with fruit/of a forbidden knowledge.*
> *THE TREE*
> *stands tall, aloof, inviting*
> *Why there?*
> *and if so*
> *why forbidden?*
> *Who is this God*
> *who sets the trap*
> *for His own creation?*

The Set-Up
1981 | mixed media on paper | 27 × 22 in | 68.6 × 56 cm

During the time I was working on *The Trials*, I was also developing a group of works based on myths and legends of the Haida and Kwakwaka'wakw (previously known as Kwakiutl) nations of the West Coast. One of the most intriguing myths was the initiation ritual. A young man goes alone into the forest where he meets the powerful Cannibal Bird who attempts to devour him. In the ensuing struggle the young man prevails, becomes a Cannibal Bird himself and finds his song. Songs are private property for the First Nations — through fighting his demons and finding his song, the young man finds himself. He then returns to his people as a wild man and regains his identity while dancing around the ritual fire.

Impressed by the profound meaning of this myth, I took the liberty of replacing the snake from the biblical story with the Cannibal Bird as a symbol of Eve's inner voice. I believe that it was not the snake that made Eve reach for the forbidden fruit, but a deliberate act of defiance against unreasonable rules — the first act of free choice by a human being. My work would place the little-known myth of the West Coast first people into the universal search for knowledge.

Two years after exhibiting *The Trials* at the Burnaby Art Gallery, I felt that the work was still incomplete and I wrote a poem for each image. The drawings of *The Trials* were shown along with the poems in a space built especially for it during the historical exhibition *BC Women Artists 1885–1985* at the Art Gallery of Greater Victoria.

The Trials took a year to complete. I spent more time thinking, reading and learning than actually working. The drawings needed to be concise, sparse and, yes, beautiful. Beauty had been women's most important asset throughout history — men measured women's worth by their looks rather than by their intelligence and, in turn, women used their beauty as a weapon to achieve power over men — therefore the drawings had to be beautiful. By doing this, I willfully ignored the trendy contemporary motto 'beauty is dead', which has led to an avalanche of ugliness in art. I was out of fashion again, but I did not care.

After examining the historical fate of women in the first two acts, I needed a resolution to the play. The third act was the most difficult to conceive since it had to reflect the changes in contemporary society. The solution, I thought, was to show Adam, who had used much of his knowledge to create weapons of death and destruction, holding a gun while the Cannibal Bird hovered over his shoulder. The Tree of Knowledge became a barrier between Adam on one side and Eve on the other. It was time to bring Eve back into the picture. Here, though still in her kitchen, Eve was reaching again for the apple — the symbol of knowledge denied her for centuries.

Despite the historic oppression of women, I firmly believe that it is wrong and counterproductive to view men antagonistically. I love the three men in my life, my husband and my two sons. Men and women need one another — as the story in the first chapter of Genesis says: "male and female created He them."

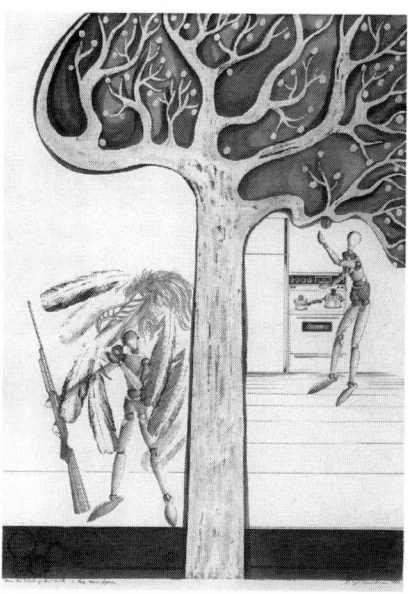

Eve Tries Again
1981 | mixed media on paper | 27 × 22 in | 68.6 × 56 cm

The last image is titled *Adam & Eve Puzzle: To Be Assembled with Love*. Benign, ghostly Cannibal Birds float in the background, encouraging both genders to share equally in life and knowledge.

So much to lose
much more to gain
Forgotten pieces of a broken puzzle
falling into place.
Two halves of one whole
one needing the other
A silent sound of fear
has reached the Heavens
The Earth cries out in pain
The time has come
to reassemble
and to complete the puzzle.
Shall we begin anew and...

Adam & Eve Puzzle: To Be Assembled With Love
1981 | mixed media on paper | 27 × 22 in | 68.6 × 56 cm

In the summer of 1986, *The Trials of Eve* had a close call with glory. This time however, Lady Luck played hide-and-go-seek with me, letting me down after allowing me a glimpse of tantalizing opportunity. Timing, as they say, is everything! Arriving in Paris for my husband's sabbatical year, I saw a poster for an exhibition at the Musée de l'Homme. (Even in the 21st Century, the name has not changed — it is still 'Museum of Man', 'man' being considered in French a generic term for 'human'.)

The title of the exhibition was *Côté femmes* (Women's Side). I couldn't wait to see it and went to the imposing museum soon after the opening. Having spent the last six years immersed in issues of women's history, I felt as if this exhibition, opening at the time of my arrival in Paris, was fortuitous.

In the introduction to the catalogue, curator Françoise Cousin explains how the use of the 'male' as a universal representative of the human species includes the female story. The exhibition aimed to show how various societies interpret the difference between the sexes from a male point of view by imposing boundaries and relegating women to a well-defined, confined place in history.

"Could we not," she concludes in her catalogue essay, "replace the idea of the natural subordination of women, symbolized in our tradition by the creation of Eve from Adam's rib, by an equal view of the human race, man and woman, men and women?"

Here she was quoting the ancient myth as the defining reason for the oppression of women just as I had done!

There were some puzzling elements in the show that were new to me, relating to African and other tribal cultures where women were also marginalized and where the Eve myth did not exist. I had been unaware of such fascinating details as the gender roles of the Tin Dama of New Guinea, based on sexual differences. I read that menstrual blood was thought of as a reservoir of life hidden in the woman's body that gets depleted each month. By the time she enters menopause, a woman's life supply is empty and she is considered dead. A funeral ceremony is held for her, she changes her name, eats a different diet and becomes a kind of medium between the living and the dead — she is now a 'ghost'.

A section of the exhibition dealt with practices designed to restrain women's movements, such as feet binding in China, corsets in Europe and the fattening of women in Hawaii that proved the husband's wealth.

I was surprised and disappointed to see a quote of Pythagoras:
"*There is a good principle that has created order, light and man; and a bad principle that has created chaos, darkness and woman.*"

Had Pythagoras read the second Creation story in the Old Testament?

I called the museum for an appointment with the curator, not really expecting her to receive a total stranger like me, but hoping to show her *The Trials of Eve* and hear her comments. Surprisingly, she invited me to her office the very next week.

I met Françoise Cousin in her office at the Musée de l'Homme. Approaching this monumental building fronted by imposing tall columns made my heart beat faster. Why was I doing this? What was I expecting? The need to hear someone of her stature comment on the work that was of such importance to me spurred me on.

Madame Cousin received me graciously and encouraged me to open my portfolio containing the twelve mixed-media drawings. She took her time, carefully looking at the imagery and exclaiming over particular points that interested her, such as the substitution of the Cannibal Birds for the snake and the use of marionettes.

"I wish that you had come earlier," she sighed. "I would have included this work in the current exhibition, but now it is too late. There is no space left and the catalogue has been printed."

At that moment, I realized that one might have two consecutive but conflicting emotions at once: sheer happiness at this warm evaluation of my work and abject disappointment at missing the unique opportunity of exhibiting in such a great institution.

As a footnote to this story, I cannot resist mentioning that some years later, I offered the work for exhibition and as a donation to the Vancouver Art Gallery. The local curator was neither interested in seeing the work nor in accepting the offer of a donation. Despite this rejection, *The Trials of Eve* has had a rich life spanning twenty-seven years, starting in 1982 with an exhibition at the Burnaby Art Gallery and finally becoming part of the permanent collection of the Glenbow Museum in Calgary in 2009. Many events, such as panel discussions, reviews, a film and many radio and TV interviews, occurred over the years.

Chapter 49

The Book

You must publish this!

Rachel Siegel
to Pnina Granirer in conversation

In 1987, Rachel Siegel, a women's psychotherapist from Ithaca, New York, came to visit. Aware of her feminist activities and her advocacy for women's rights, I showed her *The Trials of Eve*. Her reaction was unexpected.

"You must publish this as a book!" she said.

I was pleased of course, but was she really serious? Who would publish a slim book consisting of twelve images and twelve poems — and a feminist work to boot? No publisher in his right mind would risk such an adventure! Still, Rachel meant it. She truly believed that this work had to be published and widely seen. I was taken by surprise when she went on to offer me a substantial amount as seed money, suggesting I find a publisher.

"Rachel, I have never done this before. What if I lose your money?"

"It does not matter," she replied. "You have to try. This work has to be seen!"

Did she, as a psychologist, understand that it was difficult to reject such a vote of confidence? I was humbled, excited and terrified by the scope of the project she was proposing. If I refused, I would never forgive myself. But what if I failed? At least I could try to live up to the confidence she showed me.

Soon after, at an Art Books Publishers' Fair in Vancouver, I met a New York publisher who was interested in *The Trials*. We corresponded for a while after his return to New York with the understanding that I would pass on to him Rachel's gift, thus minimizing his risk. Just as I prepared to do this, he called to inform me that he was bankrupt and would not be able to publish the book. That was a narrow escape! Rachel's money would have been lost even before beginning the publishing work.

Was the project over? My optimism kept me searching for answers. Then, as if serendipity was waving its arms at me, I met my second angel. Kay Dodd, a friendly potter from Penticton, BC, was not a woman of means like Rachel, but when she saw *The Trials*, she had a similar reaction. She suggested I self-publish and offered me the same amount as Rachel to help me do it. I was worried about losing her investment and bargained her down somewhat.

My friend, Cherie Smith, gave me the final push and the courage to seize the opportunity. She cajoled, encouraged and prodded me into taking the plunge. She offered help with editing my poems or whatever was needed for the publication process.

"Just do it!" she repeated again and again.

Someone mentioned Barbarian Press, a small publishing house located in Mission, BC, that specialized in letterpress limited editions of artists' books. Determined to keep alive the craft of setting and printing by hand, Crispin and Jan Elsted had founded the press in order to practice their love for beautifully printed books.

I drove to Mission, enjoying the lush scenery on the way and wondering if this was a good idea. Crispin, a big bear of a man with a gentle voice and a soft beard, and Jan, gifted in crafting beautiful books, greeted me warmly and gave me a tour of the press. It was wonderful to see their dedication to this fine craft that produced rare and exquisite books lovingly printed on handmade paper. Each letter was an echo of times past, a declaration of faith in perfection created by human hands. For me, it was an initiation into an unfamiliar and select world where quality was paramount; a world where rarity was a preferred counterpart to mass production.

Step by step, Crispin and Jan took me through the process of designing a book that would include tipped-in reproductions of the twelve images facing the poems on the opposite page. Each detail would be carefully planned to produce an aesthetically-pleasing volume printed as a numbered and signed edition of only one hundred copies. However, when I was told that such a book would cost the buyers one hundred and eighty dollars, I was not so sure.

Who would buy such an expensive book? I was just about to learn another lesson about the world of rare books and their collectors to which I was a total stranger. I discovered the existence of special collections in libraries, universities and museums, as well as people who collect limited-edition books the way others collect works of art.

I took the plunge, despite the cost that exceeded the funds generously given to me by my friends, and tried to put the danger of failure out of mind. I became Gaea Press, designed a logo and went to work.

Two years later on December 6, 1989, I drove to West Vancouver to pick up the book from the binder. Listening to the radio on the way home, I heard the horrific news: Marc Lépine had walked into the École Polytechnique in Montreal, where he ordered the men out and then proceeded to move through the building, shooting women students wherever he found them. He killed fourteen women before he turned the gun on himself.

The Trials of Eve book, completed that very day, had acquired an even deeper reason for its existence.

As a newly fledged publisher, I had had to learn the nuts and bolts of the trade: distribution, reviews, advertising, mailing lists and much more. Marketing was new to me. It was a steep learning curve, very different from making art, but it had to be done. After *The Trials* was awarded the Alcuin Society Award for Excellence in Book Design, largely due to the superb design by Crispin Elsted and the fine hand-setting and presswork by Jan Elsted and Joy

Tataryn, orders for special collections of universities and museums began to pour in.

The Trials sold well. The first twenty-five copies, more expensive still due to an enclosed limited edition wood engraving made especially for the book, sold out. I created a second engraving for the last twenty-five copies, with the same result. Numerous events ensued, such as panel discussions examining the issues presented in the work, book launches, and radio and TV interviews.

In 1990, Gretchen Jordan-Bastow came to my studio and I showed her the original drawings of *The Trials of Eve*. She carefully examined each drawing and read the poems.

"This is a film!" she proclaimed. "This story must be made into a film!"

History does repeat itself. Rachel Siegel's words echoed in my mind. "This is a book. You must publish it!"

Having close ties with the First Nations community, Gretchen was particularly interested in the substitution of the Cannibal Bird image for the snake that brought this local West Coast cultural icon into a universal context.

This project was so important to Gretchen that she took out a mortgage on her house to finance it. It would be her first film, opening up her career in filmmaking. Despite criticism raised by some First Nations people accusing her (and myself) of appropriation, Wedlidi Speck, a well-known chief on Vancouver Island, allowed her to use the sound of his drum in the film and wrote this blurb for the back of the softcover edition:

"*The Trials of Eve is about a mythic journey where Eve meets the Cannibal Birds, the inner dark nature of the SELF, and is able to move past them onto a higher and greater peace.*"

The film was shown in Vancouver on BC's Knowledge Network and in 1992 at the FIFA (Festival International des Films sur l'Art), the UNESCO International Art Film Festival in Paris.

Having worked with many librarians during my adventure as a publisher, I came to a surprising conclusion: most librarians love books, but a great number of public galleries curators do not truly love art! All the librarians I encountered showed a true interest in and love of books, while many of the curators I dealt with did not seem to be interested in art and artists, except as tools for enhancing their own careers.

They were shackled by the unforgiving politics of art, the danger of losing their jobs if they made the wrong decision and the pressure to follow trends. Since nothing is black-and-white, I was also fortunate to meet a small number of curators working in smaller public galleries who showed a keen interest in artists and their works.

After just a few years, I had covered all the publishing costs and began making a small profit. It was a happy day for me when I mailed cheques to Rachel Siegel and Kay Dodd, repaying their generous loans, which had enabled *The Trials* to come into the world. With time, I also sent them a share of the small profit from further sales.

When the plates for the book were first printed, I had ordered five hundred extra copies of each image. Following the success of the limited-edition book, I realized that my goal of distributing *The Trials* to more people was unrealistic due to the high cost and the small print run of only one hundred copies. Why not publish a softcover edition that more people could afford?

The softcover edition was published eleven years after the first exhibition of *The Trials*. The new book included the eleven-year history of the work, an essay discussing the issues involved, a foreword by New York feminist art critic Lucy Lippard, and an introduction by Ann Rosenberg, a Vancouver artist, writer and curator. By 2016, only a few books were left from the limited edition and the softcover book was sold out.

The Trials is still creating an occasional ripple. In 2008, Mary Ann Beavis, a professor in the Department of Religious Studies at St. Thomas More College, Saskatoon, wrote in *Feminist Theology with a Canadian Accent: Canadian Perspectives on Contextual Feminist Theology* (Novalis, Saint Paul University, Ottawa):

Her implicit Eve/Job typology is original, as is her reinterpretation of the 'temptation' in terms of Kwakiutl mythology. Her identification of Eve with the stereotype of Mary Magdalene as the eternally grovelling penitent whore is also a piece of striking feminist theological interpretation. (page 301)

Thirty-five years have passed since the creation of *The Trials of Eve*. Much has changed since. The achievements of women in the Western world have surpassed the dreams of the first suffragettes in Britain or the feminists in the United States and Canada. Only the unfinished puzzle of the last chapter still has to be assembled.

Chapter 50

The Carved Stones

*Eerie sight of rocks becoming bleached
bones shapes fit for dreams . . .*

Pnina Granirer

Where do ideas come from? What mysterious chemistry in the brain lights up unexpected vistas with a sudden flash of lightning? This is probably the most frequently asked question, but the answer, as Bob Dylan so poetically put it, "is blowing in the wind." We expect logical answers, but creativity remains a mystery. Despite numerous attempts to unravel this miraculous activity of the human brain that so enriches our brief stay on earth, the answer remains hidden.

Sometimes, feeling that my work was becoming repetitious, I knew I had to change direction. After an exhibition, I would sink into despair. What would I do next? Would I ever get a new idea? Is this the end? In literature, this is known as 'writer's block', a condition as painful and distressing as a serious illness. Where would the next spark come from? Would it come at all?

An unexpected word or a chance experience may unleash ideas that provide new inspiration for the artist, such as my small son's observation about magic and the adult world that led me to the *Childhood Magic* series. With time, I learned to trust that new ideas would always surface.

One day in the mid-1980s, I was sitting on a boulder facing the ocean in Roberts Creek. As I listened to the sound of waves pulled in by the incoming tide, an extraordinary sense of the universe unfolding swept over me. An almost mystical experience of blinding clarity revealed to me eternity hiding within the solid surface of a stone. I had never before perceived rocks in that way.

The journey of *The Carved Stones* series was about to begin.

These were not simply paintings of beach landscapes. The sandstones silently lying on the shores of the Gulf Islands, washed by the tides and dried by the winds, had a profound effect on me. A modest rock with deep indentations carved on its surface would assume monumental proportions, reigning in splendid isolation on a sheet of Fabriano paper. A group of stones enclosing a small round rock would convey the image of rocks giving birth. There was no end to the wealth of ideas contained within the carved stones of the Gulf Islands.

The very first work was of a blue sandstone encrusted with white barnacles with black and blue rugged textures. I did it by lifting the wet acrylic paint with newsprint. Instinctively, I had stumbled upon a classical Surrealist technique: decalcomania. Many years later, this would qualify me to exhibit my work in exhibitions of Surrealist art in Spain, Portugal, Chile and Costa Rica.

The Bau-Xi Gallery where I had been showing my work since 1975, did not share my enthusiasm for the new works and refused to exhibit *The Carved Stones*. My long association with this well-known gallery had been a happy and successful one and had greatly helped my career. I had shown regularly and my work had sold extremely well and become better known. Needless to say, I was disappointed. I knew that these paintings were totally different from my former work, but is this not what makes art alive? New ideas, new challenges, exploring new frontiers? Should not galleries try to educate their public, explain the creative process and raise interest in new ways of expression? I am well aware that the art business is a difficult one and that galleries have to pay their expenses, but they have also, to my mind, a duty to educate the public.

The Atelier Gallery across the street did not seem to have the same concerns and offered to exhibit the new works by a special agreement with the Bau-Xi Gallery. At the time, I didn't understand what it meant to show at a new gallery, while still being represented by my old one. It was a gentle way of telling me 'goodbye'. I never showed at the Bau-Xi again.

A new door opened for my stone drawings a year later, when I found myself again in Paris accompanying my mathematician husband. This time, I had my third exhibition in Strasbourg, at the Aktuarius Gallery, showing some of the new works under the title *Les Roches Bleus* (The Blue Rocks).

Jean Christian, the local art critic whom I never met, wrote a review in *Les Affiches-Moniteur d'Alsace et de Lorraine*, ending with these words:

"Even though the artist has already exhibited twice before in Strasbourg and thus is no stranger to us, she still surprised us by this new height that more than justifies the international reputation she has developed for quite a few years now. All the more so, since far from repeating herself, she treats the most original themes with great control and sobriety, suggesting the silence of the space disturbed by the rumbling of the ocean and the piercing cries of the seagulls. And also by an overwhelming poetry."

It was good to hear this critic saluting the exploration of new ideas.

Returning to Vancouver I showed the review to my gallery, but they could not have cared less and our partnership came to an abrupt end. This experience was a traumatic one for me, the closest I ever came to experiencing the unsettling effects of a divorce. Was my career over after only a few successful years? I felt abandoned, betrayed and fearful for my future as an artist.

How was I to know that despite this experience, *The Carved Stones* would have a long and eventful history and be shown over the next five years in Vancouver, Victoria, Toronto and Penticton, then later in Spain, Portugal and Chile? How could I have guessed that in 2013, George Harris, director/curator of the Two Rivers Gallery in Prince George, who proved to be one of the rare curators who deeply cared about art, would understand these works in depth and mount an exhibition spanning twenty-seven years, titled *The Whisper of Stones*?

Working with George Harris was one of the highlights of my career. I had finally met a curator who was keenly and truly interested in the artist's work. After examining a large body of work, he carefully chose each piece for the exhibition. His catalogue essay suggests that my choice of stone images is connected with a wish for permanence, addressing issues of dislocation and uncertainty in my life. His insight was illuminating, explaining my constant quest for solidity, history and continuity.

I was humbled by the amount of time and work he dedicated to this show, from writing an extensive essay to the Cultural Property Committee for the donation of the works, to designing and publishing an attractive catalogue. All the paintings in the beautifully produced catalogue are now in the permanent collection of the gallery.

After twenty-six years, *The Carved Stones* had finally found a permanent home.

Soon after leaving the Bau-Xi Gallery, I had a dream.

I am in a crowded train, travelling with a group of people to a town I don't know. The train begins moving, slowly at first, then faster and faster. I look out the window and see a blur of fields, trees and clouds racing by with the odd house swishing along, as if a large sponge is constantly wiping out the view, leaving only faint traces of what was there a second ago. Then the train stops. There is much shoving, pushing, shouting and confusion as everyone grabs their luggage and heads for the exit. Where is my suitcase? I can't find it anywhere. I search desperately under the seat, overhead, in every corner, but I can't find it, I can't find it, I can't find it.

People leave the train; they all have their bags but mine is missing. The last of our group is leaving. The doors close and the train is moving again. I am frantic. I am alone and don't remember the name of the town we were going to. The train moves on, swaying, speeding and carrying me towards an unknown destination, away from my friends. My heart is racing. I am dizzy with panic and dread. I am left behind, alone. Where am I going? What will happen to me?

PanicPanicPanicPanicPanicPanic

I woke up, dizzy with anxiety.

The dream followed me for days as I tried to decipher its message. And then, suddenly, it hit me.

Ending my long relationship with a well-established gallery, I felt bereft, abandoned, lost. I was now literally alone, my security blanket as an artist yanked away — the price for daring to explore new ideas in a world controlled more by profit than by artistic values.

In the dream, I was leaving behind my bags and my friends, my security and my support. But, as I now understood, I was still travelling forward. The train would take me to unknown destinations — I would explore new territory without gallery constraints. From now on, I would continue working free of the fear that my own dealer would reject my vision. Scary and painful thoughts — but exhilarating at the same time.

In hindsight, I know that had I found my suitcase and joined the group leaving the train, I would have never created the work that followed.

In 1986, we spent ten months in Paris during my husband's sabbatical year. Although it was not my first time in this wonderful city, it was only then, due to my work with *The Carved Stones*, that I noticed the ubiquitous stone sculptures on the streets and in the museums of the City of Light. This new awareness of monumental shapes carved in stone triggered an idea that would complement and enhance the works inspired by the Gulf Islands sandstones.

Man-carved sculptures and monuments are common in Europe, celebrating a civilization in which culture was deemed superior to nature, while nature was portrayed as feminine, to be dominated and exploited. The rocks that I had been drawing and painting were wild nature at its purest, but despite their wondrous shapes, they were not considered as important as man's handiwork.

The thought occurred to me that I could bring these statues carved by man — and symbolizing culture — back into the stone landscape from whence they came. I could integrate the two into one imaginary landscape, thus paying homage to both nature and culture.

In her statement for the 1989 exhibition of *The Carved Stones* at the Penticton Art Gallery, curator Jane Clark acknowledged my attempt at integration with these words:

"Granirer is an optimist and through her work emphasizes the regenerative powers of harmony and richness of spirit rather than the destructive powers of conflict and the depletion of spirit."

In addition to the inspirational impact of the Paris stone monuments on *The Carved Stones* series, the city offered me other significant experiences. My early virtual art education from the *Larousse Encyclopedia* became real in this city where art was everywhere. The grey reproductions seen in my youth came to life, greeting me like old friends. In the Louvre, I recognized the superb Géricault painting of *La Liberté guidant le peuple*. In the centre of the large canvas, at the apex of a dynamic triangular composition, stands a powerful, bare-breasted woman representing France and carrying the red banner of the Revolution. Corpses lie at her feet and clouds fill the sky in strong contrasts of light and shadow. I could almost hear the noise of battle and the cries of the dying.

Nike, the *Winged Victory of Samothrace*, greeted me from the height of the grand staircase in the Louvre. How different was the actual statue from the small, almost insignificant image I remembered, crammed together with other photographs of sculptures on the black-and-white page of the *Larousse*! There she was — a towering, powerful presence dominating the crowds of tourists below. Although headless and armless, she was the strongest female figure I had ever seen, confidently striding forward, her robes billowing in the wind, her large wings spread out behind her. Most female sculptures portray women with their bodies exposed to be admired and desired, but this one was different — she was a strong and inspiring leader. She was Nike, the goddess of victory, leading her people. Her overwhelming presence followed me for years and became a major element in many of my paintings. Had she inspired Géricault when he painted *La Liberté guidant le people*?

Further travel in Europe brought me face-to-face with other paintings I had seen in the old *Larousse*. In Milan, *The Last Supper* — peeling off the walls, badly lit, but mysterious and awe-inspiring — looked very different from the reproduction I remembered. Visiting the Uffizi Museum in Florence, I saw other familiar and powerful paintings: the large, sprawling *Battle of San Romano* by Paolo Uccello, dominated by three-dimensional horses almost galloping out of the frame; Sandro Botticelli's exquisite *La Primavera* and *The Birth of Venus* commissioned by the Medici family; the *Venus of Urbino* by Titian; *The Madonna of the Goldfinch* by Raphael; and many more. In the Museo del Prado in Madrid, I encountered Velásquez, Goya and El Greco. I stood in awe in front of Rembrandt's *Nightwatch* in the Rijksmuseum in Amsterdam and Van Gogh came to life for me in the Van Gogh Museum. None of these masterpieces first seen in the old *Larousse Encyclopedia*, were strangers to me — but now they had become real.

Chapter 51

Out of The Flames

I don't think about all the misery, but about the beauty that still remains.

Anne Frank
The Diary of a Young Girl

In 1989 I became involved in the organization of an international exhibition entitled *Fear of Others: Art against Racism*. As a participating artist, I needed to create a work reflecting the theme of the show — the destructive scourge of racism. For me, there was only one choice: the Holocaust. No other event in history better illustrates the systematic annihilation of a people because of its ethnicity. I never thought that living in Vancouver, two continents away from Tuviah Friedman's Haifa office with its stacks of papers and photos documenting Nazi atrocities, I would embark on a project forcing me to revisit those images.

The work did not flow easily. How could one convey the immensity of the destruction of a people with only a few images on a flat surface? What should I include and what should I omit? How would I be able to work within the limitations of space and still express the tragedy of the Holocaust? What would the format of the work be? Most importantly, would I succeed in reaching the viewers and touching their souls without appearing self-righteous?

The story is not only a difficult one: it is personal and yet universal, painful and yet uplifting. I could not allow myself to succumb to anger and despair without the hope for a better future. Without hope, how could we go on living? My work had to address the evil, but it also had to celebrate deliverance. Searching for ideas, I found myself sifting again through photographs, poring over documents and reading books about the Holocaust. Forty-four years since the end of the war, the amount of documentation had grown to gigantic proportions. Selecting the right images would be a difficult task.

I envisaged the work as a triptych. Each panel would be part of a narrative taking the viewer through three stages: war, destruction and survival. I chose the details carefully, making anguished decisions and doing much soul-searching. Dare I feature Hitler as a central image in the first panel? His face and excerpts of his criminal, megalomaniac plans described in his infamous book, *Mein Kampf*, dominating the upper part of the painting, nauseated me. But then, how could I not include him? Wasn't he the evil architect of the largest methodically planned mass murder in history? Should we not remember him and his hysterical ravings as a warning for the future?

Out of the Flames

1988 | triptych | mixed media on paper | 3(40 × 30 in) | 3(101.8 × 76 cm)
Collection of Yad Vashem Museum, Jerusalem

LEFT: THE FLAMES OF WAR

In this panel, the flames of war engulf Europe. A jagged piece of blood-red paper collaged over the burning background symbolizes the brutal dagger of hatred that ripped the world apart. Hitler's face, his dark, open mouth spewing the poison of anti-Semitism, dominates the panel. Archival photograph transfers of captive Jews appear on torn sheets of paper; a few yellow Stars of David raggedly hang in space, soon to be devoured by the spreading conflagration. I spent many hours sifting through numerous documents, each image searing the soul and haunting my dreams in the dead of night, clamouring to be included.

CENTRE: THE COLD WINTER OF THE CAMPS

In the central panel, a second flaming arrow stabs the darkness that has descended upon the world. This terrifying threat is aimed at the helpless victims, symbolized by the drowning hands below. A large blanketed figure of a Muselmann, as these emaciated inmates were called, anchored by the image of a woman wearing the Star of David, stands as a counterpoint to the bloody arrow. The deliberate choice of the dominant blue-grey indicates the coldness and the hopelessness of the camps.

RIGHT: OUT OF THE FLAMES

As was the case with *The Trials of Eve*, I felt the need to complete the triptych on a note of hope. I spent long hours searching for a satisfactory resolution for the third panel. It had to be simple but powerful; it had to state in no uncertain terms that despite the Nazi genocide, the Jews were still here. And finally, it had to state that Israel offered them a much-needed lifeline. As the flames die out, the Nazi flags and the swastikas are receding, slowly falling out of the painting and slipping away in defeat. This last panel underscores the irony of the Nazi attempt to destroy the Jewish people that led, instead, to the Phoenix-like emergence of a new Israel. The photograph of five young girls in this panel originates from a snapshot of my cousin Gabi, three friends and myself: we are all survivors. We are all alive. We are here. We are in Israel.

I titled the work *Out of The Flames*. This was the only painting I ever did about the Holocaust. When it was finished, I was drained, depressed and exhausted — but also elated to have found a way to express this tragic event.

Out of The Flames is the second most meaningful work I ever painted, following *The Trials of Eve*.

I would have never imagined that more than seventy years after the tragedy of the Holocaust, echoes of anti-Semitism would be heard again on the streets of Europe's great cities and on university campuses in Canada and the US. Was I too optimistic to show the hatred fading away? Was I too hopeful to envisage a future with acceptance for the people who contributed so much to Western civilization?

I had seen works by Leon Golub, the American Jewish political artist, in important museums in Paris and New York. His huge paintings, that took a stand against torture in South America, showing the victims in stark, grey powerful images, were unforgettable. His series of paintings against the Vietnam war had been banned in the US, so he had moved to Paris, which was more open-minded about protest art. On his return to New York some years later, his career soared and his works were exhibited widely.

Our planned exhibition was international in nature, with an invitational component. Remembering Golub's paintings, I took the daring step of picking up the phone and calling him directly, inviting him to participate in *Fear of Others*. Imagine my pleasure when he responded positively and asked, "Could my wife join as well?" I had no idea that his wife was the feminist artist Nancy Spero. Of course, we were very pleased that such important artists would participate in the exhibition.

The Vancouver Art Gallery had initially rejected our invitation to collaborate, but hearing that these two renowned American artists would be included in the exhibition, did an about-face and hosted one of the panel discussions with both Golub and Spero as guest speakers. The gallery then invited them to exhibit and bought their work. I had become the unwitting midwife in the birth of a love affair between the Vancouver Art Gallery and these artists.

While taking Leon Golub on a tour of the exhibition, he stopped in front of *Out of the Flames* and examined it carefully.

"This is a powerful work," he said. "You should do an extensive series of paintings about the Holocaust!"

I could not, however, follow his suggestion. Painting *Out of the Flames* was an emotionally draining experience that I could not repeat.

Two disappointing footnotes — lessons on the politics of art:

Soon after the exhibition was over, I was in New York and called Leon Golub, hoping to see him again and visit his studio. I was looking forward to this, particularly after his positive comments on my work, the time I spent with him in Vancouver and the opportunity I had created for him at the Vancouver Art Gallery. Instead, he coldly informed me that he was too busy to see me.

I might have understood that he was busy, but the rudeness of his answer made it clear that there was no interest on his part to see me again. There was not even a polite attempt to acknowledge my participation in *Fear of Others*.

The second incident occurred some years later when the two artists were invited to show for the second time at the Vancouver Art Gallery. Golub gave a talk to a packed room saying, among other things: "Each artist has a deep hole within that can never be filled: the need for recognition."

How could he say this? Golub was an artist who had truly 'made it', who had exhibited in the biggest museums in the world and had achieved a great deal of fame. What more did he need? Was this unfulfillable yearning what an artist was all about? And if he understood this, how could he so rudely dismiss artists like me, who admired him and had opened the doors for him in a new city?

At the end of the talk, I went to say hello, but he did not remember me.

C'est la vie! as the French say. Life is a cocktail of joys and sorrows, success and disappointment, ups and downs, light and darkness, happiness and despair — the glass is never empty and its contents always unexpected. It is easy to get drunk when success is the best part of the concoction, as well as experience sadness when disappointment fills the glass.

A few years after the exhibition of *Fear of Others*, I offered *Out of the Flames* as a donation to Yad Vashem, the Holocaust Museum in Jerusalem, thinking that this was where it truly belonged. Half a year later, the painting was accepted for the museum's permanent collection.

Yad Vashem had been established in 1953 as the world centre for documentation, research, education and commemoration of the Holocaust, safeguarding the memory of the past for future generations. Its precursor was the small office in Haifa where I had worked for Tuviah Friedman in 1954.

The very name of the museum comes from Isaiah:

"Even unto them will I give in mine house and within my walls a place and a name [a 'yad vashem', literally a hand and a name] *better than of sons and of daughters: I will give them an everlasting name, that shall not be cut off."*

(Isaiah 56:5)

While visiting Israel in 2008, I called the curator of the Yad Vashem Museum, asking if my painting might ever be exhibited. She replied that the museum had 10,000 works of art in its collection and only if a curator would organize an exhibition with a theme that could include my painting would there be such a possibility. Disappointed, I gave up hope. I should have been more trusting.

One year later, I received an email from Jerusalem asking for more details about my war experiences. The reason? *Out of the Flames* had been chosen to be included in a large exhibition of works by survivor artists, titled *Virtues of Memory: Six Decades of Holocaust Survivors' Creativity*. This was one of the most rewarding moments of my career.

There is nothing closer to fulfilling the commandment "and thou shall tell it to your children" written in the Passover *Haggadah* than this exhibition of works by artists who survived the Nazi inferno and whose personal testimony in graphic form will last forever. The range of the art was staggering, encompassing over 300 works and accompanied by a 660-page catalogue.

I have always been uneasy calling myself a Holocaust survivor, feeling that I was blessed by chance and spared the terrifying ordeals so many others experienced. I needed to know how this important museum, which had included me in an exhibition of survivor artists, defined this term. Asking the curator what the museum's definition of a Holocaust survivor was, she answered, "Any Jew who came out of Europe alive after the war is a survivor."

My unease was resolved.

I truly understood the scope and importance of *Virtues of Memory* only when I walked into the exhibition hall at the opening. This was an awesome display of the power of art as a language unique to human beings and a true manifestation of the human spirit overcoming adversity. In addition, there was much more in this event for me personally. I was moved to tears when I saw the works of my former Bezalel teachers, Jacob Pins, who taught me woodblock printing, and Yehuda Bacon, my etching teacher and an Auschwitz survivor. Not far away, close to the entrance, hung my own work, *Out of the Flames*. It was a humbling and emotional experience to share the space with these artists whom I greatly respected.

Viewing the exhibition, it became obvious that the production of visual memories from the Holocaust had not ceased over 65 years. The earliest work in the show dated from 1945, while the latest was from 2008. Virtues of memory, indeed!

The exhibition of *Virtues of Memory: Six Decades of Holocaust Survivors' Creativity* was extended and ran for a period of eighteen months.

Chapter 52

A Visual Diary

My work reflects my life and my constant search for renewal. Yes, I know. There are artists who find a style they like that sells well and brings them recognition, but this is not my way. For me, repeating a theme without the challenge of new ideas is akin to a slow artistic death — renewal is life. Ever since I heard Werner True's brilliant metaphor about the stone that creates no ripples when thrown into a lake, I have worked in series, exploring new thoughts and ideas until they reach the last ripple — and then move on.

Mirroring my life, my art became my visual diary.

Similar to pages from a diary, each work brings back memories. The small pen-and-ink drawing of beggars and narrow alleys in Jerusalem remind me of my student years at Bezalel. I remember my first lesson in bargaining while staring at the watercolour of the teeming Mahane Yehuda market in Jerusalem, where I stopped by a mountain of green watermelons, some cut in half to reveal vibrant red flesh dotted with black gleaming seeds. My mouth watering, I craved to sink my teeth into the sweet fruit, I asked the price, but it was more than I was prepared to pay. Disappointed, I walked away, but then I heard the vendor shout, "Lady, lady, come back!" I turned around and could not believe my ears when he offered me the same watermelon for almost half the price! No haggling needed. Just walk away and presto! The price comes down.

Early drawings of David, my firstborn, bring back echoes of his childhood and my experiences of new parenthood. Others, done years later in Vancouver, are memories of him as a teenager hooked on the guitar.

The *Childhood Magic* series and our cat Caesar guarding a small sleeping boy bring back thoughts of my younger son, Dan, the inspiration for those drawings.

Dreamskeeper is a memento of the jet-black cat that demanded a place of importance in our house. Caesar was jealous of my habit of making senseless marks on paper. He didn't hesitate to let me know that it was far more important to pay attention to him than engage in this silly activity by jumping on my lap and trying to grab my pen with a quivering paw, to stop me from drawing.

Dreamskeeper
1987 | silkscreen | 16 × 26 in | 40.7 × 66 cm

One day I was reading a story to five-year-old Dan. Leaning against the wall was a framed drawing of Caesar, waiting to be delivered to its new owner. Caesar came in slowly and sat very close to the drawing, looking at me with a piercing gaze that surprised me by its intensity. After a few seconds he walked away, his tail held high, leaving an unmistakable message behind: the glass on the frame was wet.

"There!" he was telling me. "This is what I think of this thing!"

I had never imagined that one day I would live on a continent a world away from Jerusalem and that one of the courses I took at the Bezalel Art School would become relevant in my life as an artist.

Shortly after arriving in Vancouver we went to explore Stanley Park. Stopping at Brockton Point, I saw a breathtaking sight: the very totem poles I had studied under Mordecai Ardon! Chance had brought me to this place and here was the art I had so admired. Neatly stored in the folds of my memory, a few years later these forms would become the inspiration for a new body of mixed-media drawings I called the *West Coast Series*.

The ubiquitous Canada geese flying in formation above the waters of Burrard Inlet symbolized the free spirit of Canada and would become the trigger for the series following *Childhood Magic*. The drawings and prints featuring these birds were more than just a diary of my days in my new home, they had almost become my signature.

I was surprised when someone, noticing the oval designs that appeared in my drawings, observed that I was influenced by West Coast indigenous art. True or not, it was an interesting idea — and so I decided to embark on an entire body of work centered on West Coast imagery.

The years I spent working on this series were some of the most enjoyable of my career. Since my studio was too small to accommodate large paintings, I worked mainly on paper and began more and more to use the triptych and diptych format that allowed for larger works. Captivated by the beauty of British Columbia's lush forests and the poetry of the indigenous mythology, I painted imaginary vistas of nature enclosing the native culture within. My

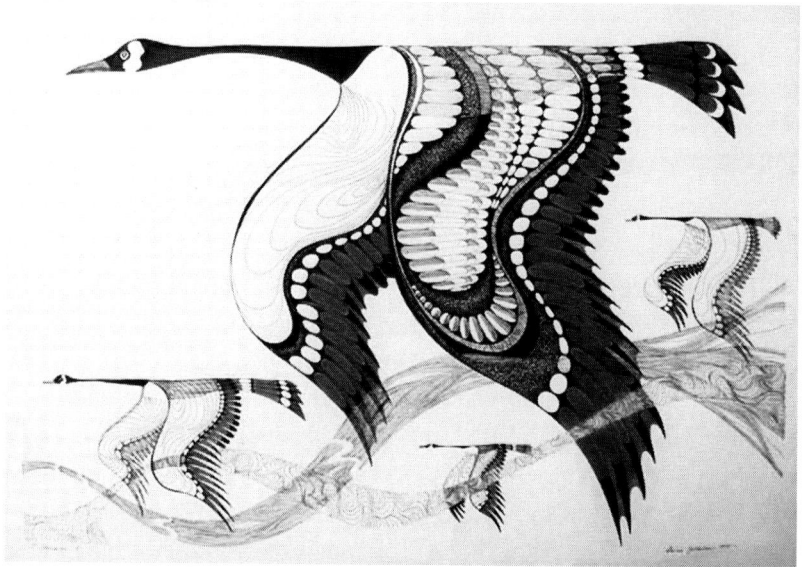

O Canada
1978 | silkscreen | 18 × 26 in | 46.2 × 66 cm

work was well received and my exhibitions at the Bau-Xi gallery almost sold out at the openings. Ideas kept flowing and new works filled my studio.

All was well until the day in 1981 when I received a commission for a diptych similar to one that had been sold. While painting it, I realized that I was just copying my own work rather than creating something new. The excitement of discovery was gone: I was just repeating myself. That brought to an end the *West Coast Series*, although my gallery wanted me to produce more of this work that was selling so well. I simply could not do it. I had to explore new ideas if I wished to call myself an artist.

I had just found out that taking such risks in Vancouver's conservative art market could have unpleasant side effects. Dealers like Ambroise Vollard and Daniel-Henry Kahnweiler, who built the reputations of great artists such as Picasso, Matisse and Braque by vigorously educating the public and promoting their work, were almost non-existent. In those days, Vancouver galleries would hang the works on the walls and little else was done to promote the artists.

269

Over the years, I travelled to Japan, Spain and Mexico. I kept short journals and took many photographs that eventually inspired series of paintings reflecting my travels — visual diaries of the places I visited.

A trip to Japan resulted in *The Kyoto Suite*. The serene stone gardens in that beautiful city connected in my mind with the *Carved Stones* series of British Columbia's Gulf Islands. These highly stylized and peaceful gardens transformed stones into a symbolic presence of beauty, serenity and worship of Nature.

A trip to Spain took me to Granada, where I visited the magical gardens of the Alhambra. The visual delights of brilliant Moorish designs accompanied by the musical sound of flowing fountains created a symphony of colour, peace and harmony that inspired the *Alhambra Series*. In 1993, these paintings were shown at the Richmond Art Gallery in the exhibition *Juxtapositions*.

On a sunny spring day the following year, the Oriental poppies in my garden had burst open, resplendent in the brilliance of their red and salmon pink petals. Yes, they seemed to say, there is darkness in the midst of beauty, but beauty is here as well.

This was when I experienced my second epiphany. The first had been a sudden awareness of the power of stones carved by nature. Now, it was the sheer beauty of flowers that triggered a glimpse of heaven. The concept of an Eden lost forever due to Eve's sin has been enshrined in Western culture by Christianity. But no, I thought. Eden is still here in our lives and in our gardens, if we only care to look. I had found the ephemeral beauty of paradise in the vibrant petals of flowers growing in my garden. *In Search of Eden* was to be my next project.

When I began working on the *Eden* series, I never thought that two major events would literally bring me into a professional paradise.

The first one was when Richmond Art Gallery Director Page Hope-Smith suggested a retrospective of my work. I had already exhibited twice at that gallery, but I was overwhelmed at the scope of such a major project and felt immensely honoured. Page Hope-Smith was one of the last of the kind of curators without the academic degrees required today, who had a true love, understanding and appreciation of art. She valued art for its own merit, without the current prerequisites of political agendas and theoretical conceptual biases. I will be forever grateful to her for trusting in my work.

The exhibition *Pnina Granirer: Celebrating a Life's Work, A Forty Year Retrospective*, encompassed some 120 works, filling the whole gallery space. The show ran from January 15 to February 16, 1998 and was curated by Gregg Simpson, a prolific Vancouver artist and curator.

The second serendipitous event happened when I casually mentioned to Ron Hatch, an old friend and publisher of the local Ronsdale Press, that I planned to publish a small monograph for the retrospective. He pleasantly surprised me by saying that at this stage in my career, a monograph would not be enough. A book would be more appropriate — and he was willing to publish it. This was almost too good to be true. Not only would there be a major retrospective exhibition, there would also be a book to accompany it. The gates of Eden had truly opened for me!

Writer and curator Ted Lindberg was asked to write the text. Following many hours of interviews and discussion, *Pnina Granirer: Portrait of an Artist* was published in 1998, just in time for the opening of the exhibition.

In May 1998, life brought us a priceless gift; our first grandson was born to David and Bea. Now we were blessed with two delightful grandchildren: beautiful, golden-haired Samantha and little red-haired Jonathan. To celebrate his arrival, I painted a large work entitled *Generations*.

In this painting, four generations peer out of windowpanes framed by old-fashioned lace curtains. Photograph transfers of my grandparents and their large brood and of Eddy's grandparents with Eddy's father and his siblings appear in the windows. There are pictures of our young selves holding our two sons and then our sons with their families. Maya, Dan's lovely daughter was introduced later, behind a window left open for the new arrival. And below, greeted by vibrant spring poppies growing in a watery womb, baby

Jonathan arrives into the world. May all our grandchildren find the Eden I have been searching for.

Diaries are witnesses of events experienced and of thoughts and feelings easily forgotten without the words that capture them on the blank pages. Even though painting is "another way of keeping a diary," as Picasso is reputed to have said, in writing the process is inversed. The event itself, an encounter, an observation, a voyage to a new landscape, all these are recorded as they happen. They germinate in the artist's imagination until they are ready to burst into visual form.

In 2009, my husband and I visited Guanajuato, Mexico, where I captured many of the picturesque colonial streets on my digital camera. While downloading the photos into the computer, I realized that I could manipulate these images and create a new and exciting world that presented a view totally different from reality. Transforming conventional photos of these narrow streets into abstract, colourful and impossible landscapes became an exciting exercise in imagination. Working on the computer was new to me, an almost guilty pleasure. Much as I felt that being in the studio and getting my hands dirty with paint was what I wanted to do, this was a new challenge that achieved fast results for an unbridled imagination. I called the series *Imagination Games*.

Most of my work for the past 15–20 years had been figurative. In these digital photographs the figure was absent, as brightly painted colonial houses were transformed into abstract shapes of colour. In the past, I had developed figurative works based on ideas. Now, I let myself be immersed in the pure pleasure and yes, the real fun of playing with form and colour. Escape from real life? A Mexican holiday revisited in this novel kind of diary? Why not? Visual art provides these islands of joy just as music does and we are fortunate if we can all partake in the feast.

Chapter 53

The Dancers' Suite — Hello Again to The Human Figure and Surreal Events

Dance is the hidden language of the soul, of the body.

Martha Graham
interviewed in the *New York Times*

My return to figurative art in the mid 1990s was due to a chance occurrence. When a friend expressed her difficulty with drawing the human figure and asked for help, I suggested the life-drawing sessions at a nearby community centre. As she was too shy to go alone I offered to accompany her — and was hooked again! My love for drawing and the beauty of the human body captured me anew. Young and old, slim and fat, short and tall, male and female bodies filled one sketchbook after another with pencil, charcoal, watercolour and ink drawings. And then, one evening, while attending a performance of Ballet BC, I had a new idea.

On the stage of the Queen Elizabeth Theatre, strong spotlights revealed a group of dancers standing as still as statues. Slowly, dramatically, bodies came to life, exploding into a frenzy of legs, arms, heads leaping, falling, rising. Having worked for so long with sedentary models, I was mesmerized by the grace, the beauty and the ability of the human body to move in space. I had to paint and draw these dancers!

I was happy when I was allowed to photograph the dancers of Ballet BC during rehearsals. The photographs shot in the dance studio over a period of almost ten years, resulted in an extensive number of paintings and drawings titled *The Dancers' Suite*.

As dancers' bodies materialized on spackled canvas painted in rich earthly tones, I realized that dance was one of the oldest forms of human expression — as was drawing. Ever since humanity initiated the rituals that were to ensure its survival, people have swayed and moved to the rhythms of music, using their bodies to appease the gods and express their joys and sorrows, and their drawings on rugged walls deep inside dark caves became the earliest form of visual art. Through *The Dancers' Suite*, I could explore the link between these two non-verbal forms of art: dance and painting.

I watched the young dancers in rehearsal as they twisted into un-natural shapes, forcing their muscles into leaps and movements one would not think the human body was capable of. Their days were long and strenuous, driven by the desire to move gracefully and powerfully. The goal was to appear on stage and dance — then bask in the final, delirious ovation. I admired their determination and willingness to compel their bodies into difficult movements that achieved a sublime beauty. Poorly paid and prone to injury, these young people dedicated their lives to what they loved best: dance.

A very different group became a second source of inspiration: the Kokoro Dancers. *Kokoro*, meaning 'soul' in Japanese, is based on the Butoh 'dance of darkness' that came into being in Japan in the late fifties. This dance style expresses the horrors of war and the misery it inflicts on human beings. The dancers shaved their heads and danced naked, after covering their bodies with a white powder. They moved in slow motion like statues come to life, their gestures expressing the angst of the human condition.

Kokoro's founders Barbara Bourget and Jay Hirabayashi, were friendly and welcoming. I spent many hours photographing their rehearsals and exhibited some of the paintings at the Roundhouse during their International Dance Festival. Arriving at the end of the festival to take down my works, I immediately noticed two empty panels. The paintings were gone — the only proof of their existence was in the lonely nails and the small tags with the titles left on the wall. I had been honoured yet again by art-loving thieves who craved to become art collectors for free.

Eventually a new thought occurred to me: what would it be like to see a life-size drawing of a dancer floating in space with no visible support?

I bought a large roll of clear Mylar and cut it into six-foot sheets. Dipping the brush in black or blue paint, I drew the body of a dancer on each sheet. The drawing had to be simple, with no additional background detail. Spotlights shining above those transparent sheets, hung one behind the other with a space in between, multiplied the figures, creating shadows of the drawings on the wall. I called these works *Floating Dancers*.

Floating Dancers were shown for the first time from August 8 to October 6, 2002 at the Yukon Art Gallery in Whitehorse, as a component of *The Dancers' Suite* exhibition. I was amazed to find such a beautiful and spacious gallery in this small town so far North. Not only was there a thriving arts centre, but also an active, close-knit artistic community of painters, dancers, actors and musicians.

The gallery offered the luxury of a professional installer who hung the works and when I saw the installation I was thrilled beyond words. These paintings, Mylars and painted photographs that had been crammed in my studio, had suddenly acquired a presence and an authority that surprised me. The Mylar panels of *Floating Dancers*, alternating between the paintings and moving gently with the air currents, gave the impression of the dancers having stepped out of the canvas and dancing freely along the walls.

Before sending the works to Whitehorse, I had wondered how interesting it could be if a live dancer moved inside the Mylar sheets, becoming a living component of the visual work. I called the Yukon Art Gallery asking whether there were any dancers in Whitehorse and they mentioned Gail Lotenberg, founder of LINK Dance. When I invited her to collaborate with me on this project, she readily accepted.

At the opening, as the public waited patiently for the show to begin, Gail and her partner Bodra Aliyah, slowly approached the

Floating Dancers. At the precise moment they entered the space between the two transparent sheets, there was a gasp from the audience. By adding their movements to the drawn figures, they had become an integral part of the art. The *Floating Dancers* was exhibited again at the Seymour Art Gallery in North Vancouver, at the Burnaby Art Gallery and at the Sidney and Gertrude Zack Gallery in Vancouver during the Chutzpah! Festival. For those exhibitions, the sheets of Mylar were hung from the ceiling, giving the eerie impression of drawings floating in space. For a special performance at the Burnaby Art Gallery, dancer Cori Caulfield gracefully moved among these ephemeral dancers, following their movements with her own, to the eerie sound of the musical saw played by Andrea Minden.

I rarely discussed my art with our friends. When I first worked as an illustrator in Jerusalem, it was the paid work that gave me status.

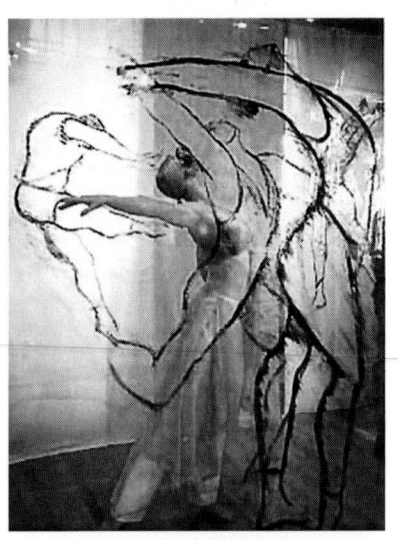

Cori Caulfield with *Floating Dancers* at Burnaby Art Gallery

After arriving in Urbana, Illinois, making art for its own sake became just 'nice'. Only later, when my work began to be exhibited and reviewed, did my friends take it more seriously.

The shift occurred one day in Urbana when a short question from an acquaintance changed the perception of my self-worth as an artist.

"May I buy this drawing?"

Someone wanted to live with my work and was willing to pay for it! This was the moment I knew that my work was more than just 'nice' and gave me an insight into the importance of money. By putting a price tag on a painting, a 'nice hobby' becomes a respected profession.

I have never received support from 'important' people in my journey as an artist. When opportunities arose to develop relationships with persons of influence, I would freeze, feeling awkward and intimidated, aware of the importance of cultivating this or that particular contact who could help my career. I learned that in the art world, talent and hard work were not enough. Politics and connections counted sometimes more than the quality of the art itself. Making a career in the arts requires a thick skin and a willingness to accept rejection.

Then, when I least expected, serendipity visited me again.

In 1992, Gregg Simpson, who paints huge abstract paintings and has a heart of gold, invited me to participate in a group exhibition at the Gallery Alpha in West Vancouver. Early in his career, Gregg had been involved with a number of Surrealist artists and had established connections with some of them in Europe. I should add that, although many artists use Surrealist imagery and Surrealism is thriving in Europe and South America, Vancouver is chillingly hostile to it.

Gregg extended an invitation to me again in 2005, this time to participate in an exhibition at the Museo Fundación Eugenio Granell, the only museum in the world dedicated to Surrealist art, located in Santiago de Compostela, Spain. The exhibition was titled *Surrealismo Costa Oeste: Una Perspectiva Desde Canada* and included Martin Guderna, Gordon Payne and Gregg Simpson. I had never considered myself a pure Surrealist, but there were many Surrealist elements in my works, including the decalcomania technique, and I was happy to be included. This exhibition brought me to the attention of the Surrealist artists and curators in Europe and in South America, resulting in more invitations to international exhibitions in Coimbra, Portugal, Santiago, Chile and Costa Rica. I owe Gregg this connection with an art world that I had been unaware of. Some of my works are now in the permanent collections of the Museo Fundación Eugenio Granell in Spain, the Museo Nacional de Bellas Artes de Chile, and the Fundación Camaleonart in Costa Rica.

I discovered that the Surrealist artists and curators were a warm and welcoming crowd, friendly, supportive and respectful and appreciative of one another.

Thank you, Gregg, for introducing me to this world!

Chapter 54

The Lonely Path

If art is to nourish the roots of our culture, society must set the artist free to follow his vision wherever it takes him.

John F. Kennedy
remarks at Amherst College, October 26, 1963

The world would have been a better place for artists had the art establishment paid attention to John F. Kennedy's words. Humans being what they are, the herd instinct becomes evident even in the arts, shunning creators who do not follow fashionable trends. The politics of 'if you're not doing what we do, you're out!' have marginalized many artists who were not interested in theories prescribed by critics, trends and academics, preferring to follow their own vision. This is nothing new — the outright rejection of Gauguin by the Impressionist artists of his time is well known. As for myself, I had no interest in trends and no ambitions as lofty as the Turner Prize. All I wanted was to create images that felt right for me and would hopefully communicate with and touch others.

In hindsight, I understand my art practices better. Was it the memory of Mother Alfonsa tearing up the portrait I had so lovingly offered her that kept me from painting portraits? Could my total lack of interest in Op Art be due to its association in my mind with the detailed sketches for commercial posters done at the Bezalel Art School? And why was abstraction leaving me unfulfilled, needing more than just paint on canvas? Was my training in drawing and figurative art an obstacle for following fashionable new trends or was it my interest in more universal ideas?

Whatever the reason, I chose to create my own visual world instead of being part of the herd. Having lived through the oppressive totalitarian régimes of fascism and communism, I have a deep mistrust of official policies, particularly in art. The strict imposition of social realism under both these systems is an example of the destructive effect of enforced rules. Art is at its strongest when addressing universal issues. The inane slogan 'beauty is dead!' that opened the floodgates to an avalanche of coarseness and revolting ugliness only compelled me to use as much beauty as I could. Art as journalism, discussing and highlighting current affairs, does not interest me. Early in my career, I decided to follow my own course regardless of the cost.

I did not care about the pedantic theories that turned art into a dry, theoretical academic discourse. The rampant genuflections of the tsars of art criticism toward socio-critical theories repelled me. Sadly, I realized that being different was not considered an asset, but a liability. There is lavish praise and great success in today's art world for artists who follow the trends, using items of shock value such as bodily fluids, garbage and ugliness — the list is a long one.

Examples abound, particularly among the winners of London's Turner Prize. *My Bed*, a work by a British artist consisting of her bed covered in dirty sheets, bloodstained underwear, discarded condoms and empty bottles, became a sensation described as an 'unconventional self-portrait' — and sold for £2.54 million! I still think that the untidy bed of our Jerusalem landlord would have been much more deserving of that prize . . .

The famous shark in formaldehyde, *The Physical Impossibility of Death in the Mind of Someone Living*, by another British artist, featuring a 13-foot tiger shark in a glass tank of formaldehyde, was extolled by curators and museum directors, as well as by art critics, and described as 'seminal'.

Only a few sane voices, such as writers and art critics Tom Wolfe and Robert Hughes, dared to call out, "The Emperor is naked!"

Chapter 55

I Can't Believe I'm Eighty!

Today, let us make haste to enjoy life. Who knows if we will be tomorrow?

Jean Racine
Athalie

On April 11, 2015, I turned eighty years old — but I don't feel the connection between this ominous number and myself. Eighty? I can't believe it!

Believe it or not, it is true. Numbers have a way of solidly anchoring life — they frame the days, the years and the decades in a rigid structure, a window through which we watch our lives fleeting by. Even so, as Hans Christian Andersen says, "there's plenty of time to be dead!" — instead of setting our sights on the final exit, we should enjoy the view from the window.

Special milestones require special celebrations. Not only was it my eightieth birthday, it was also the fiftieth year since I arrived in Canada with my family. This second milestone needed to be celebrated in style. Both anniversaries would highlight the thread that has stitched my life together into the quilt that has warmed and sustained me day after day and year after year: my art.

As a faithful serendipity worshipper I was not surprised when a brilliant idea occurred to me: for this birthday, I would forego any gifts. Instead, I would be the one to offer gifts to my friends and collectors and I would do this in an unusual way.

From my long experience with art galleries I was only too familiar with the way that business worked. Established galleries usually charge the artist a 50% commission for each work sold in exchange for space and promotion. Why not invite the public to become my gallery for ten days and offer the commission to my collectors instead? As my gallery, they would be able buy my works for half the price while I would receive the customary 50%.

Everything worked out well. I rented a gallery space where the works were hung as a survey, with an appropriate title: *Timelines*. The following weekend, I opened my studio during the yearly Open Studios of *Artists in our Midst*, the very first art walk in the city, which I initiated in 1993 with my friend Anne Adams. Over the years, this event has inspired many other artists to open their studios in various neighbourhoods, creating an awareness of the importance of art in people's lives.

Planning for this celebration was all consuming. I felt alive, happy and full of energy. Following this show, I would dedicate all my time to writing.

People flocked to the exhibition and red stickers bloomed like poppies in spring. Beatrice, my wonderful daughter-in-law, took care of the business side, busily writing receipts. She was so excited about the response to the show that she kept telling me to do this again, soon.

Two days before the show ended, Yolaine Mottet of Radio-Canada, the local French-language radio station, who has known me for years, responded to my press release and interviewed me. She arrived with a cameraman and did an interview that I later sent around to all my friends. The response was overwhelming.

The weekend in my studio was just as lively. I was touched by the remarks about my work, by the keen interest in the paintings and by the feeling of excitement that filled the air. A few small drawings from my student years in Jerusalem were bought, along with other large works. The dates did not matter — art is forever! A 1964 painting of Lulu Belle done in Urbana, Illinois, leaning against the wall behind other paintings, was pulled out and adopted with great enthusiasm. Some people couldn't resist the bargains and bought two, three or even more works. Beatrice could barely keep up with writing receipts for the eager art collectors.

During these ten days new thoughts entered my mind like red flags fluttering in the brain. What does art mean to people who are not moving in the stratosphere of wealth, prestige and art auctions where grotesque amounts of money are spent? What was more important to me as an artist: fame and having my work bought as an investment, sold and re-sold like stocks, or seeing people genuinely falling in love with a work of art?

Yes, I won't deny that recognition is extremely important and all artists crave it, as Leon Golub so forcefully said. On the other hand, meeting someone who loves a painting and wishes to live with it, who wants to learn the details of its creation and is convinced that owning it will enrich his or her life, is the most rewarding experience for an artist. Another red flag had 'sale' and 'bargain' written on it. Was I doing the right thing by offering this large discount? Did this not devalue my work? Was I trying to prove a point about the large fees charged by galleries that inflate the price of art?

Then I stopped asking myself these questions. I realized that reaching the ripe old age of eighty had liberated me — I did not care anymore about the conventions of the art world and I did not feel the need to fight for acceptance and recognition. I was free to do what I pleased and write my own rules. The hard, difficult work of the artist trying to build a career was behind me. What a relief!

Sunday afternoon was drawing to a close and there were still people coming and buying. We were exhausted, exhilarated, happy and tired. It was a memorable event.

Chapter 56

Full Circle

Two days after the exhibition and sale, we are on our way to Romania.

The plane rises smoothly and I settle into the narrow seat on which a pillow and a plastic-wrapped blanket remind me that this will be a very long flight. From Vancouver to Munich and then on to Bucharest. Yes, it is truly happening: Eddy and I are on our way back to Romania. The distance of time is much greater than the tedious hours of the long flight — the sixty-five years that have passed since we left Romania have gone by like a flash and now we are returning to the country of our birth.

Our first stop will be Bucharest, where Eddy spent his childhood from the age of six. Now he is eagerly looking forward to seeing his old home on Calea Moșilor.

And me? Thinking of the beautiful image of my old house in Brăila printed from Google Earth, I can't wait to see it again. On my computer screen it looked exactly as I remembered it: an elegant one-storey stone building wrapped around the corner where two streets met. What shall I find?

After four nights in Bucharest, we boarded the bus to Brăila. It was a long four-hour ride with a stop for refreshments. The bus rolled through endless fields of corn and small decrepit villages. Strangely, we saw pumping oil derricks here and there, a bizarre and puzzling sight among expanses of corn and potatoes.

It was very warm. The sun was steadily baking the monotonous landscape in relentless and stifling heat. Here and there, passing through small villages, I saw church spires topped with the ubiquitous Orthodox cross. After the ousting of Ceauşescu, the Communist dictator, in what people now refer to as 'the Revolution', religion has returned to Romania in full force. The efforts of the Communist dictatorship to erase the old beliefs with terror have come to naught.

We finally arrived in Brăila and were dropped off in front of a large Orthodox Cathedral. We weren't sure where to go when a flurry of taxicabs arrived. We climbed into one after the driver practically grabbed our luggage and told us to get in.

Riding taxicabs is amazingly cheap in Romania, just slightly more expensive than riding the bus in Vancouver. In about ten minutes, we arrived at our small hotel on the corner of Strada Goleşti and knocked at the door. A woman wearing an apron arrived smiling profusely and told us that, today being Sunday, the owners had gone to the park with the children and would soon return.

I glanced across the street and my heart skipped a beat. There, just a few steps away, was the house where I had spent nine years of my youth! In the few seconds that unfolded in slow motion, I noticed the changes that did not show on the Google Earth photograph: crumbling stone, basement windows that weren't previously there, a metal ladder in the corner leading — where? What I saw was different from the smooth, crisp image downloaded from my computer. I turned my head and walked into the hotel lobby with a heavy heart. I decided I would wait an hour or so. I was not quite ready for the reality that awaited me after sixty-five years across time . . .

THE HOUSE — A REQUIEM

An hour later, I stood on Strada Goleşti at the back corner of my old house. From a distance and through narrowed eyes, the details disappeared and the massive building seemed to be as I remembered it, but when I opened my eyes, I saw the ornate stonework with its elegant rows of short columns, fluted protrusions and arch-like indentations, crumbling away. This building of elegance and grace was now pitted with holes, reminding me of a pear, once beautiful and smooth, now overripe and covered with unsightly spots of decay.

Plunked on the sidewalk, an ugly brown steel ladder with a small platform stood next to the corner wall, into which a door had been inserted.

As I stared at the unfamiliar sight, an older, overweight man wearing a sleeveless undershirt stretched tight over a bulging stomach came out. I told him that I lived in this house a long time ago. He asked me if we had owned the place and seemed relieved to hear that we had not.

This question was repeated time and again by people who lived in the house now and who feared that the original owners might come to claim their old properties confiscated by the Communists.

"A *jidan* used to live in the basement at one time. Did you know him?" the man asked.

I shuddered. This derogatory word describing Jews brought back unpleasant memories. It has become a part of the language, like *Tzigan*, meaning 'Gypsy', or any other reflection of prejudice and hatred — and is still in use.

I noticed that a few of the decorative stone panels had been cut out and windows installed in their place for new basement suites. Uneven green mould had spread on the carved base of the house like a careless paint job. The original pavement stones on the street were now bulging in places as if afflicted by a cancerous skin disease, many of them broken or missing. The roots of the long-gone acacia trees that had once spread their leafy canopies and heavenly perfume over the sidewalk had pushed the smooth ornamental pavement stones upwards into tortured shapes. One had to be careful walking here — it would be easy to twist one's ankle and fall.

I turned the corner towards the main entrance on the Grădina Publică, the public garden where I had spent many happy hours playing on the grass and luring snails out of their shells with a song. Yes, the garden was still there — the same wrought-iron fence, trees and cobblestone sidewalk. The street was clogged with cars parked everywhere on the sidewalk and on the road, like shiny beetles swarming the pavement. It was Sunday and everyone was heading to the park to escape the heat.

As I neared the entrance to the house, I saw a couple getting out of a car and walking towards the wrought-iron gate. I approached, explaining why I was there. At first, they were suspicious and asked me the ubiquitous question — did we own the house? No, I told them, we had only rented it from a Greek woman, Madame Litzika. They visibly relaxed and invited us in.

I hoped that my pleasant smile hid the turmoil within. Was this really happening? The past came rushing in: images, feelings, memories, sounds, words and more memories. Then the gate opened and I stepped into the courtyard. For a short second, I felt disoriented and confused. This was not the place I remembered. Could this be the large yard with flowering irises encircling a roundabout in its centre? Where were the white and red climbing roses thickly covering the neighbour's wall? Decrepit wooden shacks lined the yard now; some trees had been planted and the place looked like a neglected country place. My camera could not show this squalid reality. The lens erased the holes and the dirt on the rotting shacks and hid the prevalent sense of decay.

The man and his wife, both in their mid-forties, invited me into their flat. There were now seven families living in the house, they told me and they asked how many people lived in the house when I was young.

"Just my family," I said, "and I was an only child."

I could see the shock on their faces. The man told us that he worked in the business of marketing natural Romanian teas, mostly from the ubiquitous and fragrant linden trees. He seemed to know more about the history of the Romanian Jews than I had expected and was familiar with the selling of the Jews that enabled so many of us to leave Romania for Israel, filling the country's empty coffers with foreign currency.

In a daze, I walked under the window of my old room to the main entrance. The five marble steps leading to the front door with the ornate sandblasted glass designs were cracked, sadly and silently whispering of their days of glory. The front doors were still there, but now a new coat of brown paint cheapened their look. A large coil of electric wires hung on one side of the door and two blue-handled mops dangled on the other.

I paused slightly.

Did I really want to see what was behind this door?

We entered the vestibule — once the abode of our tall bronze Aphrodite. I imagined my cousin Gabi and myself standing at the door, handing programs to the guests arriving for our special performance. *Come in, the show will begin shortly!*

My family at the front entrance (1947–48)

Silence. In the shabby looking vestibule now shared by two families, a table and two chairs were set on one side and a door I did not remember on the other. The old shiny wooden floor had been covered in cheap brown vinyl and the ceiling had been dropped, conveying a cramped look.

My hosts kindly invited me into their apartment through the door that had not been there before. Eerily, it was exactly where my room and my parents' bedroom used to be. Though I did not recognize it, I was amazed at the coincidence. Rather than encountering some other tenants, serendipity had made it possible for me to meet this hospitable couple who offered me the unexpected opportunity to revisit the very rooms where I grew up, although everything was changed. Walls painted in dark blues and greens had been erected, transforming the rooms into small cramped spaces. A kitchen now occupied a corner of my parents' bedroom and only the two tall windows with the wooden shutters facing the park across the street were the same as before. Proudly, my hosts showed me the 'original' ornate brass door handles, left intact only in their apartment.

I walked into the next space: my room! Apart from the old light green tile stove built in a corner (used now for gas instead of wood), I didn't recognize a thing. The couple's sons lived in the midst of the usual mess teenagers thrive on and the room seemed much smaller. I tried to imagine my carved wooden desk in the corner and the green wardrobe along the wall. Was coming here a good idea or should I have kept the old memories of what used to be?

Our host was talkative and friendly. He said that everyone was unhappy with the rampant corruption in the country, which paralyzed any progress or development. I would have liked to talk with him longer, but didn't want to intrude more than I already had, so I took my leave.

Chapter 57

Serendipity

The heroes were always making discoveries, by accidents and sagacity, of things they were not in quest of.

Horace Walpole
in a letter to a friend about the fairy tale
The Three Princes of Serendip

Had I a magic lamp to convey a helpful genie who could grant me three wishes, these are the ones I would have asked for:

1. To visit my childhood home
2. To find someone who remembered me
3. To find someone who knew my family

But I had no lamp and no genie to assist me. However, there was something else that I had come to trust over the years: serendipity. Serendipity — or luck — protected my family during the war, helped me get my art education and finally brought me to one of the best places on earth: Vancouver. And over the years, when I feared that I had used all the winning cards in my deck of creative ideas and would be sentenced to the wilderness of a life without art, unexpected fresh insights would always occur.

Serendipity had granted my first wish on the very first day. Not only had I seen my old house, I had also met the people who lived exactly where my room used to be and they had invited me in. Had I arrived a few minutes later, I would have missed them. Would I have dared to walk up and knock at their door?

Before leaving for Romania I had unsuccessfully attempted to find information about the remaining Jewish community in Brăila. Now that I was there, I tried calling the president of the Jewish community, but to no avail and my hope of finding anyone from the community collapsed. I gave up.

It was a holiday, the Day of the Child. The streets were almost deserted in the heat of the morning as I walked towards the Piaţa Traian, the city square we used to call the 'little garden'.

How small the town looked to me now! The French-style ornate buildings surrounding the park, their tall windows overhung by triangular or rounded lintels were the same as before. I noticed long banners hanging on the building that was the city's history museum, announcing an exhibition of the history of minorities in Brăila. The museum was closed that day and, as I peered through the window, a woman dressed in a blue smock and carrying a broom opened the door and said that it would be open tomorrow. She could not help me with any information about the Jewish community although the exhibition dealt with multicultural minorities — of which there were many: Turkish, Greek, Armenian, Roma, Jewish, and more. We chatted for a few minutes. Like other people I talked with, she complained bitterly about the corruption and the unemployment and told me that life was better under Ceauşescu, the Communist dictator, and that belonging to the European Union was bad for the country's economy. It was the second time I had heard such an opinion. For working-class people, the Communist régime had been preferable, offering secure employment and housing confiscated from the bourgeoisie.

I crossed the street into the little garden, where a carpet of flowers led to the well-remembered statue of Emperor Trajan. There was his bust, atop a white stone column. I remembered the history lessons about the Roman legacy in Romania, the conquest of the early Dacians, the introduction of Latin and the bloody wars and rebellions.

I continued towards the Strada Regală, where we used to walk up and down the sidewalks on Sundays, boys on one side, girls on the other, ogling one another and letting the gossip fly wild. I didn't recognize the street. Its name had been changed to Mihai Eminescu, one of the best-known Romanian poets, even though on the historical landmark sign, it was still called the Strada Regală.

The leafy, tall acacia trees I knew had been replaced by young trees and the street looked smaller. The wide side-

Emperor Trajan monument

walks were still there, but the road had become a pedestrian area with some outdoor restaurants set in the middle. A few of the buildings had been restored, while others were falling apart. One large boarded-up building was covered with graffiti in the same universal style one sees all over the world. I didn't recognize a thing.

Walking along, I stopped to read an historical monument sign. The words jumped out at me: "Temple Coral built in 1862". Could this have been the synagogue that my grandfather used to frequent during the High Holidays? I followed the arrow indicating the location of the temple on a side street paved with cobblestones and narrow sidewalks clogged with cars — and there it was!

Historical sign

Temple Coral

The white wrought-iron gate decorated with Stars of David was closed. With trepidation, I tried the handle — and it opened. What was waiting for me behind this gate? The place looked deserted and eerily quiet. I followed the narrow passage to the back of the building and saw another gate. Opening it, I took a few steps into a small courtyard when I heard voices coming through an open door. A group of elderly people was sitting around a table laden with food, drinks and books. Surprised, they looked up as I stood in the doorway.

I felt as if I was in the midst of a Fellini film where bizarre events occur and impossible situations take place without warning. Reality became fantasy and fantasy became real. Words tumbled out of my mouth like marbles spilling out of a bag as I told them who I was, how I had returned to the city after a sixty-five-year absence, where I had lived, who my family had been. This was their study session, they said and asked me to join them, offering me tea and cakes and showering me with questions. I noticed a small woman, her grey hair cut short, staring intently at me. She asked again what my name was and I told her my birth name: Paula Solomon.

Her face drew a blank. I told them that my father had changed the family name to 'Savin' during the time of the Communists and that now my name was Pnina Granirer. I realized that I had a problem with too many different names tied in a complicated knot.

"Yes, yes," the woman said, "but what did they call you?"

"I had a nickname," I answered. "It was 'Puica'."

The woman jumped up, her face aglow, an ecstatic smile on her face.

"Puica!" she shouted. "We were together in Gordonia! I am Marcela Kalman!"

The moment she said her name, it was as if a mask fell off her face and I saw her, young again with jet-black hair and glasses, standing next to me during the flag ceremony at Gordonia, the Jewish youth organization. She ran to me with outstretched arms and we hugged and laughed and giggled like two silly school-girls, while everybody around laughed with us.

Marcela and I in Brăila, 2015

My second wish had been granted: I had found someone who remembered me.

During this time, the vice-president of the Jewish community was speaking excitedly on her cellphone to her 87-year-old mother, who said that she had known my mother as a friend and would like

Marcela first on the right, Gabi behind her and myself fourth from the right. with a group of friends from Gordonia, 1950

to speak to me. The voice coming out of the small device sounded younger than expected, telling me that she had loved my mother and had known her well. Her name is Marcela Dermer. We set up a time for a visit the next day.

My old childhood friend Marcela Kalman-Goldenberg offered to show me Gabi's old house on the Cuza Boulevard and we walked off together along the old Strada Regală until we reached the boulevard. Across the street, a couple of buildings looked vaguely familiar. I recognized the Cinema Trianon, where Gabi and I used to spend Sunday afternoons watching two movies in repertory with the coins Grandma had given us. Next to it, separated by the same dirty lane from which long ago a scary man had emerged dangling his penis, was the Gordonia building where Marcela and I met.

Gabi's house was unrecognizable. The heavy gate was still there, now tightly locked. The wrought-iron balconies on the second-floor windows, where we used to sit and watch the entertaining and colourful funeral processions on the boulevard below, were gone. The sad transformation of Gabi's house left a void that echoed emptily through a severed past. Despite finding my old house in such a bad state of repair, at least it looked much the same as in the past. The thread connecting my childhood memories with the present had frayed, but it still existed.

THE THIRD WISH

Aurelia, Marcela Dermer's friend and caregiver, drove me to Marcela's apartment. On the way, the streets became a blur of houses with cars whizzing by and trees lining broken sidewalks. Somewhere, very soon, I would meet an unknown woman who would open a box of memories from a long gone past. Fate was about to offer me an unexpected gift.

We arrived at a large apartment complex built during the Communist era. These sad, grey concrete buildings, ugly monsters of cold and unfriendly mien, looked more like prisons than homes. The lobby was dark — one would never guess that the sun was shining brightly outside. We took the tiny elevator to the fourth floor and Aurelia rang the bell. A small woman with short silvery hair, a twinkle in her eyes and a beaming smile lighting up her round face opened the door. She wore a dress with white flowers printed on a black background and walked with difficulty. Marcela was eighty-seven years old, but her face was smooth and young.

She hugged me with great warmth and invited me to sit at a round table in the kitchen. The apartment she shared with her widowed daughter reminded me of similar places in Israel in the 50s and 60s, comfortable and old-fashioned.

This is Marcela's story:

Marcela was born in 1927 to a Jewish family of modest means. During the war her father had been sent to a labour camp and the family had struggled to make

Marcela Dermer and I, 2015

ends meet. After studying at the same Scheffer Elementary Jewish School that I went to in second grade, she had gone to the Industrial Lyceum, a school specializing in art and design. During the war, public schools were forbidden to Jewish children — she had completed her studies only due to a supportive teacher who realized that two of her Jewish students were gifted and took a personal risk by letting them stay. The drawing class had been her favourite and soon she was copying fashion designs from French magazines and changing them according to her taste, creating new ideas.

When she was seventeen — I could not believe my ears — Marcela began selling her designs to a seamstress whose name was Madame Feinstein. Madame Feinstein? This was our very own family seamstress! As Marcela spoke, I saw again the large atelier where I had spent many uncomfortable hours standing still while Madame Feinstein, her mouth full of pins, tried a dress on me, adjusting here, pulling there for what seemed like an eternity.

Eventually, Marcela learned to try dresses on clients and began earning more money to help her family. It was in Madame Feinstein's kingdom that she had met my mother, who had befriended her, impressed by her imagination and beautiful designs.

"I remember you sitting on a little chair when I came to your house," she said. "I loved Carola. She was kind and friendly and so was your father."

I never imagined that I would meet someone who knew my mother and some of my family. I must have met Marcela in the past, but my memory failed me, while hers was as sharp as the pencil that created her fashion designs.

Marcela opened a flood of memories that rang true. It was as if she had been waiting sixty-five years in that drab, dark concrete building for the moment when time and serendipity would bring us together so she could offer me this bright bouquet of mementoes about my family.

Marcela told me a story about my mother that I had never heard before. After the war, many women had a hard time eking out a living. Carola came up with the idea of collecting used clothes and teaching women to restore and then sell them through the cooperative store where my father worked as a board member. This enabled some of the women to support themselves. Little did she know that one day, in Israel, she would do similar work for a living!

Marcela had never left Brăila. She had developed a successful career as the director of the House of Fashion and worked for the cooperative of popular arts, winning awards and invitations to Moscow. Elena Ceaușescu, the infamous dictator's wife, had been in charge of these co-ops. Some of the expensive dresses gifted to Madame Ceaușescu for her lavish birthday parties were tried on her by Marcela.

Soon enough, it was time to go. Reluctantly, I said goodbye. We hugged and kissed and hugged and kissed again. I had forgotten how warm and loving Romanians were!

The third and last wish had come true: I had found someone who knew my family.

My childhood memories had come full circle.

Chapter 58

Wake-Up Call

Would it hurt to die?

J.K. Rowling
Harry Potter and the Deathly Hallows

On July 20, 2015, I find myself in the Emergency Unit at the Vancouver General Hospital.

I try to ignore the pain tearing my stomach apart while waiting to be seen by a doctor. How can this be? Only last night we went out to dinner with friends. Was it something I ate? I am lying on a gurney while being wheeled around for tests. A few young doctors speak to me about something dire called diverticulitis. What exactly is it? Two days go by, but I lose track of time.

"You are going to surgery now. Don't worry," they say.

I attempt to be cheerful as I am wheeled to the elevator and down a long hallway.

"Look, there is my painting!" I exclaim.

The orderlies and the nurse stop and admire the large canvas I have donated to the hospital's art collection. It is titled *Definition of Eden*. At least this is real, I think.

And then — nothing.

I am lying in bed in Intensive Care, connected to a monitoring unit with tubes coming from everywhere in my body. My mind is a blank. I am thirsty but not allowed to drink, only to moisten my parched lips. Then I am on a gurney again. Back to the operating room — a second surgery.

I wake up for the second time in the IC unit. There are only four beds and a nursing station in the centre of the room, with two nurses on duty. The care provided to the patients by the gentle and competent nurses is outstanding. I am floating somewhere in a realm never visited before, where nothing matters except breathing, but breathing is difficult. There is a clock on the wall opposite my bed — I need to see it, need to know the time to make the day real. I beg the nurse to leave the curtains open.

Days go by. My family comes to see me, but I must be a terrible sight — the look in their eyes . . . I try to hold on to the lifeline of their love and concern for me despite a sense of utter and overwhelming loneliness. Their love and caring presence sustains me. I have a strange feeling of detachment, as if this is not happening to me. I watch the nurses efficiently move through their long shifts and let myself be nurtured like a helpless baby.

Very slowly, my body begins to recover. Day by day, I get stronger until finally I am allowed to eat and drink. Eddy brings *Pnina Granirer: Portrait of an Artist* and shows it to the nurses, who are interested and excited. At least now, I am not just a battered body hovering between two worlds. I have regained my identity as a painter.

After sixteen days in the hospital, it was time to go home. I had been close to the land of no return and life would never be the same for me. The words I wrote in the introduction to this book have acquired an ominous meaning:

"Suddenly, alarmingly, the future is but a short path ahead, while the past casts its long shadow behind. Simple words like 'later', 'next year', 'tomorrow', 'not now', become risky, unsure and speculative. Words such as 'now' acquire a gravitas not considered before."

A few months after my brush with eternity, I was getting stronger but could not shake the sensation of fragility and finality of life. I had been lucky to emerge from the shadows back into the light. I counted my blessings and told myself how much worse it could have been. What if it had happened while I was in Romania?

It may take dramatic events such as the one I had just experienced to bring long held thoughts into focus. Remembering the words of Pat Martin Bates and Judy Chicago about the obstacles posed to the career of a woman artist by having a family, I realized that while they might have been right in that respect, they were totally wrong to negate the human element of the family's importance in the artist's personal life. My caring and supportive husband Eddy, who is still working on his math, David, my oldest son and his wife Beatrice, Dan, my youngest son and my beloved grandchildren Samantha, Jonathan and Maya have always been in the forefront of my thoughts and a source of inspiration for my art.

From a guitar-playing teenager with uncouth humour, David has morphed into a fine stand-up comedian. With his *Stand Up for Mental Health* organization, David has turned his own difficult experience with depression into an inspiring creative endeavour. He is teaching people with mental health issues to perform comedy on stage, which helps them do away with the stigma associated with their kind of illness. *His Stand Up for Mental Health* program is reaching people across Canada, the US and Australia, empowering those who are ignored and marginalized by society.

Dan, who much to my delight is an avid art lover, graduated from Harvard and then received a PhD in Political Economy from Princeton University. After spending many years in New York successfully working in the financial sector, he returned to Vancouver and is now, after a long, drawn-out divorce, a half time single parent to Maya. I am blessed to have them all here; my life would have been empty without their presence.

Both Eddy and I have seen our parents move to Vancouver and pass away, leaving our family smaller and more precious than ever.

I was lucky again when, only one month following my two surgeries, my doctor gave me the green light to go on a trip to

Alaska in celebration of our 61st wedding anniversary. Not bad! The two youngsters who had embarked on a lifetime journey with empty pockets full of dreams were still together! And topping Eddy's mathematical achievements and my modest success in making art, the best masterpiece of all was there to celebrate with us: our two sons and their families.

Despite the harrowing experience of my surgeries, there were things to be done that reminded me that there was much I could still look forward to. Two exhibitions were on the agenda: an international show in Costa Rica in March and an exhibition next year at the Museo Granell in Santiago de Compostela, Spain. Works had to be chosen, lists had to be made, shipping to be organized. I was very much alive indeed! Now that I understood how easily the thread of life might be severed, I felt the urgency to finish this memoir. I hurried through the busy work of organizing my paintings — other chores would have to wait.

There is so much in my life that I am thankful for. My fairy godmother has not let me down and serendipity has been a faithful companion.

But for now — writing comes first.

My painting with words is waiting for the last brushstrokes.

Hanukkah dinner at our house, 2016. From left to right: Maya, Dan, Samantha, myself, Eddy, David, Bea, Jonathan

Fountains
1992 | triptych | mixed media on paper | 3× 40 x 30 in | 3× 101.6 x 76 cm
Collection of the Segal Centre for Mental Health, Vancouver, BC

Sand Garden
1991 | mixed media on paper | 30 x 40 in | 76 x 101.5 cm
Kyoto Suite

Definition of Eden
1994 | mixed media on canvas | 48 x 60 in | 122 x 152.5 cm
Collection of the Vancouver Jewish Community Centre

Gift of Laughter
1995 | mixed media on canvas | 48 x 36 in | 122 x 91.5 cm
Private Collection

Apex
2001 | mixed media on canvas | 36 x 48 in | 91.5 x 122 cm
Collection of Laurie and Bob Molday

Blue Dreams
2004 | mixed media on canvas | 20 x 24 in | 51 x 61 cm

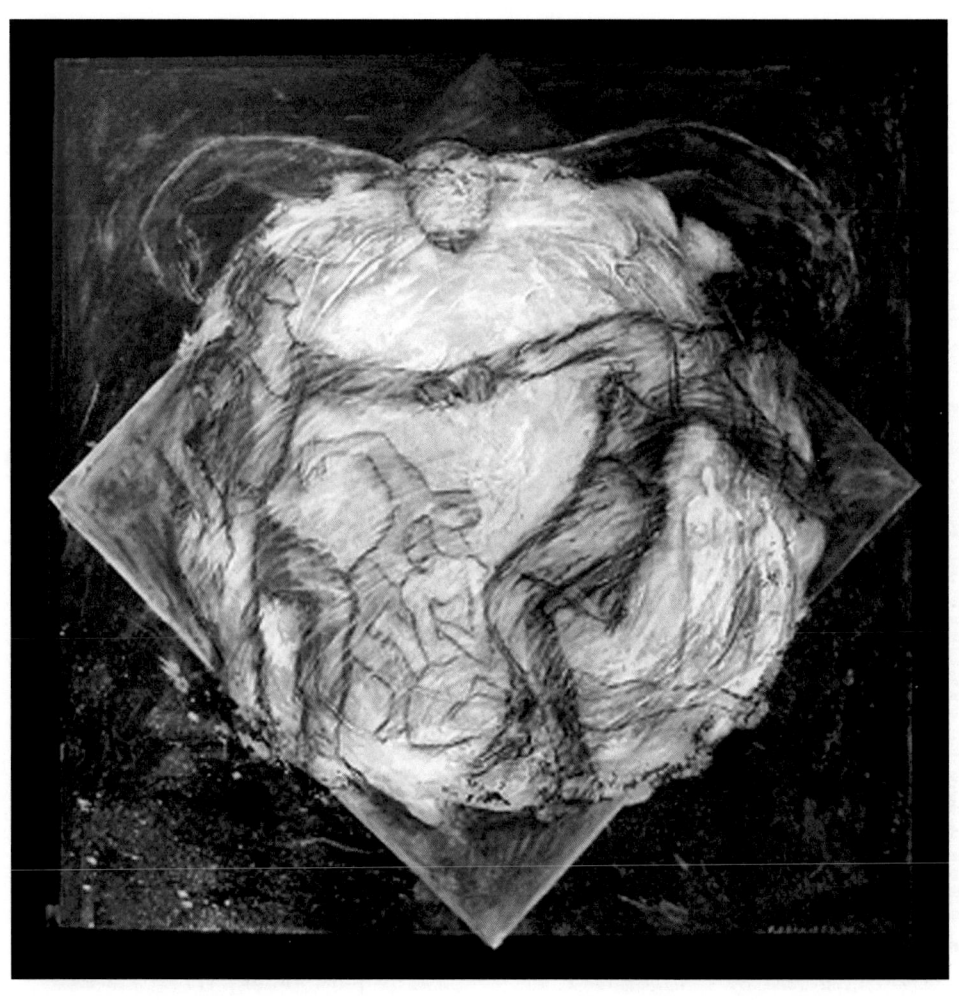

Fate
2005 | mixed media on canvas | 36 x 36 in | 91.5 x 91.5 cm
Collection of Tim Salcudean

Floating Dancers — installation
for dance performance Choreo+Graphe
2005 | Burnaby Art Gallery | Burnaby, BC

Silent Spectator and Floating Dancers — installation
2001 | Yukon Art Gallery | Whitehorse, YT

The Dancers' Suite — installation
2001 | Yukon Art Gallery | Whitehorse, YT

Guanajuato Variations
2011 | digital photography | 15 x 24 in | 38 x 61 cm

Dreamscape
2011 | digital photography | 15 x 24 in | 38 x 61 cm

Chapter 59

In Search of Meaning
—Epilogue

A painter should begin every canvas with a wash of black, because all things in nature are dark except where exposed by the light.

Leonardo da Vinci
cited in *The Rule of Four*
by Ian Campbell and Austin Thompson

The white canvas stares at me like an empty page waiting for words, but I hesitate to touch its blank surface. I need the mystery of darkness to help me bring it to life. Quickly, in broad strokes, I cover the entire surface with black gesso. Now I am ready to bring forth the story hiding in the dark. Moving figures appear on the textured surface covered with warm reds, oranges and browns — they are confined, or perhaps trapped, within the limits of a geometrical diamond shape, symbol of the rigid boundaries we are born into. Still, something is missing and I can't quite see what it is. I set the work aside for a few days, take it out again and stare at it for a long time. What is wrong? There are no rules to follow. I wait for the painting to guide me. And it does.

Without thinking, I pick up a stick of charcoal and, in a few strokes, a head appears at the top of the diamond, looking down at the figures below. My heart is beating faster, as if I am about to experience a mystical revelation. My hand follows an unspoken command and quickly traces two arms that embrace the diamond and its occupants in a sweeping gesture. What is it? Why has this mysterious, bodiless figure appeared out of nowhere? Puzzled, I stare at the work.

And then — in a flash, I understand. The mysterious figure is Fate.

God may not play dice with the Universe, as Einstein is believed to have said. Still, does not Fate/God play a game of luck with the personal universe of human beings by allowing them no choice of parents or of the time and place of their birth? We live within these rigid and haphazard boundaries as best we can. The smallest change in the place and the time of birth or the identity of our parents may mean the difference between life and death, poverty or wealth, misery or happiness. We have no choice but to search for the meaning of our lives within those given structures.

Ten years ago, through this painting, Fate had given me a deeper understanding of life and issued a stern warning about the future, imposing an unplanned and unexpected ending to this memoir.

A time to be born — and a time to die.
I have been granted more time to live.

Acknowledgements

This memoir might never have been written without the people who urged me to tell the story of my 'interesting' life. I would like to thank all those who provided support, offered comments and assisted in the editing, proofreading and design.

I can't thank enough my dear friends Linda Shulman and Maureen Chacon for reading the much too long, unedited first draft. Their positive feedback was a huge encouragement. I am most thankful to Phyllis Reeve, who has always supported my art and offered astute editorial suggestions. My heartfelt thanks to my gym companions Suzanne James and Rosabella Prasad, who took the time to read the second draft and told me how much they enjoyed it. Ronsdale Press publisher Ron Hatch, who had published *Pnina Granirer: Portrait of an Artist*, gave me an unsolicited gift by not only reading the second draft, but also adding editorial notes. Thank you Ron! I'd like to thank my husband Eddy, my sons David and Dan and my daughter-in-law Beatrice, for giving me their much-needed insights and encouragement. After all, they are part and parcel of my story. My gratitude to my cousins Gabi Mozes, Lily Sigler and Ditta Herscovici in Israel and to my cousin Nomi Zingher in New York, for sharing important insights about our family.

Many thanks to Omar Gallegos for his beautiful book design and for his patience in dealing with the never-ending changes, to my second editor Kyle Hawke, who tightened some of the loose ends, and to Daniel Colmont, for keeping everyone on track. My gratitude also goes to Peppa Martin, who took my photograph at such short notice. Thank you Susan Dobie, for introducing me to your amazing daughter, Pat Dobie. As my first editor she gently, but ruthlessly, cut down the memoir to a more publishable format. Thank you Pat, I consider myself fortunate to have worked with you.

Last but not least and keeping in step with the serendipity that I have been blessed with, I am delighted to have had the pleasure of reconnecting with Jo Blackmore, owner of Granville Island Publishing, who decades earlier had published my art on a UNICEF poster and who has the uncanny ability to notice the smallest of details needing correction. Thank you Jo, for helping me make this memoir a reality! Working with you has been a most rewarding experience.

Index

Discussion Questions for Book Clubs

- How does the love marriage of Pnina's parents and their constant support of her while growing up influence her outlook on life?
- During Pnina's early childhood, when Romania was dealing brutally with its own Jewish population, her native town of Brăila was safer than most other cities. How and why do you think this was?
- This memoir describes the strong socialist beliefs of many young Israelis, particularly the new immigrants from Communist-dominated countries. How do you think their views influenced the building of Israel?
- How does the author use humour to deal with the challenges of living in Israel?
- One of her themes is of alienation and the desire to belong. Have you ever experienced such feelings in a new place where the language and culture are different? How does her story help you better understand the immigrant experience?
- The artist describes in detail her process of creating a work of art. What effect has this had on you and how does it influence the way you look at art now?
- When the family arrives in Vancouver, Pnina concentrates more on her art. Do you identify with her struggle between commitment to her family and to her art? To what extent is it possible to do both?
- Do you think that Pnina should have continued doing the same kind of work if it sold well in order to retain her prestigious gallery representation? Can you think of other ways the gallery and artist could have tackled this age-old dilemma?
- How do you feel about her being so outspoken about certain trends in art?
- Why do you think some people, like Pnina, experience more serendipity in their lives?

About the Author

Pnina Granirer has exhibited her work locally, nationally and internationally in Paris, Strasbourg, the US, Prague, Santiago de Compostela (Spain), in Coimbra (Portugal) and in Santiago (Chile).

A forty-year retrospective of 120 works at the Richmond Art Gallery in January 1998 reflected the artistic development over her long career. The lavishly illustrated book *Pnina Granirer: Portrait of an Artist* by Ted Lindberg (Ronsdale Press) was launched at the opening of the exhibition and in 2005, a film about Granirer's work by Mehdi Ali was launched on Bravo!TV.

The Trials of Eve, a major work of 12 mixed media drawings and 12 poems, now in the collection of the Glenbow Museum in Calgary, Alberta, was published as an award-winning limited edition book and a softcover. A film by Gretchen Jordan-Bastow based on this work was first shown at the FIFA in Paris, on Bravo!TV, on Knowledge Network and other venues.

In 1993 Granirer co-founded *Artists in Our Midst*, the first ongoing Open Studio Walk in Vancouver, BC. She organized and hosted discussions about art via many Philosophers' Cafés, sponsored by Simon Fraser University.

Her works can be found in numerous private and public collections, nationally and internationally, such as the Glenbow Museum in Calgary, the Yad Vashem Centre in Jerusalem, the Art Gallery of Greater Victoria, BC, the Two Rivers Gallery in Prince George, BC, the Richmond Art Gallery, BC, the Art Gallery of Hamilton, ON, the Museo Eugenio Granell in Santiago de Compostela, Spain, the Museo Nacional de Bellas Artes in Santiago, Chile, and many more.

In 2014, her work was included in the encyclopedia of international Surrealism by Arturo Schwarz, *Il Surrealismo — Ieri e Oggi* (Italy) and in a 5-page chapter in José Miguel Pérez Corrales's anthology, *Surrealismo: El Oro del Tiempo* (Spain).

Granirer's work has always reflected her personal experience. She works in series and her interest lies in unifying shape with content.